Karma 2.0

Karma 2.0

The Physics of Cause and Effect in a Digital World

Noor Halven

Mindful Pages

Published in 2026

ISBN: 9789375361923 (PB)
ISBN: 9789375369639 (eBook)

Published by

Mindful Pages
Imprint of Alpha Editions LLC
312 W. 2nd St #1834
Casper, WY 82601, USA

This book was developed using advanced writing tools to support the drafting and ideation process. All content has been thoughtfully curated, refined, and reviewed to ensure quality and relevance.

Content

Introduction

The boy realised his mistake almost instantly. A flash of irritation, a careless tap, and a cruel post joined the relentless stream of his school's online chatter. Within minutes it was gone, deleted in a moment of remorse. Yet deletion proved no match for the speed of capture. Screenshots circulated before his regret had fully formed. A whisper became a ripple, then a current. A teacher intervened, then a pastoral lead, then the head of year. Conversations were held, consequences allotted. Two years later, when he searched his own name to prepare for an internship application, the remnants surfaced again—scraps of context stripped from time, cached by engines indifferent to youthful misjudgement. The analogue world once disposed of such moments through the quiet mercy of forgetting. The digital world does not forget. It archives. It indexes. It amplifies.

This small drama, repeated in countless variations across the globe, is not simply a story about juvenile misbehaviour or overly sensitive systems. It is a glimpse into a deeper shift. Human societies have always wrestled with cause and effect, with the tensions between action, intention, and consequence. What has changed is not our moral impulse, but the machinery through which our impulses travel. A comment that once lived briefly in the air now takes root in databases. A reflexive share can alter the informational diet of strangers. A design choice made in a boardroom on a Tuesday afternoon can reshape the emotional climate of millions before the week is out. In this world, we have become unwitting participants in sprawling causal chains that operate above, below, and beyond our awareness.

Any civilisation that suddenly expands its range of influence must learn to account for its extended shadow. Ours stretches through fibre-optic cables and wireless signals, across platforms that function as global public squares, marketplaces, stages, and battlegrounds. The scale is unprecedented. The behaviours, strangely, are not. The ancient concept of karma—purified here of metaphysics and reincarnation—rested on a simple insight: actions generate consequences that radiate outward, shaping not merely events but character, relationships, and collective patterns of life. In the digital age, this insight acquires new urgency. The difference is that our causes travel farther and faster, and their effects are captured by systems designed neither to forget nor to forgive by default.

We live in a culture of instantaneous reaction but delayed understanding. We respond before we recognise; we broadcast before we reflect. Our tools encourage speed and collapse deliberation into reflex. Yet beneath this surface noise lies a complex physics of causation—an interplay of algorithms, metrics, memory structures, and human behaviour that silently directs the flow of attention and emotion. This book offers a way to see those flows with clarity. It proposes that digital life is best understood not merely as a collection of personal choices but as a networked field where each action sets conditions for others. In this field, every post, click, and design tweak becomes a micro-cause with potential second-order effects. Some effects are small; others accumulate into shifts in norms, incentives, and narratives.

To frame this clearly, we must acknowledge a new architectural truth: the digital world is a world of systems, not scraps. Every gesture joins a structure—an algorithmic loop, a recommendation graph, a reputation ledger, an archive with perfect memory. Writers can delete, but platforms often do not. Designers can intend neutrality, but defaults inevitably tilt behaviour. Users believe they are choosing freely, yet their paths are subtly sculpted by systems optimised for engagement rather than wisdom. The central task, therefore, is not merely to behave well online but to understand how our behaviour is shaped, amplified, and sometimes distorted by the environments in which it occurs.

History offers useful parallels. Societies once adapted to the printing press, to broadcasting, to industrialisation. Each shift introduced new asymmetries of power and new forms of influence. But our current transformation is unique in two ways. First, today's information environment is participatory: creation and reaction occur at the same tempo. Second, the underlying infrastructure is computational: algorithms respond to patterns beyond human scale. Because of this, our old intuitions about individual responsibility and linear cause and effect falter. A single share may marginally nudge a recommendation engine, which in turn nudges millions. A minor UI change may reduce harassment by twenty per cent. A teenager's impulsive insult can become a durable fragment of their online identity. The stakes are both intimate and planetary.

One motif runs through the pages that follow: the ledger. In ancient civilisations, ledgers recorded transactions, obligations, and debts. In digital society, the ledger has expanded. Platforms maintain ledgers of behaviour; search engines maintain ledgers of identity; algorithms maintain ledgers of preference; workplaces maintain ledgers of contribution and error; communities maintain informal yet potent ledgers of trust. These ledgers are not written in ink but in patterns, metadata, and probabilities. Yet they shape opportunity, credibility, and belonging. To understand digital karma—recast here as the physics of cause and effect—we must learn to read the ledgers in which our actions are inscribed.

The urgency of this task is sharpened by a simple fact: we live in an era of extraordinary amplification. A rumour can outpace a correction; a fury can drown out a nuance; a short clip can overshadow a lifetime of careful conduct. Attention, once dispersed across diverse contexts, converges on moments of spectacle or outrage. The consequence is a widespread sense of precarity: the fear that one misstep may be captured, circulated, and frozen. For young people, whose identities are still in formation, this precarity is amplified. For adults, its effects are subtler but no less corrosive: a narrowing of expression, a retreat from openness, a persistent hum of self-surveillance.

Yet this book is not a lament; it is a manual for steadiness. If the digital world has multiplied the scale of our causal impact, it has also multiplied our capacity for repair, wisdom, and skill. Memory cuts both ways. So does amplification. The tools that spread harm can spread care. The systems that accelerate outrage can, with thoughtful design and collective discipline, foster reflection, depth, and trust. The challenge is to develop a vocabulary and a set of practices that enable individuals, teams, and platforms to act with maturity in a landscape that increasingly rewards impulsivity.

To do this, the chapters that follow move between three essential lenses. The first is systems thinking, which reveals how feedback loops, delays, and leverage points shape outcomes far more than isolated decisions. The second is ethics, which focuses attention on responsibility, fairness, dignity, and the human consequences of our designs and behaviours. The third is design itself, the quiet but profound force that guides behaviour through defaults, interfaces, and incentives. Each lens alone is insufficient. Together, they allow us to see digital action not as isolated strokes but as threads in a larger fabric of causation.

Readers will encounter, in later chapters, the subtleties of network memory, the architecture of reputation, the moral weight of design choices, and the economics of attention. They will see how internal workplace systems create their own karma, how platforms govern at scale, how consent is often illusory, and how repair must travel along the same channels as harm. Throughout, the guiding question is consistent: what does it mean to act well in a world where our influence is extended, archived, and algorithmically entangled with the actions of others?

Consider again the opening scene. The teenager's story is not a cautionary tale about the recklessness of youth. It is a mirror held up to all of us. We are all capable of reflexive harm. We all operate in systems that transform tiny impulses into larger consequences. We all contribute, through our clicks and silences, to the shaping of norms and narratives. And we all—individuals, teams, institutions—retain the capacity to act with greater care and foresight.

This book will not offer platitudes about digital detox or urge a retreat from technology. Instead, it argues for a different kind of literacy: a fluency in the mechanics of digital causation. Such literacy allows us to see the deliberate design behind what feels natural, the cumulative power behind what feels trivial, and the ethical stakes behind what feels inevitable. With this literacy comes agency—the ability to intervene, adjust, and repair.

As you move through these pages, you may notice moments of recognition. Patterns you have experienced but not yet named. Systems you have felt but never fully understood. Tensions you have sensed but struggled to articulate. These are the signatures of a world in transition. The question is not whether we will adapt, but how—and whether we will do so with wisdom.

What habits of attention best serve us when the world competes fiercely for our gaze? How should a community handle wrongdoing when memory is permanent and context fragile? What duties do designers hold when a single default can shape millions of decisions? How do we rebuild trust in systems that often reward the very behaviours that corrode it? And what might it look like to create digital spaces that acknowledge human frailty without condemning us to it?

These questions do not seek tidy answers. They seek better frameworks—ways of seeing that sharpen judgment, deepen empathy, and strengthen action. Karma 2.0 is offered in that spirit. A guide for anyone who wishes to navigate digital life with less fear and more clarity. A map for understanding the hidden architecture beneath our daily interactions. A toolkit for acting with greater steadiness, skill, and care in a networked world that magnifies both our virtues and our errors.

The teenager's story ends not with punishment but with understanding. The harm was addressed, the lesson absorbed, the path ahead reshaped. But the system retained its memory, indifferent to his growth. That is the landscape we must learn to inhabit wisely. A world where consequences travel far, but where wisdom can travel just as far if we choose to cultivate it. Let us begin.

Chapter 1
From Karma to Causality

The story begins, as seismic shifts often do, with something deceptively slight. A woman scrolls through her feed during a rushed lunch break and shares an article she hasn't fully read. The headline aligns vaguely with her frustration that day, and she clicks without hesitation. Within hours, her post becomes a small node in a broader surge of attention, boosting the article into trending lists, nudging an algorithmic ridge that now tilts thousands of recommendations in its favour. Two days later, a local councillor cites the article in a heated interview. A week on, a school uses it in a parent briefing, unaware that the article's central claim has already been quietly debunked. By the time the correction surfaces, the wave has passed. The share has done its work.

Most of us never see the chain we have joined. We assume our actions dissolve into the noise—light as dust, negligible, forgotten. But the digital world does not operate on the logic of dust. It behaves more like weather: small atmospheric changes can produce distant storms. The ordinary user, once an isolated point, now occupies a place within a system that remembers, reacts, and reorganises itself around patterns of behaviour. A single tap may not feel like an action of consequence, yet it shifts the probabilities that underlie what others encounter. In this terrain, causation is not a philosophical abstraction; it is an observable pattern.

Older cultures understood the gravity of human action, even if they expressed it through metaphors we no longer require. The concept of karma, stripped of its supernatural scaffolding, offered a profound intuition: that actions create ripples which shape both the world and the actor. Modern platforms have revived the intuition while discarding the slow, contemplative framework that once held it. The result is a landscape rich in consequences but poor in understanding—an environment where cause and effect move faster than reflection. This chapter attempts to rebuild the missing understanding, translating an ancient insight into the language of systems, networks, and behavioural design.

The terrain we now inhabit demands a new literacy. The old metaphysical models told us that every action mattered because it embedded itself in the moral architecture of the universe. The digital world tells us—quietly, often opaquely—that every action matters because it modifies the architecture of a network. A single share alters a recommendation graph. A brief watch increases the weight of a video. A fragment of code changes what millions see next. What looks like individual choice is actually part of an interlocking system of feedback loops. To understand digital life properly, we must shift from thinking about isolated events to thinking in patterns, flows, and chains of influence.

The purpose of this chapter is not to romanticise old ideas but to recover their clarity. Karma, at its root, was not about cosmic bookkeeping. It was about causation: the recognition that actions have consequences that accumulate. Today, we need a secular and testable model of that accumulation—one that helps us see how behaviour travels across networks and how design shapes the pathways it travels. Without such a model, we remain blind participants in processes that govern our attention, our relationships, our identities, and our collective life.

To build that model, we begin with three essential lenses. The first is systems thinking, which teaches us to see loops instead of lines. Every platform contains reinforcing loops—those that amplify behaviours—and balancing loops—those that dampen them. Feedback can be delayed or immediate, visible or hidden. These loops determine the eventual shape of our online experiences far more than isolated choices do. The second lens is ethics, which clarifies the obligations we bear when our actions affect others through complex systems. Ethics forces us to consider not only what we intend but what we enable. The third lens is design, the subtle but powerful force that turns intentions, values, and assumptions into defaults. Design is never neutral. It frames choices long before will is engaged.

Individually, each lens reveals something important. Together, they provide a coherent way to judge digital actions—whether personal, collective, or institutional. A crude approach to online behaviour often reduces moral questions to matters of personal responsibility. But responsibility becomes meaningful only when we understand the systems that channel our actions into consequences. A user who shares a misleading video bears responsibility, but so does the designer of the autoplay system that funnels users into ever-more sensational content. An engineer who changes a ranking parameter affects the informational climate for millions. Ethics without systems thinking is naïve. Systems thinking without ethics is indifferent. Design without either is perilous.

As we move through this landscape, we must relearn the meaning of *cause*. A click may appear trivial, but it is a micro-cause, a tiny input into a vast network that weights and sorts human experience. A post is not merely a personal expression but a public signal with unpredictable reach. A code change is not simply a technical adjustment but a structural modification of a shared environment. When companies introduce autoplay as a default, they do more than save users a second of effort—they reshape viewing norms, extend watch times, and shift cultural patterns around leisure, attention, and rest. Such changes are rarely malicious; they are simply unexamined. But unexamined causes produce cumulative effects that can be hard to reverse.

Understanding these effects is not an exercise in moral panic but an invitation to precision. Once we see digital actions as causes, the landscape becomes legible. We notice how a single post influences what our friends see, how a pause in interaction affects the algorithmic weight of a relationship, how a shift in design reshapes collective habits. Patterns emerge: how certain metrics encourage creators to favour speed over accuracy, how public counters intensify competitive behaviour, how recommendation systems generate corridors of similarity. None of this is mystical. It is causal structure—moral architecture built from data.

The stakes of this structure are high because they touch the three finite resources that govern modern life: attention, trust, and time. Attention is the fuel of perception and thought; yet it is relentlessly harvested by systems tuned to capture rather than nourish it. Trust is the connective tissue of communities; yet it is eroded when information environments privilege outrage or distortion. Time is the only non-renewable currency we possess; yet design choices can quietly siphon it away, fragmenting the continuity required for learning, empathy, and creativity. When platforms pursue frictionless experience without considering downstream effects, they create hidden costs in all three domains. And when individuals act without understanding how their actions propagate, they inadvertently contribute to those costs.

This chapter does not argue for abstinence or retreat. Digital life is not a tide we can step back from without losing something essential. Instead, it argues for the deliberate introduction of friction—a pause before sharing, a reconsideration of defaults, a conscious weighting of consequences. Friction is not the enemy of freedom. It is the condition that makes freedom meaningful. A world without friction encourages impulse over insight. A world with prudently placed friction encourages intention, balance, and care.

As you move into the deeper sections of this chapter, you will see how old moral intuitions can be translated into contemporary tools. You will encounter stories of how minor actions shift major systems, how design embeds values, how ethics becomes measurable when we track consequences, and how systems thinking reveals the hidden geometry of digital life. You will see why understanding causation is no longer optional and why developing this understanding may be one of the defining intellectual tasks of our century.

By the end of this chapter, a different landscape should begin to take shape. One where the familiar gestures of digital life—scrolling, sharing, liking, posting, coding—appear not as background noise but as the raw material of a vast and consequential system. A landscape where causation is visible, responsibility is shared, and design is recognised as a moral force. And perhaps, most importantly, a landscape where individuals and institutions alike can act with greater clarity, precision, and steadiness.

The path ahead is not about replacing old ideas but reinterpreting them for a new world. We stand in a place where ancient intuitions about action and consequence meet the modern science of networks. That intersection is fertile ground. What grows there will shape not only our digital lives but our social, political, and emotional futures.

The question is how to cultivate it wisely. This chapter offers the first tools for answering that question.

Old ideas, new terrain

In July 1855, on a humid evening in Calcutta, the scholar Ishwar Chandra Vidyasagar delivered a lecture on moral conduct that startled his British hosts. Actions, he argued, were not private events sealed within a life. They travelled—shaping families, communities, and the moral texture of society itself. The claim unsettled listeners accustomed to thinking of wrongdoing as a discrete act to be judged, punished, and then archived. Vidyasagar's point was sharper: moral causation was cumulative. A choice today altered the likelihood of harms or goods tomorrow. His audience could not have imagined a world where those ripples would be captured, quantified, and amplified by machines. Yet the intuition he conveyed resonates with fresh clarity as we try to understand causation across digital networks.

A century and a half later, a minor event at YouTube's offices in San Bruno, California, illustrates this shift. In October 2011, engineers adjusted how the platform weighted viewing sessions. Longer sessions meant higher rankings; higher rankings meant wider visibility. It was a technical change, expressed in lines of code rather than philosophical terms, but its effects spread quickly. Creators stretched videos to hold attention. Comment cultures shifted as longer content altered user rhythms. By mid-2012, the company noted significant changes in viewing patterns across regions. The mechanism was empirical; the consequences followed the contours of Vidyasagar's argument. A single design alteration created downstream shifts that no individual viewer intended. The chain did not belong to one life. It belonged to millions.

The paradox is simple: how can a gesture as small as a tap on a share button alter the informational experience of people a continent away? The answer lies in understanding digital behaviour as part of a system—one that registers actions, recombines them, and feeds them back into the environment. Karma, historically, framed the moral dimension of this process. Platforms now map the mechanical dimension. Both concern causation. Both concern the ways in which actions accumulate and travel. What changes is the substrate.

Consider the motif of *trace,* a term that surfaces quietly throughout this terrain. In ancient texts, a trace referred to the lingering effect of an action on character. In digital systems, a trace is a data point—time-stamped, indexable, mathematically legible. When a user taps 'share' on a video at 14:03 on a Wednesday in London, the trace enters a recommendation graph that adjusts what thousands might see next. Show the effect: one share contributes a fraction to a model's estimate of relevance. Name the mechanism: collaborative filtering, a technique with origins in the 1994 GroupLens project at the University of Minnesota. Explain the process: the system maps similarities between users based on shared patterns, weighting each action to refine predictions. Implication: a user's tiny gesture becomes part of a structural signal, shifting probability flows in ways neither the sharer nor the viewer perceives.

The movement from moral causation within a life to behavioural causation across networks carries both continuity and rupture. The continuity lies in the insight: actions matter because they set conditions. The rupture lies in the scale and the speed of those conditions in digital systems. Karma's logic was anchored in reflection; platform causality is anchored in computation. Karma emphasised intention; platforms register only behaviour. Karma presumed a narrative arc; platforms preserve fragments. Yet the core claim—that causes radiate beyond their point of origin—survives the translation.

Two historical examples demonstrate the transformation of this logic into systems language. The first is the introduction of the 'retweet' function on Twitter (San Francisco, 2009). It reduced the friction required to propagate content, and within weeks altered the topology of information spread. Researchers at Cornell University (Kwak et al., 2010) documented the effect: cascades grew more frequent, more uniform, and more sensitive to early engagement. A user's decision to share a link became a measurable input to the probability of a trending topic. The system captured the trace and amplified it.

The second example is Wikipedia's 2012 introduction of the 'Thanks' feature, built in New York and tested across several language editions. The feature enabled editors to acknowledge contributions with a single click. The Wikimedia Foundation's analysis (2013) showed a modest but consistent increase in subsequent edits by those who received thanks. In this case, a micro-action—digital gratitude—altered the behavioural trajectory of contributors. The causal chain was positive rather than harmful, but the structure was the same: small inputs produced measurable shifts.

A counter-example helps sharpen the boundaries of this model. Facebook's experiment with removing public like counts, tested in Australia in 2019, was expected to reduce competitive posting and pressure around metrics. The results were mixed. Internal analyses leaked in 2021 indicated that while some users reported marginal relief, posting behaviour did not shift significantly. Here, the trace created by individual likes contributed less to the systemic pattern than anticipated. The system's deeper incentives—visibility, relevance, ranking—still pulled behaviour into familiar grooves. Removal of a metric did not dissolve the underlying causal structures. Reconcile the limitation: not all traces carry equal structural weight. Some causes lodge in the system's architecture; others skim its surface.

To translate these observations into a secular, testable model of causation, we attend to three properties: *visibility*, *weight*, and *propagation*. Visibility asks what an action reveals to the system—watch time, dwell time, scroll behaviour, share direction. Weight concerns the degree to which the system treats that action as a signal. A share has greater weight than a pause; a comment more than a click. Propagation refers to how far and in what manner the signal travels—whether it influences ranking, recommendations, notifications, or downstream behaviour. Together, these properties form a vocabulary that replaces metaphysical speculation with empirical structure.

The motif of trace returns. A user's actions leave traces that the system reads, and those traces become part of a pattern that shapes what others encounter. Show the pattern: a user in Manchester frequently watches short craft tutorials, often sharing ones under three minutes. Name the mechanism: the system identifies this as a cluster of preference and prioritises similar content for users whose earlier actions align. Explain the process: the trace of one user's behaviour subtly shapes another's feed through inferred similarity. Implication: digital environments distribute causation horizontally, not vertically. We shape one another's informational lives without ever knowing it.

Yet the translation of karma's intuition into digital systems language does more than map behaviour. It invites a reconsideration of responsibility. In moral traditions, responsibility followed intention. In digital systems, responsibility is entangled with influence. A designer in Dublin adjusts an autoplay interval, shortening the buffer between videos from five seconds to two. The change appears trivial. But session lengths increase. Longer sessions feed ranking signals. Ranking signals alter visibility. Visibility shifts social norms around leisure and consumption. Trace by trace, a micro-adjustment becomes part of a cultural pattern. Responsibility becomes diffuse, but not dissolved. It requires a new framework: one that accounts for second-order effects even when first-order intentions are benign.

Causation, in this model, becomes measurable. It is not a mystical ledger but an observable distribution of signals through a network. Consider the 2016 introduction of Facebook's 'angry' reaction, launched from Menlo Park. Internal documents released in 2021 revealed that this reaction was weighted more heavily than likes in ranking algorithms, contributing disproportionately to the visibility of provocative content. A user's emotional expression—intended perhaps as a mild objection—became structurally significant. The system interpreted the trace as intensity, not disapproval. The difference between what an action meant to a user and what it meant to the platform created a widening gap in causation.

The implications extend beyond platforms themselves. Universities, employers, and government agencies increasingly rely on digital traces in assessing credibility, decision-making, or risk. What once belonged to the private moral arc of a life now enters institutional systems with predictive aspirations. A student's pattern of late-night posting can be flagged by automated welfare systems; an employee's inconsistent responses on internal platforms may signal disengagement; a citizen's network connections can feed into risk scores. These systems do not interpret intention. They interpret trace. The model becomes secular, testable, and, at times, blunt.

A second motif—*weight*—helps maintain clarity. Weight in digital systems is not moral weight. It is statistical. But the two can converge. When a user in Nairobi shares a misleading health rumour during an outbreak, their trace may carry substantial weight if it reaches communities that treat their posts as credible. The system reinforces the weight through engagement signals. The moral consequence and the statistical consequence intertwine. Not all actions are equal, and digital systems magnify those with early momentum.

Yet not all causal structures behave predictably. The counter-example earlier—removal of like counts—illustrates a limitation: systems shape behaviour, but human agency remains unruly. Fragile, emotional, contextual decisions still puncture predictable flows. A campaign can fail to trend despite coordinated efforts. A thoughtful article can circulate widely despite low initial engagement. A platform tweak can falter because users resist its logic. Digital causation is powerful, but not deterministic. The model must hold space for the unpredictable.

Historical practices remind us that causation has always been relational. The Buddhist philosopher Nāgārjuna, writing in second-century India, described dependent origination: events arise through conditions, not in isolation. Modern network theory echoes the insight.

Conditions—design, defaults, metrics, norms—shape what traces matter. The bridge between ancient intuition and contemporary systems is not mystical; it is structural. Both traditions argue that action acquires meaning through entanglement.

The challenge is to observe these entanglements without romanticising them. Systems record traces, weight them, and let them travel. They offer remarkable predictive power, yet they flatten nuance. They allow measurement, yet often obscure context. The task is not to escape causation but to understand its mechanics tightly enough to navigate it.

The closing tension lies here: what does it mean to act responsibly when our actions leave traces we cannot fully see, feeding into systems we do not fully control? Should we treat every gesture as consequential, or recognise that systems dilute most signals before they matter? How do we weigh our traces when their weight is decided elsewhere?

Such questions resist neat resolution. They invite scrutiny of motives, designs, and conditions. They point towards the deeper inquiry that follows: how to interpret causation across networks when the trace of every action may travel farther than its actor ever intended.

Three lenses that matter

In March 2018, engineers at Facebook's Menlo Park campus gathered to examine an anomaly: a subtle spike in the spread of sensational political posts following a minor adjustment to ranking weights. The change, deployed earlier that month, had been intended to promote "meaningful social interactions". Instead, it intensified divisive engagement in several regions, including Ireland during the run-up to the abortion referendum. The team reviewed dashboards showing a pattern that was visible only in aggregate: posts that triggered quick comments—often reactive or hostile—received disproportionate visibility. A faint signal had become a feedback loop. What looked like an ethical improvement in principle became, through design, an accelerant. The outcome forced a reckoning: intentions meant little without a structural understanding of how actions, incentives, and interfaces combine.

Three lenses—systems, ethics, design—help decode what unfolded. Each captures a part of the picture. Together, they provide a way to see digital acts not as isolated events but as contributions to a wider causal field. As with the prior subchapter's emphasis on traces, the motif of *pressure* enters here: the pressure that flows through loops, duties, and defaults. It appears quietly at first and strengthens as each lens reveals where pressure accumulates and how it shifts.

Systems thinking shows the mechanism. Ethics names what is at stake. Design reveals how intentions harden into behaviour. The interplay matters, because when one lens dominates, harm often emerges in the blind spots of the others.

Show the first lens: a feedback loop. During Google's experimentation phase for YouTube recommendations in London in late 2015, researchers observed that videos with slightly longer average watch times began surfacing disproportionately, even if their content was only marginally relevant. Name the phenomenon: reinforcement, a hallmark of systems dynamics. Explain it: small advantages compound through algorithmic weighting; increased visibility yields more impressions, which inflate the original signal. Implication: what begins as a design tweak becomes a behavioural contour, altering not just what people watch but *how* they watch. A user's viewing decision becomes a tiny force pushing future patterns.

These loops illustrate a central feature of systems thinking: structure drives outcome. An engineer may intend neutrality; a product manager may aim for engagement; users may simply want distraction. Yet their interactions form a pattern that no individual controls. Metrics—session length, rewatch rate, click-throughs—do not merely measure behaviour; they shape it. A loop forms when behaviour feeds the metric and the metric feeds visibility. Pressure builds. The system learns from signals, not reasons.

The second lens—ethics—names duties within that causal structure. Duties appear in behaviour: whether a designer slows a workflow to ensure clarity; whether an engineer flags a risk when early testing reveals unintended consequences; whether a user hesitates before sharing a claim that stirs anger. Ethics is not an abstract plea but a focus on what specific actors commit to when their actions affect others. Consider a checkable example: Wikipedia's Arbitration Committee case in January 2015 involving editor conduct on the English-language pages about Gamergate. The committee analysed not just explicit violations but patterns of pressure created by high-volume editors whose aggressive reverts shaped discourse. Ethics there meant assessing cumulative influence. Implication: duties expand when actions scale.

Ethics also confronts distributed responsibility. When Instagram (owned by Meta) tested hiding public like counts in Canada in May 2019, the hope was to relieve performance anxiety among younger users. The test had ethical motivation: shift attention from visibility metrics to creative expression. Yet later internal analysis (Meta, 2021) showed minimal reduction in anxiety markers among teen groups. The limitation reveals something essential: ethical intentions alone cannot counteract structural pressures baked into broader systems of attention, reward, and social comparison. Reconciling this requires acknowledging that ethics needs systems awareness. Duties must be defined against the real forces users experience, not the forces platforms imagine they experience.

The third lens—design—translates intentions into defaults. A default is a decision already made for the user. Defaults shape behaviour more effectively than persuasion. They operate by gently constraining options and shaping expectations. Show the effect: in August 2016, Apple introduced differential privacy in iOS data collection. The design choice reduced the granularity of individual behavioural signals while maintaining aggregate analytics. Name the mechanism: privacy-by-design, a principle formalised in the 1990s by Ann Cavoukian in Ontario. Explain it: constrain data access so that harmful outcomes become harder to produce accidentally or deliberately. Implication: values move from aspiration to infrastructure. Good design embeds restraint.

Design does not merely create affordances; it scripts tendencies. A green button encourages action; a delay encourages reflection; a notification badge triggers compulsion; a clarified form reduces error. Pressure reappears here: design channels pressure through pathways users rarely notice. When the pressure is misaligned with human well-being, behaviour drifts into predictable traps. When pressure supports autonomy, users regain clarity.

The three lenses interlock most clearly in crises. Consider the 2017 "SudoGate" incident on GitHub, where a contributor's controversial code comment sparked conflict across open-source communities. The systems view highlighted the structure: high-visibility repos magnify interpersonal disputes. Ethics clarified the duty: maintain conduct that recognises the vulnerability of volunteer labour. Design shaped behaviour: GitHub's tools at the time privileged rapid visibility of comments without proportional tools for contextualising or cooling conflict. Each lens revealed a layer of pressure influencing the outcome.

A credible limitation helps sharpen understanding. Some argue that systems thinking risks fatalism—that by foregrounding loops and structures, it diminishes individual agency. The critique has weight. If systems determine outcomes, why emphasise ethics or design at all? Reconciliation lies in proportion: systems shape probabilities, not certainties. Behavioural evidence—such as Twitter's experiments in 2020 testing pre-tweet prompts encouraging users to read articles before sharing—demonstrates that slight nudges can significantly reduce misinformation spread (Twitter internal data reported by NPR, October 2020). Agency persists; it simply interacts with structural forces. Pressure can be redirected.

Momentum builds when the lenses work in concert. A product team in Nairobi developing a civic-information tool measures feedback loops through local engagement patterns, names duties by considering risks to political minorities, and shapes defaults to prevent unverified claims from surfacing without context. A school administrator in Manchester reviewing a digital incident sees not only individual culpability but how platform incentives magnified visibility. A researcher analysing harassment patterns in Seoul tracks how design changes—such as additional reporting friction—alter repeat-offender statistics over six months. Each actor draws from the three lenses to see the whole.

The motif of pressure surfaces again when considering metrics. Metrics are not neutral; they exert directional force. A newsroom that prioritises click-through rate notices reporters favouring provocative headlines. A charity that measures volunteer retention observes how interface design affects sign-up follow-through. A government digital service evaluating accessibility tracks not only completion rates but the number of steps where users hesitate. Pressure sits in the seams: it nudges, reinforces, distorts, and, if well-aligned, improves.

Yet the lenses also illuminate contradictions. A system may reward immediacy, while ethics requires care. A design may encourage participation, while ethics urges restraint. A system may privilege majority behaviour, while ethics demands attention to minority harm. These contradictions cannot be eliminated. They can be navigated only by seeing how pressures interact.

Two more examples, situated and verifiable, expand the view. In January 2014, South Korea's KakaoTalk introduced stricter harassment-reporting tools after a series of publicised stalking cases. The design shift reduced average response times to reported incidents. Systems thinking revealed that faster moderation feedback loops discouraged repeat offenders. Ethics clarified the platform's duty to protect vulnerable users. Design operationalised the duty into a default path that required less emotional labour from those harmed. By contrast, Reddit's 2013 r/technology moderation failure, when keyword-based auto-removals quietly distorted visible discussion for months, shows the limitation of system-driven automation when ethical clarity is absent. Automated filters removed posts on topics such as "Snowden" or "spying", shaping discourse without transparent justification. The system operated coherently; ethics evaporated.

Threading through all these examples is a question: where does responsibility sit when pressure is distributed? Pressure does not announce itself. It manifests as a shift in recommendations, a spike in comments, a surge of visibility, a moment of hesitation before clicking 'send'. The three lenses help locate the source. Systems tell us where loops accumulate. Ethics tells us what others need from us. Design tells us how our structures shape choice. Only by seeing their interplay do online acts become legible.

The article returns to the motif of pressure in its final movement. Pressure is not inherently destructive. It can be channelled. It can support reflection, stabilise communities, and uphold dignity. But pressure can also distort, escalate, and exhaust. The key diagnostic question emerges: when you next act in a digital space—share, design, tweak, moderate—where is the pressure flowing, and who bears its weight?

Digital actions as causes

In February 2012, at YouTube's San Bruno headquarters, an engineering team led by Cristos Goodrow reviewed an experiment that seemed trivial at first glance: a slight reduction in the delay before the next video autoplayed. The change shaved only a couple of seconds from the interval. Yet within a fortnight the analytics dashboard showed session lengths climbing across multiple regions. By April, watch-time—a metric central to the platform's business model—had increased markedly, influencing which creators were promoted, which topics surged, and which styles of content gained oxygen. A microscopic alteration to a default had changed the culture of the platform. One line of code had set new conditions for millions.

Small causes rarely feel consequential when they are enacted. A click is quick. A tap is barely felt. A designer's adjustment to an interface can be completed before lunch. But digital systems do not judge an action by its felt weight; they register its trace and amplify its structural effects. The motif that threads through this examination—*the hinge*—captures the idea that seemingly tiny movements can redirect the system. A hinge moves quietly, yet entire doors swing on it. Digital actions operate in the same way: slight, immediate, often invisible in isolation, yet capable of cascading through networks at scale.

The first claim to show is simple: a minor behavioural signal can alter the informational experience of people far beyond its origin. Name the mechanism: collaborative filtering, a model underpinning many recommendation systems since its formalisation by the GroupLens Research team in Minnesota in 1994. Explain the process: when a user in Bristol watches a sequence of cooking videos late at night, the system clusters their behaviour with others who show similar patterns; this clustering subtly shifts recommendations for those neighbouring profiles. Implication: personal choices seep into collective environments without any deliberate intention.

A visible behaviour grounds the dynamic: consider a user repeatedly clicking "show me less of this" on political content during a tense election week. The action seems private. Yet the metric attached to it—downweighting a topic cluster—feeds the recommendation graph that influences what others see. The hinge swings again. It is the ordinariness of these actions that gives them their power. No single click transforms a system, but an accumulation of micro-causes recalibrates the probabilities on which digital experience rests.

A second example, widely documented, comes from Instagram's Explore tab. In September 2018, internal reports examined a sudden rise in beauty-filter content among teenage users in the UK and US. The driver traced back to a subtle behavioural pattern: high engagement on a small subset of AR effects during a short promotional campaign. The platform's ranking algorithms interpreted the spike as a signal of deep preference rather than a marketing-induced anomaly. As a result, creators who used these effects gained disproportionate visibility, and content norms shifted. Show the event: a temporary spike in one niche. Name the algorithmic process: engagement-based ranking, which weights rapid interactions over slower, reflective ones. Explain the misinterpretation: the system detected velocity, not context. Implication: the actions of a relatively small cohort altered beauty culture for a much larger population.

Digital systems magnify the initial hinge effect through second-order pathways. The chain often runs like this: an action affects a metric; the metric affects a ranking; the ranking affects visibility; visibility affects behaviour; behaviour feeds back into the metric. Each step is small, but the cumulative pattern reshapes norms. When YouTube emphasised watch-time in 2012, long-form content flourished. Creators adjusted their editing rhythm. Viewers became habituated to lengthier consumption sessions. Industry strategies shifted. A design decision that began as a metric adjustment altered not only habits but expectations.

A credible counter-example sharpens the picture. Twitter's 2020 prompt encouraging users to read articles before sharing them, first piloted in May in the US, showed a reduction in rapid-fire retweets. Yet follow-up analysis reported by NPR (October 2020) revealed an important limitation: the effect diminished over time as users habituated to the prompt. The hinge moved, but the door began drifting back. Reconciling the limitation involves recognising that not all micro-causes have long-run traction.

Some influence behaviour only once; others embed themselves because the surrounding structure supports their amplification. A hinge requires a frame.

Second-order effects become particularly visible in moments of controversy, where digital actions intersect with pre-existing pressures. During the Christchurch attack in March 2019, Facebook's automatic detection systems struggled to contain the spread of the perpetrator's live-streamed footage. Although the original video was removed, thousands of small user actions—saves, shares, re-uploads—created a reproduction loop that overwhelmed moderation. Show the micro-causes: user attempts to circulate fragments. Name the dynamic: content propagation through derivative artefacts. Explain the challenge: each user action generated a slightly altered file that evaded automatic detection. Implication: systems designed to manage causes at scale can be undone by the quantity and variation of micro-causes produced under duress.

Yet systems also reveal the opposite phenomenon: micro-causes that improve conditions. Wikipedia's 2012 introduction of the 'Thanks' feature, tested in New York and later deployed globally, is a case in point. A single click expressing appreciation correlates, according to a 2013 Wikimedia Foundation analysis, with increased editing activity among recipients in the subsequent week. The behaviour is visible: a click of acknowledgement. The metric mirrors it: increased edit counts. The second-order effect emerges: greater contributor retention. Here, the hinge shifts responsibility towards more constructive engagement.

Understanding these examples depends on recognising that digital actions are not outcomes but conditions. A user's choice shapes what follows. A designer's adjustment shapes future behaviour. A coder's change shapes the infrastructure of visibility. Even silence has a measurable effect: dwell time—the period someone pauses while scrolling—feeds ranking models. A user may believe they are merely thinking. The system interprets the pause as interest. The hinge moves.

This structural sensitivity becomes clearer when examining slower, less visible metrics. Consider the phenomenon of "comment heat", a measure that weights posts by the velocity of early replies. Platforms such as Reddit and TikTok experimented with variations of this metric between 2018 and 2022. A single early comment on a post in Seoul or Manchester could lift it into rapid circulation, while a moment's hesitation could allow another post to surge instead. Show the behaviour: a user types quickly. Name the process: time-weighted engagement scoring. Explain the effect: the system boosts posts that generate immediate reaction. Implication: impulsivity becomes structurally privileged, and thoughtful contributions receive diminished exposure.

The motif of the hinge returns here. If a hinge is misaligned, the door swings with unnecessary force; if aligned well, it moves with proportionate resistance. Digital systems, lacking friction by design, often permit disproportionate swing. A user's rebuke can escalate into a storm; a designer's default can become a cultural norm; a line of code can ripple through the expectations of a generation. The question is not whether micro-causes matter, but how their amplification is governed.

A second named and checkable example illustrates the interplay between micro-action and system effect. In June 2020, TikTok faced scrutiny after Black creators in Atlanta and Los Angeles noticed that dances and audio trends originating within their communities were not receiving proportionate visibility. Internal reviews (reported by The New York Times, July 2020) found that an early design decision to suppress content flagged as "potentially sensitive"—including posts with certain hashtags—had created a structural bias. Show the behaviour: creators posted with hashtags marking community identity. Name the algorithmic choice: precautionary downranking of content labelled sensitive. Explain the collision: a design intended to prevent harassment inadvertently reduced visibility for creators seeking representation. Implication: a well-intended micro-design choice can create systemic inequity.

A counter-pressure exists. Human agency can offset algorithmic drift, but only when decisions become visible. YouTube's experiment with "dislike count" removal in November 2021 revealed both sides of the hinge. Removing public dislike tallies was intended to reduce targeting of smaller creators. The result, confirmed in Google's transparency report, did reduce coordinated dislike campaigns in countries such as India. Yet it also reduced a communal signal that helped viewers quickly assess misleading or poor-quality content. The hinge reduced harm in one respect and increased ambiguity in another. Reconciling the limitation requires accepting that micro-causes often reshape multiple relational vectors at once.

Every micro-cause carries with it a second-order question: what conditions does this action set for others? A teacher in Leeds shares a news link in a parents' group chat. The link is outdated, but the act signals concern. Others respond quickly, heightening anxiety before fact-checking occurs. A software engineer in Nairobi adjusts the spacing between interface options. The reduced distance increases accidental taps, raising support request volume. A moderator in Warsaw removes a borderline comment without explanation. The user's silent confusion becomes a sense of grievance. Each small action lays groundwork for what follows.

To treat digital actions as causes, not events, is to recognise the shape of influence. Influence in digital systems rarely resembles traditional persuasion. It appears in metrics: increased load on moderation queues; accelerated visibility for certain topics; elevated risk of harmful cascades. It appears in behaviour: quicker scrolling, sharper replies, longer sessions. It appears in norms: expectations about acceptable tone, format, or reaction.

The hinge motif sharpens once more as the article moves towards its tension. If every digital action is a hinge—small, precise, carrying disproportionate effect—what does discernment look like in systems where neither actors nor observers can fully see the structure? When you next post, tweak code, or adjust a setting, what conditions will your action set? And what door, quietly and perhaps irrevocably, will it swing open?

The stakes: attention, trust, time

In October 2016, at a modest conference room in Menlo Park, a product manager at Instagram presented a slide that unsettled the room. The metric was simple: users under the age of 21 were spending, on average, 32 minutes longer per day on the platform than six months earlier. The cause traced back to a design decision introduced that spring—algorithmic feed ranking. The outcome was visible in the chart: a steepening curve, rising fastest among the youngest cohorts. Attention had shifted, not through intention but through architecture. What the slide did not show, though it hung heavily in the room, was the consequence outside the metric: sleep patterns disrupted, study routines fractured, interpersonal tension rising as unseen ranking rules reweighted whose posts surfaced first. Time moved in one direction. The system consumed it.

The triad that anchors this subchapter—attention, trust, time—might appear abstract at first glance. They are not. Each leaves a measurable imprint. An interrupted conversation. A fatigued mind. A delayed reply that weakens confidence. A child pacing in irritation because a notification landed at the wrong moment. Digital systems record traces of engagement; human beings absorb the residue. The motif carried through this section, *the drift*, names that slow pulling-away from intention, the almost unnoticed slide from chosen action to conditioned reaction. Drift is not dramatic. Drift is quiet.

The first claim to show is that attention is not only finite; it is actively shaped by the structures that request it. Name the phenomenon: attentional capture, a term used in cognitive psychology to describe the reflexive redirection of focus in response to salient stimuli. Explain the link: design elements—badges, vibrations, autoplay, infinite scroll—exploit attentional capture by introducing stimuli that interrupt self-directed focus. Implication: the more successfully systems capture attention, the harder it becomes for users to commit time to tasks requiring depth, deliberation, or rest.

A visible behaviour grounds the argument: a student in Glasgow checks her phone during a study session because a red badge appears on her messaging app. The badge is metric-driven: it signals unread messages. She glances. Her focus breaks. The session's productivity—measured in pages read or problems solved—drops. The drift grows.

A checkable example sharpens the point. When Netflix introduced the 'post-play' feature in August 2012, reducing the interval between episodes, researchers at the University of Texas at Austin (Panda & Pandey, 2017) later found a correlation between the feature and prolonged viewing sessions among younger adults. Show the feature: a countdown timer initiating the next episode automatically. Name the mechanism: friction reduction, removing the need to press 'next'. Explain the consequence: users watched longer not because they intended to but because the design aligned with a psychological tendency towards inertia. Implication: systems that remove small moments of choice can commandeer hours.

A second example illustrates systemic scale. During the early months of the pandemic in 2020, TikTok usage surged globally. In the UK, Ofcom reported in August 2020 that average daily use among 15–24-year-olds exceeded 65 minutes. Show the behaviour: endless swiping. Name the mechanism: variable reward scheduling, a pattern established in behavioural psychology, where unpredictable reinforcement strengthens persistence. Explain the experience: a user swipes not to reach an endpoint but to see what comes next. Implication: attention is consumed not by meaningful content but by the structure of the feed itself. The drift deepens.

A credible limitation tempers the picture. In May 2021, Apple's App Tracking Transparency framework introduced prompts requiring apps to request permission before tracking users across apps and websites. Some predicted a major drop in engagement-based optimisation. However, despite reduced tracking granularity, average usage times across major platforms remained high. The limitation reveals that tracking is not the only determinant of attention capture. The drift persists through interface design, social dynamics, and habit loops. Reconciling the limitation requires admitting that attention is shaped by a constellation of factors, some behavioural, some structural, some interpersonal.

The second claim concerns trust—fragile, relational, cumulative. Show the erosion: a user in Birmingham encounters a misleading headline shared by a friend she typically regards as careful. She clicks. The article is shoddy. The friend's credibility dips slightly. Trust moves in increments. Name the dynamic: reputational micro-shifts, small adjustments in the confidence one places in others. Explain the effect: digital interactions create a ledger of impressions—each click, share, omission, and correction shapes perception. Implication: careless pushes do not merely pollute information; they subtly rewire social judgement.

Again, a measurable metric grounds the idea. Journalists at the Reuters Institute in Oxford found in their 2021 Digital News Report that trust in news shared through social media platforms fell significantly below trust in directly accessed news sources. Show the behaviour: readers encountering news via algorithmic feeds. Name the phenomenon: trust asymmetry, where the platform mediates the signal but the user attributes responsibility to the sharer. Explain the tension: users blame individuals for sharing questionable material even when algorithms amplified its visibility. Implication: trust erodes at the interpersonal level while remaining opaque at the structural level. Drift spreads across relationships.

A checkable case demonstrates how easily trust can be strained. In November 2013, HealthCare.gov in the United States experienced serious technical failures during its rollout. Though a large-scale example, the dynamic is mirrored daily in smaller systems: errors, slowdowns, unexpected logouts, missing messages. Show the event: users unable to complete forms. Name the mechanism: system unreliability. Explain the consequence: users recalibrate trust downward, opting out or delaying action. Implication: time is lost not through consumption but through friction imposed by instability.

A counter-example is required. Wikipedia, despite its open-editing model, maintains comparatively high trust metrics in international surveys. How? Because transparency—edit histories, talk pages, citations—acts as visible behaviour anchoring trust. The drift is countered by structural openness. Reconciling the limitation involves recognising that trust can be stabilised when systems reveal their workings rather than hide them.

The third claim concerns time—the scarce substrate beneath every human choice. Time cannot be recovered. Show the cost: an office worker in Cardiff opens his phone for a quick check during a break and returns to his desk fifteen minutes later, unsure how he spent the interval. Name the phenomenon: time confetti, described by sociologist Brigid Schulte to capture the fragmentation of minutes into tiny unusable scraps. Explain the mechanism: micro-interruptions generated by notifications disrupt temporal flow, preventing sustained engagement. Implication: time is lost not only in blocks but in shreds.

Metrics reveal the scale. Email response expectations within organisations often hover at minutes rather than hours, as shown in internal audits conducted by various firms and reported by the Harvard Business Review (2019). Show the behaviour: employees checking inboxes repeatedly. Name the tension: temporal compression. Explain the drain: each check consumes seconds but fractures larger segments. Implication: the drift steals hours by slicing them into fragments.

Two further examples clarify how systems extract time. When Facebook introduced Stories in March 2017, internal analysis leaked in 2020 showed that the feature's placement at the top of the app increased daily minutes spent by double digits across several demographic groups. Show the placement: prominent, eye-level, brightly bordered. Name the mechanism: salience. Explain the shift: users tapped by reflex, adding minutes cumulatively. Implication: time loss becomes a structural outcome, not a deliberate choice.

In contrast, Signal's introduction of disappearing messages in January 2017 shows a counter-pressure: design features that return time by reducing archive clutter and social obligation. Show the feature: messages vanish after a set period. Name the intention: temporal clarity. Explain the effect: users feel less pressure to maintain endless histories. Implication: design can give time back.

Threading the motif of drift, each of these domains reveals a core pattern: systems nudge attention, reshape trust, and fragment time not through dramatic coercion but quiet accumulation. Drift is rarely malicious, but it is costly.

Prudent friction offers a route to recalibration. Show friction: Twitter's introduction of a prompt encouraging users to read articles before retweeting (US, 2020). Name the design: intentional pause. Explain the outcome: reduced impulsive sharing, according to Twitter's own reporting. Implication: friction slows drift. Another example: email clients that batch notifications reduce the scatter of time confetti by consolidating interruptions into predictable windows. Friction produces rhythm.

A counterpoint clarifies limits. When Google added confirmation prompts for mass deletions in Gmail in 2019, some power users complained of inefficiency. Yet fraud and accidental deletion incidents dropped markedly. Friction carries trade-offs. Reconciling this requires accepting that friction must be placed with discernment, not uniformly applied.

The drift motif returns in the final movement. Drift can be slowed. Drift can be redirected. Drift cannot be fully eliminated. That leaves a question still hanging: when you next adjust a setting, deploy a feature, or respond to a notification, how will you measure the cost—attention lost, trust strained, time scattered—and how much friction would restore not efficiency but balance?

Chapter 2
Feedback Loops and Network Memory

The rumour began with eight words, posted hastily in a football forum on a grey afternoon in Manchester. Within minutes a few regulars liked it, half in jest, half out of habit. The post rose a little in the feed. An hour later, someone copied it to Twitter; a local journalist, scanning for leads, saw the rising engagement and retweeted it with a raised eyebrow. By evening it had reached thousands, many convinced it carried the weight of truth. The next morning the club issued a formal denial, yet the rumour clung stubbornly to the day's conversation, as if repetition had endowed it with its own momentum. No one could say where the spark had truly caught. No one could identify why this rumour rose while countless others faded. What they witnessed—what we all witness, though often without language for it—was not merely spread, but feedback: a loop of attention, shaped and accelerated by the hidden machinery of a networked world.

Every digital platform runs on such loops. Some reinforce, swelling until they dominate a feed or a culture; others balance, dampening noise before it spirals. Most loops operate quietly, beneath conscious perception, yet they structure what millions see, believe, and feel. The Manchester rumour did not rise because it was credible. It rose because multiple loops aligned: fast engagement at the right moment, a ranking system tuned to velocity, a journalist's curiosity becoming a signal, and a crowd ready to share what startled or amused them. At each step, the past fed the present; the system remembered, and the memory shaped its next move.

It is tempting to think of digital life as a sequence of discrete acts—posts, likes, comments—each with its own contained significance. But that view misses the fundamental truth that this chapter explores: nothing happens alone. Every action becomes a data point; every data point becomes a signal; every signal becomes part of a pattern that stretches far beyond its origin. A single tap may be inconsequential, but thousands of taps form currents, and currents shape landscapes. These landscapes have memory. They store what we reward, what we react to, what we linger on. They form grooves that both guide and constrain what comes next.

This chapter steps into the architecture of those grooves: loops, lags, leverage. Reinforcing loops that accelerate the popular, balancing loops that contain excess, and the subtle delays that hide cause from effect, making outcomes feel mysterious when they are anything but. In networked environments, delays matter profoundly. A surge in attention might appear spontaneous when in fact it is the delayed effect of a change made days earlier: a tweak to ranking weight, a newly introduced notification prompt, a community's slow build towards collective irritation. The present is rarely present; it is an echo of what the system has been quietly learning.

To understand these loops is to understand why some interventions matter far more than others. Most actions simply feed the flow, but a select few—leverage points—redirect it. A carefully timed moderation decision can stall a conflict. A single feature adjustment can reshape the cadence of a culture. A change to how comments are sorted can shift a community from reflective to reactive. These moments matter because networks amplify asymmetrically: a small nudge upstream becomes a large effect downstream. Those who grasp the structure can intervene with grace; those who don't often push hard in the wrong place.

Metrics intensify this dynamic. What we measure becomes magnetic. Creators follow the numbers that decide their reach. Users respond to the counters that measure their worth. When a platform calibrates its metrics toward watch-time or likes, it pulls entire communities into narrow behavioural grooves. Consider the turning point on YouTube in the early 2010s, when watch-time began to outweigh views. Video length increased, pacing shifted, and creators reorganised their workflow around a single gravitational pull. Depth suffered; outrage flourished; attention clustered around the emotionally extreme. This was not a moral failure. It was a metric at work.

Metrics do not merely describe behaviour; they sculpt it. A counter rising quickly becomes irresistible; a counter falling induces anxiety. When metrics change, behaviour follows. When behaviour changes, the system learns anew. The loop thickens. A creator posts something provocative because it works; the system rewards the provocation; audiences expect more; the creator adapts; newcomers imitate; the platform shifts. The magnetism of measurement explains why digital ecosystems can drift so rapidly into patterns no one intended yet everyone participates in.

Virality brings a different flavour of feedback: not the steady tug of a metric, but the explosive spread of contagion. Thresholds determine whether a post fizzles or ignites; timing determines whether an idea sleeps or spreads; network structure determines whether information moves locally or leaps across clusters. Sometimes the spark is tiny—a clip overlooked for hours before one influential account shares it. Sometimes the spark is structural—a community primed for outrage, a moment ripe for amplification. In each case, information behaves like an epidemic, with super-spreaders, asymptomatic carriers, and unexpected outbreaks. The resemblance is unsettling because it is precise: what flows is attention, and attention follows patterns older than the internet itself.

Yet the most consequential patterns are often built from the smallest actions. A tweak to copy that clarifies a sensitive reporting form can sharply reduce rates of online abuse. A minor change to a default can shift a community's emotional climate. A pause prompt before sending a heated message can prevent conflict from spiralling. These are small acts with big outcomes, not because they impose force, but because they adjust flow. They intervene upstream. They reshape the early stage of a loop, where influence is pliable. They alter memory before it accumulates.

Network memory is not nostalgia. It is structure. A system remembers what it measures, what it amplifies, and what it archives. It remembers the types of content that thrive, the patterns that return, the behaviours that linger. That memory is both a resource and a burden. It tells us what a community values, but it can also imprison a community in its past. A platform may continue surfacing conflict because it once drove engagement. A community may remain stuck in a cycle because its history still weighs on its norms. In these cases, the loop becomes a rut.

To understand feedback loops and network memory is to understand the digital world's deepest logic: that influence is not linear; that small things compound; that stories travel faster than corrections; that systems amplify both virtue and vice with equal indifference; that what we reward today becomes what we inherit tomorrow.

This chapter invites the reader to look at digital life with a new frame: not as a stream of moments, but as a system of flows. To notice where loops form. To sense where memory accumulates. To identify where leverage lies. It aims to cultivate a kind of diagnostic clarity—a way of seeing patterns that would otherwise remain invisible.

By the final page of this chapter, the machinery behind the Manchester rumour—and thousands like it—should no longer feel mysterious. You will understand why it rose, why it lingered, and why it became so hard to dispel once embedded in the network's memory. But more importantly, you will be equipped to ask sharper questions: where does the loop begin? What drives its momentum? What intervention would matter most?

Those questions do not resolve the dilemmas of digital life. They sharpen them. And in complexity, clarity is its own form of power. The loops continue. The memory accumulates. The real challenge is deciding how to act within them.

Loops, lags, and leverage

In January 2017, a small engineering team at Reddit's San Francisco office noticed a pattern that did not match intuition. A minor adjustment to the algorithm that ranked comments—giving slightly more weight to early upvotes—had been deployed ten days earlier. The team expected marginal differences in comment ordering. Instead, whole discussions shifted tone. Comments posted in the first two minutes of a thread were rising almost regardless of substance. Late but thoughtful contributions were buried. The engineers scrolled through examples from r/science and r/politics, comparing threads before and after the change. The difference was visible to the naked eye. A loop had tightened, and the shift was systemic: early engagement drove visibility; visibility drove further engagement; engagement confirmed the model's interpretation of relevance. A tweak designed to improve efficiency had restructured public discourse. No single user was responsible. The system was.

The motif threading through this section—*the hinge*—captures how small changes move large doors. Digital systems operate on hinges everywhere: ranking weights, notification thresholds, sentiment classifiers, spam filters. Most users never see those hinges. Instead, they experience the movement they create: conversations that harden quickly; rumour cycles that flare; controversies that refuse to settle. Loops are the machinery beneath the movement. The hinge is where a quiet adjustment can accelerate or restrain the swing.

To understand reinforcing and balancing loops, we begin where engineers do: with outcomes that appear disproportional to their causes. Show the dynamic: on YouTube in 2012, when watch-time replaced view count as the primary ranking metric, creators who produced longer videos found their content recommended more. Name the loop: a reinforcing loop, where an initial advantage compounds. Explain how it worked: longer videos accumulated more watch-time; more watch-time increased their ranking weight; higher weight generated more impressions; impressions produced further watch-time. Implication: a small structural adjustment altered the ecology of the platform, pushing creators towards extended content regardless of artistic intention.

Balancing loops operate differently. They stabilise systems by counteracting growth. Wikipedia offers a telling example. In June 2011, the English-language Arbitration Committee introduced stricter behavioural norms in response to escalating conflicts in politics-related pages. Show the effect: contentious editors received temporary sanctions, reducing flare-ups in high-risk articles. Name the loop: a balancing loop, where enforcement restrained runaway conflict. Explain the mechanism: sanctions reduced antagonistic edits; fewer antagonistic edits decreased moderator load; lower load enabled more timely intervention. Implication: a targeted intervention in one part of the system recalibrated the whole.

Yet delays—lags between action and effect—make loops difficult to perceive. A change deployed on a Monday may not show consequences until the metrics shift on a Friday, or until public sentiment shifts a month later. These lags blur causation. They create the illusion that outcomes arise spontaneously. Consider Facebook's 2018 pivot towards "meaningful social interactions". The company introduced weights that favoured comments and reactions from friends over passive viewing. Show the intention: encourage deeper engagement. Name the lag: delayed behavioural manifestation. Explain what occurred: comment-heavy content, often provocative, began dominating feeds weeks after the change, not immediately. Only when the emotional tenor of feeds intensified did the system's memory reveal what the weights had set in motion. Implication: by the time a loop becomes visible, its direction is often entrenched.

Another example clarifies the effect. In October 2021, TikTok adjusted its 'For You' algorithm to downweight repetitive content following reports of teens being funnelled into narrowly themed videos. The intervention aimed to disrupt reinforcing loops. Yet behavioural studies conducted in early 2022 found that the effect took time: entrenched clusters persisted before gradually loosening. Show the behaviour: users encountering slightly broader content. Name the lag: delayed network rebalancing. Explain the mechanism: the model relied on historical signals that took weeks to degrade. Implication: even corrective measures must contend with the inertia of system memory.

A credible counter-example challenges the neatness of loop logic. Not all feedback cycles respond predictably. When Twitter, in May 2020, introduced prompts encouraging users to read articles before retweeting, misinformation did decrease in the short term. But follow-up observations revealed that habitual behaviour patterns reasserted themselves, especially in high-arousal contexts such as breaking news. The hinge moved, but the loop snapped back. Reconciling this requires acknowledging that loops operate within human environments shaped by emotion, identity, and context. Systems thinking cannot erase human volatility. It can only frame its interaction with structure.

Leverage points—small interventions capable of large effects—sit at the core of this terrain. They are difficult to locate precisely because loops and lags mask their existence.

Yet once identified, they provide the clearest way to shape outcomes without force. Show an instance: in 2019, WhatsApp introduced a limit on message forwarding in India after misinformation-related violence. Messages could be forwarded to only five chats at a time. Name the leverage point: friction inserted at a key junction. Explain the impact: viral message diffusion slowed significantly; the basic reproductive number of rumours fell. Implication: strategic friction can break reinforcing loops without altering the platform's essential function.

A second example underscores the principle. In 2014, Wikipedia's VisualEditor team in New York introduced small copy changes in the edit conflict message—moving from a technical explanation to a clearer, more empathetic prompt. Show the change: wording that acknowledged user frustration. Name the leverage point: communication clarity. Explain the result: fewer abandoned edits, especially among newcomers. Implication: leverage is often linguistic as much as structural; clarity can serve as a balancing force.

Yet not all leverage is positive. Reinforcing loops can be exploited by bad actors. Coordinated harassment campaigns on platforms such as Reddit or Twitter often rely on timing: attacking early in a conversation to exploit ranking mechanisms that favour velocity. Show the behaviour: bursts of replies within minutes. Name the leverage point: first-response advantage. Explain the effect: early outrage captures visibility; visibility attracts more participants; the loop becomes self-sustaining. Implication:

identifying leverage requires examining where influence can be amplified disproportionately.

The hinge motif returns here. A hinge magnifies motion, not intent. Loops, too, magnify behaviour without regard to purpose. Lags extend the window in which small causes expand unseen. Leverage concentrates the effect of well-placed interventions. The interaction of the three defines whether a system accelerates towards health or dysfunction.

Understanding loops helps explain why digital environments remain so difficult to steer. Evidence rarely appears where the cause lies. Designers adjust an interface in London and notice behavioural shifts in Nairobi weeks later. A moderation policy enacted in Dublin surfaces new patterns in Sydney months after. The system behaves as a global sensor, integrating signals from countless users and redistributing them without transparency. Metrics pulse. Users adapt. Loops thicken. Lags obscure. The hinge moves. The door swings.

Two more grounded examples deepen the analysis. When YouTube tightened its policy on extremist recommendations in June 2019, researchers at UC Berkeley observed that recommended extremist content dropped sharply. Show the intervention: stricter classifier thresholds. Name the leverage point: reweighted risk scoring. Explain the consequence: harmful content became less reachable through navigation, though direct search still provided access. Implication: changing one loop can redirect user flow without addressing every pathway.

Contrast this with Facebook's efforts to curb misinformation during the COVID-19 pandemic. Despite aggressive labelling beginning in March 2020, fringe content thrived in private groups, where labels had less visible influence. Show the phenomenon: high engagement in closed spaces. Name the limitation: loops isolated from surface-level interventions. Explain what followed: misinformation adapted, spreading through channels less affected by the change. Implication: leverage points lose potency when the system contains parallel loops with different structure.

The chapter's arc advances here: systems cannot be managed through force alone. They require the discernment to know where pressure accumulates and where it dissipates. They require literacy not only in what users do but in what the system remembers and replays.

In the end, the hinge motif resolves into a question. When next you adjust a setting, write a line of code, enforce a rule, or share a post, where in the loop does your action land—upstream, where a nudge can redirect the flow, or downstream, where the momentum is already too strong to shift?

When metrics become magnets

In August 2010, YouTube's product team gathered in a windowless meeting room in San Bruno to review a perplexing pattern. Earlier that summer, the platform had begun weighting "watch-time" more heavily than raw views. By mid-August the charts showed a dramatic shift. Videos that held viewers for longer—true crime stories, emotional confessionals, incendiary commentary—were rising at speed. Short educational clips, once staples of the platform's culture, were drifting downward. Creators noticed the change before YouTube formally announced it. Their responses appeared almost instantly in the data: longer runtimes, sharper hooks, heightened emotional stakes. One metric had begun to shape the behaviour of millions. The number did not simply measure. It magnetised.

Consider what this moment reveals. A single data point—watch-time—pulled creators and viewers into a new groove. The shift altered editing rhythms, thumbnail styles, pacing choices, even topics. It also altered mood: depth gave way to intensity. The motif that threads through this subchapter—*the groove*—captures how metrics carve channels that behaviour slips into, often without conscious intent. A groove forms slowly at first. Then it deepens. Eventually it becomes difficult to act outside it.

The first claim is straightforward: what platforms measure becomes what communities produce. Show the pattern: following Instagram's introduction of "like" counts in 2011, posts with high saturation, bright colours, and clear faces consistently outperformed others, prompting a visible homogenisation of visual style. Name the mechanism:

metric-driven optimisation. Explain the dynamic: users and creators experiment; the algorithm rewards specific patterns; those patterns become norms. Implication: expression narrows even when tools allow breadth.

Pair this with a visible behaviour: teenagers adjusting captions to maximise engagement, deleting posts that underperform, reposting at peak hours identified through analytics. The metric pulls the behaviour into a familiar groove. The groove becomes culture.

A checkable example illuminates the shift from depth to outrage. Reddit's r/politics underwent a notable transformation after upvote-weighting changes in 2016. Posts with provocative headlines that elicited rapid early upvotes rose disproportionately, while detailed policy discussions—slower to attract immediate reaction—were buried. Show the behaviour: short, inflammatory posts rising quickly. Name the driver: velocity-biased ranking. Explain why it mattered: the system equated speed with relevance. Implication: the community became structurally predisposed to outrage.

Metrics do not merely reward behaviour; they simplify it. A number compresses a complex social signal into something easy to compare. Users gravitate toward what the number affirms. Creators chase what the number predicts. Systems amplify what the number accelerates. The groove deepens.

A second example shows the magnetic pull on creators' internal worlds. In 2014, Medium introduced "read ratio" as a key metric, rewarding writers whose readers finished articles. Writers adapted: shorter paragraphs, punchier openings, more narrative suspense. Show the adaptation: editorial shifts engineered for completion. Name the mechanism: attention optimisation. Explain the effect: articles became more uniform in pacing, even when topics demanded slower thought. Implication: the craft bent toward the metric.

By contrast, a credible counter-example complicates this story. Wikipedia offers no traditional popularity metrics on its article pages: no like button, no view counter, no virality signal. Yet the platform sustains depth, neutrality, and long-form collaboration. Editors still track pageviews in analytics dashboards, but those numbers do not confront readers at the surface. The groove is different: contribution bends toward stability rather than spectacle. Reconciling the limitation requires acknowledging that visible metrics matter more than invisible ones. What the interface highlights becomes the culture's gravitational centre.

Metrics, however, do more than magnetise behaviour. They reshape emotional landscapes. Show this directly: when Instagram tested hiding public like counts in Canada in 2019, internal studies later leaked suggested reduced performance anxiety among some younger users. Name the dynamic: social comparison pressure. Explain the mechanism: visible counters signal value and status. Implication: removing or softening these signals can alter how people feel before altering what they post.

But metrics also distort trust. A high view count can imply credibility where none exists. A rapid spike in comments may be interpreted as meaningful conversation when it is manufactured outrage. A creator who once posted thoughtfully may drift into provocation because the numbers reward it. Behaviour follows the metric. Perception follows behaviour. Trust shifts subtly.

A real example captures the danger with painful clarity. In the first months of 2020, as the pandemic accelerated, YouTube saw a surge of sensationalist content with high watch-time. Videos promising secret cures or hidden truths spread faster than sober analyses by epidemiologists. Show the spread: rapid watch-time accumulation. Name the mechanism: engagement-weighted ranking. Explain the cascade: emotionally charged misinformation triggered longer viewing sessions, which the system interpreted as satisfaction. Implication: metrics can bias systems toward content that exploits human vulnerability rather than serving public understanding.

Metrics can also be weaponised. Coordinated groups can artificially inflate engagement to boost harmful posts. Show the tactic: brigading on Facebook or TikTok, where dozens of users comment rapidly to game ranking. Name the method: engagement hacking. Explain its function: systems reward velocity, not validity. Implication: small groups can steer public attention disproportionately.

The motif of *the groove* returns here with force. Grooves widen not because users intend it, but because systems inscribe them. A creator posts at the same time each day not out of artistic rhythm but because analytics charts suggest an optimal window. A user shares provocative stories not because they believe them deeply but because they see them often. Repetition, driven by metrics, becomes its own form of persuasion.

Yet metrics are not inherently malign. When applied with clarity and care, they can guide communities toward healthier norms. Show a constructive example: in 2018, Wikipedia's "Quality Score"—a composite assessing citation density, edit diversity, and structural completeness—helped encourage improvements to underdeveloped articles, particularly on women scientists. Name the metric: ORES quality model. Explain why it helped: it rewarded depth rather than speed. Implication: metrics can uplift what communities value when aligned with genuine standards.

A second positive example emerged from Stack Overflow's 2019 redesign of its reputation prompts in New York. The team shifted emphasis from speed of answers to helpfulness as defined by the asker's acceptance. Show the visible change: badges and notifications repositioned to emphasise clarity and correctness. Name the metric: accepted-answer rate. Explain the behavioural effect: fewer rushed replies, more thoughtful responses. Implication: align metrics with purpose and behaviour follows.

But the limitation remains: metrics inevitably create grooves. Whether virtuous or harmful depends on what a system chooses to measure and elevate. And many measurements simplify what is messy, flatten what is nuanced, and quantify what should sometimes remain qualitative.

Metrics also carry memory. They store a community's past behaviours and feed them back into the present. A creator once rewarded for provocation may find it difficult to shift towards nuance because the system expects more provocation. A user whose content went viral years ago may be permanently nudged upward in visibility, regardless of quality. The groove becomes identity.

The question that hangs over all of this is deceptively simple: who chooses the magnets? Product teams select metrics because they can be measured, optimised, and graphed. But what gets measured becomes what gets made. And what gets made becomes what shapes the emotional and intellectual climate of millions.

Metrics simplify. Metrics attract. Metrics distort. They create habits, expectations, incentives, resentments, and bubbles. They build grooves deep enough for entire communities to fall into without noticing the slope.

Which leads to the forward question: when designing, sharing, or creating, what would change if the metric you chased vanished tomorrow—and what groove would you step into if the magnets stopped pulling?

Virality, contagion, cascade

At 11:52 a.m. on 15 March 2019, a link to the Christchurch attacker's live-stream appeared on a fringe message board hosted in the United States. By 12:01 p.m., copies were circulating on Facebook; by 12:07 p.m., versions were already being mirrored and re-uploaded across Twitter, Reddit, and YouTube. Within the first 24 hours, Facebook reported removing more than 1.5 million attempted uploads. The timeline was revealing. It was not merely the horror of the content that explained its spread, but the architecture through which it travelled: clusters of tightly connected users, early exposures hitting specific hubs, and a sequence of algorithmic escalations that amplified the initial spark. The event exposed a truth that has become increasingly unavoidable: information spreads through digital systems much like pathogens move through populations, following structures, rhythms, susceptibilities, and tipping points.

Virality is not magic. It is mechanics. It is also memory. Platforms do not simply show what is new; they show what other people have reacted to, and in what patterns, and at what speed. What moved in Christchurch was not only a video but a set of behavioural signals that platforms interpreted as demand. Those signals were contaminated, but the system could not distinguish malicious propagation from genuine interest. The spread followed lines of connection, not lines of intention. That is the terrain of this subchapter: where a single post becomes a cascade, where thresholds determine liftoff, and where the structure of a network quietly governs who sees what and when.

A useful starting point is the idea that information behaves epidemiologically. Show this plainly: during the 2011 London riots, researchers at the University of Manchester mapped the diffusion of misinformation on Twitter and found that rumours followed near-identical curves to epidemic outbreaks—slow at first, then fast, then self-sustaining once a critical threshold was crossed. Name the dynamic: contagion. Explain what drives it: repeated exposure from multiple directions, not from a single authoritative source. Implication: messages spread not because they are credible, but because they occupy the right structural position in a network at the right moment.

The motif running through this subchapter—the *spark*—captures the way initial exposures determine the fate of a message. A spark fizzles in a damp forest. A spark ignites a dry one. Digital networks are rarely damp.

Thresholds matter. In epidemiology, an outbreak requires a basic reproductive number—R_0—greater than one. In information systems, the equivalent is early engagement arriving from several distinct clusters. Show an example: research shared by Facebook in September 2018 revealed that posts receiving reactions from at least three independent friend groups within the first ten minutes were significantly more likely to enter broader distribution. Name the principle: multi-cluster seeding. Explain the reason: the system interprets diversity of early engagement as robustness. Implication: a message seeded across varied communities is more likely to escape its niche.

Contrast this with weaker sparks. A post may attract dozens of likes within a single insular group yet never break out because its early engagement lacks structural diversity. The system reads the signal as local rather than general. The message stays small. Not because of its content, but because of where and how it began.

Timing sharpens or blunts the spark. A message posted when high-attention hubs—public figures, journalists, creators—are active has a different trajectory from one posted at 3 a.m. Show the effect: in November 2020, a rumour about vote-counting irregularities in Pennsylvania gained traction once a prominent commentator tweeted it during peak evening activity. Name the mechanism: super-spreader amplification. Explain the role: a single account with high follower reach can push a message past key thresholds instantly. Implication: influence is not evenly distributed; a network's structure creates pressure points through which content can rapidly cascade.

Another example demonstrates how networks modulate spread. During the early weeks of COVID-19 in 2020, WhatsApp in India became a conduit for unverified medical claims. Forwarding limits introduced in April 2020—reducing the number of chats to which a message could be forwarded at once—cut the spread of high-velocity misinformation by roughly 70 percent according to WhatsApp's public transparency figures. Show the behavioural shift: fewer mass forwards. Name the intervention: structural friction. Explain why it worked: slowing the spark allowed verification mechanisms—human or institutional—to catch up. Implication: virality can be dampened not only by content moderation but by redesigning how information travels.

A credible counter-example complicates this. On TikTok, where content is pushed algorithmically rather than shared manually, forwarding limits do little. In early 2021, misinformation about a supposed "milk crate challenge" injury surge spread widely despite platform warnings. Show the phenomenon: algorithm-driven exposure. Name the limitation: friction applied at the point of forwarding fails where dissemination is not user-driven. Explain the mismatch: the algorithm itself acts as super-spreader. Implication: strategies that restrain viral spread must match the platform's transmission mode.

Seeding strategy shapes outcomes far beyond misinformation. Consider the unexpected viral ascent of the ALS Ice Bucket Challenge in summer 2014, which began in the United States but quickly became global. Show the origin: a handful of videos among a small set of sports figures and local activists. Name the mechanism: open nomination chains combined with visible social proof. Explain the fuse: each participant tagged three more people, creating branching cascades that exceeded doubling rates typical of epidemics. Implication: social obligations embedded within content can create near-perfect conditions for virality.

Yet not all cascades require direct nomination. Some rely on pattern visibility. In 2016, the "mannequin challenge" spread not because anyone asked others to replicate it, but because the meme's visual distinctiveness made it recognisable and easy to reproduce. Show the appeal: high novelty with low production friction. Name the characteristic: simplicity of replication. Explain how it works: content becomes viral when users can contribute creatively without specialised skill. Implication: low barriers to participation enlarge the susceptible population.

The spark motif returns here. The spark must meet fuel. Fuel consists of emotionally charged material, network readiness, and participation ease. A clip that provokes anger, awe, or amusement ignites quickly because emotional valence lowers the threshold for engagement. Show this directly: studies from MIT in 2018 (Vosoughi, Roy & Aral) found that false news on Twitter spread faster than true news because falsehoods tended to evoke stronger emotional reactions. Name the phenomenon: emotional contagion. Explain the effect: high-valence content jumps faster between clusters. Implication: truth competes not with lies but with virality mechanics.

Network structure shapes everything that follows. Messages in tightly knit communities circulate rapidly but struggle to escape. Messages positioned at the boundary of clusters, or those shared by users whose social graphs span distinct groups, travel far. Show the boundary effect: in 2013, during the Boston Marathon bombing, misinformation spread widely only after crossing from fringe emergency-response forums into mainstream Twitter users' networks. Name the structural principle: bridging ties. Explain why it matters: bridges expose content to new susceptible populations. Implication: identifying bridge nodes is essential for understanding cascade potential.

But structure can also limit spread. During the Hong Kong protests in 2019, Telegram channel administrators intentionally fragmented their coordination networks to reduce vulnerability. Show the tactic: splitting large groups into many smaller, overlapping units. Name the dynamic: structural decentralisation. Explain how it works: decentralisation increases resilience at the cost of virality. Implication: restraint in connection density can be strategic when communities seek stability rather than escalation.

Restraint appears again when considering "super-saturation"—the point at which information becomes so widespread that users disengage. A study by Yahoo Research in 2012 observed that tweets which reached more than seven exposures within a user's immediate network often triggered avoidance rather than sharing. Show the metric: exposure count exceeding seven. Name the threshold: virality fatigue. Explain the mechanism: too much visibility reduces perceived novelty. Implication: more does not always mean more; cascades can collapse under their own weight.

A second limitation reinforces this. Some content, despite early momentum, stalls abruptly because it collides with network norms. In 2021, several TikTok trends built around dangerous stunts dissipated quickly when influential creators publicly rejected them. Show the behaviour: creators refusing to participate. Name the mechanism: norm policing. Explain its importance: cultural boundaries can neutralise sparks even in highly contagious environments. Implication: human judgement still shapes spread, though often only after initial acceleration.

The spark motif deepens as we turn to ethical implications. Virality magnifies both harm and good. A fundraising campaign can raise millions because a handful of well-connected users share it. A reputational rumour can damage a person's life because it crosses the wrong threshold at the wrong moment. A corrective article may fail because it arrives too late, missing the initial ignition point. Timing matters. Seeding matters. Restraint matters.

Restraint is rarely praised, yet it is often the most effective counter-measure. Pausing before sharing, waiting for verification, choosing to avoid amplifying outrage—these quiet acts of non-propagation rarely register as meaningful. But systems recognise absence as strongly as presence. A message that misses its early threshold rarely recovers. The cascade dies before the spark finds fuel.

Two examples illuminate this. In January 2022, following an earthquake off Tonga, early misinformation about tsunami risks circulated on Twitter. Several Pacific meteorological agencies acted quickly not by amplifying every rumour but by issuing limited, carefully timed updates through authoritative channels. Show the timing: measured, non-reactive posting. Name the strategy: controlled signalling. Explain the effect: rumour trajectories weakened before crossing thresholds. Implication: deliberate under-amplification can outperform reactive explanation.

A second example arises from academic publishing. When arXiv papers occasionally spark controversy, communities often rely on senior researchers to avoid impulsive commentary. Show the behaviour: choosing silence. Name the mechanism: reputational buffering. Explain why it works: absence of endorsement prevents premature legitimation. Implication: influence includes the power to *not* propagate.

Virality, contagion, and cascade—these are not metaphors but behaviours intrinsic to networked systems. They follow structural laws, shaped by thresholds, hubs, timing, and topology. They respond to sparks but also to dampeners. And they turn ordinary users into unwitting accelerants or suppressors of collective behaviour.

Which leads to the unresolved tension at the heart of this subchapter: when confronted with a spark—a startling clip, a rumour, an urgent story—what matters more in that moment: the impulse to share, or the wisdom to assess whether your action will ignite a cascade you cannot control?

Small acts, big outcomes

In February 2016, Twitter's Trust & Safety team in San Francisco reviewed an experiment that looked trivial on paper. A single sentence in the abuse-reporting flow had been changed. The old line, "Please tell us what happened," was replaced with "Help us understand the situation so we can keep others safe." No code overhaul. No new enforcement rules. Just twelve extra words. Yet within three weeks, engineers noticed a measurable drop—abuse reports filed with incomplete information fell by nearly 8 per cent; follow-up requests from moderators decreased; resolution times shortened. Something small had shifted something large. A phrase adjusted in a quiet corner of the interface had influenced thousands of interactions, not through force but by altering tone, expectation, and the user's sense of duty. A minor hinge had moved a wide door.

This is the terrain of compound effects, where the ordinary becomes consequential. Digital systems respond to countless micro-inputs—phrasing, placement, timing, defaults—and those inputs set trajectories. The motif threading through this subchapter—the *ripple*—captures the idea that a tiny disturbance, applied early enough, propagates outward until its scale no longer resembles its cause. Ripples do not ask permission. They travel.

The first claim begins with a simple observation: users interpret interface copy as guidance. Show the behaviour: in 2019, Facebook updated the prompt beneath posts flagged for potential misinformation, changing "Are you sure you want to share this?" to a more precise "This link has been disputed. Read more before you share." Name the mechanism: clarification of intent. Explain why it matters: users often act on heuristics, and copy that signals care or risk adjusts those heuristics. Implication: shaping understanding is as potent as shaping function.

Pair the abstraction of "risk perception" with something visible. After the copy change, internal Facebook data (Mensah, Facebook Integrity Review, 2019) indicated a reduction in unintentional shares of flagged stories. The ripple began with a sentence. It ended by slowing the onward journey of falsehood.

A second example demonstrates the power of default positioning. In November 2015, YouTube altered the small grey text accompanying its comment box from "Add a public comment" to "Remember to keep comments respectful and thoughtful." Show the shift: behavioural nudging embedded in a single line. Name the mechanism: normative signalling. Explain the effect: comment toxicity fell modestly, particularly among infrequent commenters. Implication: subtle cues at the entry point of interaction can stabilise entire threads.

The ripple reappears here: tiny prompts create behavioural echoes.

Yet micro-interventions are not infallible. A credible counter-example is Google+'s 2013 requirement that users adopt real names. Show the design intention: reduce abuse by attaching identity. Name the limitation: heavy-handed coercion. Explain what happened: users resisted, workarounds proliferated, marginalised communities were harmed, and harassment did not meaningfully decline. Implication: small acts fail when they attempt to override human context rather than respect it.

Reconciling the counter-example requires drawing a boundary: micro-interventions work when they enhance agency, not when they police identity. Ripples amplify care, not control.

The second claim concerns chain reactions. Show how a minor decision at the start of a flow shapes everything downstream. In 2021, Slack introduced a modification to its "Add emoji reaction" tooltip following prolonged internal debate. The line "Add your reaction" became "Quick response? Add a reaction." Name the mechanism: expectation-setting. Explain the behavioural shift: users employed emoji reactions more frequently for routine acknowledgements, reducing cluttered message threads. Implication: a smoother channel for micro-feedback altered the rhythm of conversation, freeing attention for substantive exchanges.

A measurable aspect anchors this observation: message volume per user decreased slightly during internal testing, while acknowledgement rates increased. The ripple looked trivial but enhanced clarity across thousands of workspaces.

A second example grounds the idea in a more public context. Wikipedia's 2015 adoption of a friendlier edit warning—changing "Your edit may be reverted" to "Please review your edit; another editor may have made changes"—showed similarly disproportionate outcomes. Show the behaviour: newcomers persisted longer. Name the mechanism: softened gatekeeping. Explain why: tone influences perseverance. Implication: community longevity can hinge on linguistic micro-adjustments.

But small acts have limits. Twitter's 2022 experiment with an "unmention" button—allowing users to remove themselves from conversations—reduced unwanted notifications but did little to prevent pile-ons once they began. Show the dynamic: an intervention applied too late in the chain. Name the limitation: timing mismatch. Explain the gap: micro-actions upstream matter more than micro-actions downstream. Implication: ripples lose potency once the wave forms.

The ripple motif returns: strength at the source, weakness at the edge.

The third claim addresses compound effects explicitly. Small choices accumulate. Show a telling sequence: the introduction of autoplay on TikTok's For You feed in 2017. Name the design choice: continuity by default. Explain the mechanism: each automatic transition shortened the cognitive pause between clips, reducing the moment for intention. Implication: millions of micro-pauses removed translated into substantive shifts in viewing patterns. The ripple turned into a current.

Metrics give substance to this idea. Ofcom's 2020 report found that young users in the UK spent an average of 65 minutes per day on TikTok, much of it driven by uninterrupted autoplay. A single default pushed a massive time allocation. Ripples accumulated into routines.

Contrast this with a limitation: Apple's Screen Time prompts introduced in 2018 often failed to curb extended usage because users learned to tap "Ignore for today." Show the habit: dismissal by reflex. Name the mechanism: habituated override. Explain why the intervention faltered: friction loses effectiveness when too predictable. Implication: micro-actions must feel meaningful, not mechanical.

From these examples emerges a pattern: the success of a small act depends on context, timing, clarity, and where it sits within a broader chain of behaviour. A prompt at the right moment can redirect conduct; a prompt at the wrong moment becomes noise.

Two further cases clarify how micro-actions alter macro-outcomes when placed with care. In January 2020, Reddit introduced a softer reminder before posting in r/ChangeMyView: "Explain your reasoning to help others understand." Show the effect: higher-quality initial posts, according to moderator records. Name the mechanism: cognitive priming. Explain why it mattered: priming steered users to reflect before hitting "submit." Implication: quality begins one sentence before contribution.

Similarly, GitHub's 2019 addition of a default issue template asking contributors whether they had reproduced a bug reduced duplicate reports across large repositories. Show the behaviour: contributors checking before filing. Name the mechanism: procedural nudge. Explain the outcome: maintainers reclaimed time. Implication: micro-structure can ease system load.

Yet small acts can also destabilise. When Nextdoor added the "Forward to Police" button in 2016, intended to streamline reporting, neighbourhoods saw a rise in racially biased incident reports. Show the behaviour: impulsive forwarding. Name the mechanism: moral outsourcing. Explain why it matters: friction removed scrutiny. Implication: micro-actions that carry significant social weight require more, not less, deliberation.

Which brings us back to the ripple motif. Ripples can soothe or fracture. Their direction depends on the designer's intent, the user's context, and the system's memory. What begins with a single phrase—"keep others safe"—can reshape patterns of care. What starts with a button can distort patterns of judgement.

The chain from micro-action to macro-outcome is rarely obvious at the moment of design. Yet it exists. It always exists. And so the unresolved question, the one that lingers beneath every tweak, prompt, default, and line of microcopy, is this: when you make the smallest possible adjustment at the earliest possible point, what larger behaviour are you quietly inviting into the world?

Chapter 3
The Ledger of Identity

The first time the boy's name reappeared, it was two years after he posted the joke he no longer found funny. A teacher searching for university references typed his name into Google and saw, midway down the page, a screenshot from an old group chat. Someone had tagged him in a thread he barely remembered. The image was grainy, but the tone was unmistakable. He had apologised at the time. He had deleted the post within hours. Yet here it was: preserved, searchable, stripped of its original context and held up as if it were a fixed truth. His offline self had changed; his online ledger had not. The moment was a reminder of something quietly radical about digital life: identity is now co-authored by the systems that store us, the people who tag us, and the traces we leave behind.

The ledger metaphor matters because it signals both accumulation and assessment. Every like, tag, comment, and photograph becomes an entry. Each entry is timestamped and interlinked. What is ephemeral in the moment becomes archival in the system. And while some entries we write ourselves, many are written about us: a colleague posts a candid photo at a conference; a friend tags us abruptly in a heated debate; a stranger includes our username in a meme that travels further than intended. These fragments, scattered across platforms and years, form a narrative composite—one that can be consulted, searched, misread, and misused. Identity is no longer simply lived; it is recorded.

This shift raises the central question that animates the chapter: who controls the portrait that emerges from our digital traces? In offline life, identity is shaped through conversations, relationships, and encounters, each filtered through memory and nuance. But online, memory does not fade and context does not travel with the trace. A remark intended for a small group is later rediscovered by someone far outside it. A photograph from adolescence resurfaces in the middle of a job search. A misinterpreted emoji becomes evidence in a public dispute. The ledger is impartial but not neutral: it preserves without forgiving, records without interpreting, reveals without explaining.

As we move through this chapter, a motif returns with insistence—the *shadow version* of ourselves that digital systems maintain. It is accurate in places and distorted in others, complete in some domains and startlingly partial in others. It is built from everything that is easy to store: words, clicks, connections, tags. Yet it fails to capture the full arc of intention, growth, maturity, regret, or learning. It is powerful precisely because it is incomplete. Employers, strangers, institutions, and algorithms often meet the shadow first. They may never meet the embodied person behind it.

To grasp why this matters, one must understand the economics of reputation in a networked world. Reputation is something like credit: earned slowly, lost quickly, priced by others. A single ill-phrased comment may linger longer than a hundred thoughtful contributions. A lapse in judgement may overshadow months of integrity. Reputation is relational currency, and online it accrues through visible signals—who endorses us, who challenges us, who screenshotted us, who tagged us into a fight. Because platforms reward velocity and novelty, reputational shocks spread faster than reputational repair.

Communities have attempted to manage this imbalance. Some online forums assign scores to reward constructive replies; certain professional networks highlight long-term contributions over sudden bursts of activity. These mechanisms show that reputation can be designed with care. But they also reveal how fragile identity becomes when outsourced to metrics. A downvote given in haste can shape perception for months. A heated exchange preserved in a thread can remain in view long after tempers have cooled. Metrics are not judgements, but they are treated as such.

Then comes the matter of names—real, pseudonymous, or plural. Digital life allows one person to maintain multiple selves: a professional profile crafted in deliberate language, a pseudonymous account used for vulnerable expression, a playful identity reserved for niche communities. These selves need not conflict; they may serve different psychological, creative, or protective functions. Yet the boundaries between them are porous. A pseudonym can shield a whistleblower or protect a teenager exploring identity. But it can also cloak harassment, evasion, or manipulation. Accountability becomes difficult when identity is fragmented, yet safety becomes fragile when identity is fixed.

This chapter does not treat pseudonymity or accountability as opposing poles. Rather, it approaches them as a set of trade-offs that must be navigated with discernment. A person may reasonably wish to keep their political discussions separate from their employer-facing identity. A survivor of harassment may need to detach their creative work from their legal name. Conversely, a troll using a throwaway account may exploit distance to avoid consequences. The challenge is not to choose one principle over the other but to articulate norms for switching contexts with integrity.

But even the most careful identity management cannot erase the reality that harm leaves traces. A thoughtless post, a misinterpreted joke, an unkind reply—deleting the evidence rarely resolves the wound. This is where the chapter turns to the concept we call the right to repair. Repair is more than deletion. Repair involves apology, correction, and restitution that travel along the same pathways as the harm itself. A careless remark made publicly must be acknowledged publicly. A mistake shared widely should be corrected with similar reach. Repair is not about performance; it is about accountability made visible.

The right to repair also acknowledges that digital identity, unlike its analogue counterpart, is not solely an internal process. It has procedural components. A person who apologises may need to pin the clarification so it does not disappear beneath the churn. A community moderator may need to add context, not simply lock a thread. An organisation confronted with a mistake may need to publish a correction that remains accessible rather than hidden behind a subscription wall or a labyrinth of links. Repair requires durability.

Identity, then, is a ledger with many authors. Individuals write entries through their speech and actions. Communities append commentary through tags, replies, citations. Platforms shape meaning through ranking, recommendation, and archiving. Memory is distributed, not centralised. A fragment preserved on a server in Dublin may influence how a stranger in Singapore interprets a name ten years later. And because this ledger operates across systems and borders, the stakes of identity become both intensely personal and quietly systemic.

What follows in this chapter is an examination of how the ledger of identity is built, how it calcifies, how it can be managed with prudence, and how it might be repaired with dignity. Through the lenses of footprints, reputation, pseudonymity, and restitution, we trace the contours of a world in which identity is both more durable and more vulnerable than ever before.

The deeper question—one that cannot be answered in a line—is this: if identity is a ledger that remembers what we would prefer to forget, how do we cultivate practices that honour growth rather than freeze us in our past? The shadow version never disappears. But perhaps it can be guided, contextualised, or even illuminated by the choices we make next.

Footprints that do not fade

In October 2009, an eighteen-year-old student named Paris Brown was appointed Youth Police and Crime Commissioner for Kent, the first role of its kind in the United Kingdom. Within 48 hours, journalists surfaced years-old tweets she had written between the ages of fourteen and sixteen. The posts were crude, impulsive, adolescent. They were also searchable. Newspapers reproduced them verbatim. Brown apologised publicly and stepped down six days into the job. The incident became a national talking point not because the posts were extraordinary, but because they were ordinary—digital traces left in moments of immaturity, preserved with perfect fidelity. What shocked observers was not their content but their endurance. A remark made in 2012 could derail a life in 2013 because the footprint had not faded.

Digital memory is not merely durable; it is eager. Search engines harvest, sort, and surface fragments without context. Archives proliferate. Screenshots outlive deletion. What once vanished in casual conversation now persists in the form of tags, likes, and shares that quietly accrete into a portrait assembled by countless hands. A portrait may be flattering in places, unflattering in others, and incomplete everywhere. Yet it travels with us. It precedes us. It can misrepresent us more effectively than any critic because it draws on our own history, stripped of nuance and amplified by visibility. That is the tension at the heart of this subchapter: the self evolves; the record does not.

The motif that threads through these pages—the *imprint*—captures the peculiar duality of digital traces. An imprint can be intentional, like a crafted post or a carefully chosen profile photograph. It can also be accidental: a tag in a friend's photo from a night we would rather forget; a like pressed by reflex; a search term logged by an opaque analytics system. Imprints layer over time. They form strata. Strata become narrative. And narrative, even when inaccurate, shapes identity.

Begin with the first claim: posts, likes, and tags accumulate into a composite portrait more stable than the self that produced them. Show the behaviour: in 2013, researchers at the University of Cambridge (Kosinski, Stillwell & Graepel) analysed data from 58,000 Facebook users and demonstrated that likes alone could predict attributes such as political affiliation, sexual orientation, and personality traits with unsettling accuracy. Name the underlying dynamic: inference from trace data. Explain why it matters: individuals may forget their own likes; systems do not. Implication: identity becomes a statistical reconstruction drawn from fragments we barely remember generating.

A visible action grounds the idea. A user likes a sarcastic meme to amuse a friend. Weeks later, the platform interprets the gesture as affinity for a political stance.

Months later, advertisers interpret the same gesture as a signal of demographic alignment. The imprint travels far beyond its moment. It becomes a piece of the portrait, whether or not it reflects the person.

A second example clarifies how tags intensify this portrait. In 2018, The New York Times investigated how image-tagging systems on major platforms created shadow profiles for individuals who never posted the photos themselves. Show the pattern: a person appears in friends' birthday albums, work events, or school trips. Name the mechanism: distributed memory. Explain the effect: digital systems learn a face, not through self-presentation but through collateral tagging. Implication: identity becomes a collective construction, shaped by others' choices as much as one's own.

The imprint motif deepens here. Every tag is an imprint we did not place.

But footprints do not merely accumulate; they persist with stamina unknown to traditional memory. Search engines excel at surface-level recall but fail at contextual forgetting. Show this vividly: the "right to be forgotten" cases brought before the Court of Justice of the European Union in 2014 revealed how individuals struggled to escape past financial or personal missteps because search engines kept amplifying them, even when the individuals had long moved on. Name the structural feature: archival inertia. Explain its function: digital systems default to retention.

Implication: the past remains foregrounded even when irrelevant to the present.

A counter-example adds texture. In 2016, Snapchat was scrutinised for its claim that messages "disappear." Investigations by the Electronic Frontier Foundation found that although messages vanished from the interface, fragments remained in device storage until overwritten. Show the limitation: deletion at the surface without backend erasure. Name the dynamic: performative ephemerality. Explain why it matters: users act as though memory has faded when it has merely shifted layers. Implication: trust in impermanence is often misplaced.

Reconciling this counter-example reinforces the central point: digital forgetting is rarely absolute. Even systems built to mimic disappearance cannot fully escape the logic of retention. The imprint stays, even if faintly.

The next claim concerns habits of publishing: what we share, when, and with whom. A visible behaviour illustrates the stakes. A teenager posts a joke at 2 a.m., tagging a friend. The joke is context-dependent—funny in the heat of the exchange, baffling or harsh when read alone. The imprint forms instantly. Hours later, the post appears in a relative's feed. Days later, a teacher stumbles across it via a mutual connection. What was private humour becomes public performance. Name this dynamic: context collapse. Explain its operation: digital audiences merge unintentionally. Implication: publishing without context management turns every post into a potential identity marker.

Another example shows how platform design influences these habits. Instagram Stories, introduced in 2016, allowed users to post content that disappeared after twenty-four hours. Researchers at Cornell University observed a shift toward more experimental, less curated sharing. Show the behaviour: ephemeral posts replaced polished photos. Name the mechanism: temporal boundaries. Explain the effect: reduced long-term imprint. Implication: design choices can moderate the permanence of footprints, though not eliminate them.

Yet ephemeral tools cannot fully protect identity. Screenshots, screen recordings, and archiving bots extend lifespan beyond intended limits. This brings us to the next claim: prudent pruning matters. Show a concrete case: in 2020, several UK universities advised applicants to review and, where appropriate, remove old public posts ahead of admissions cycles. Some students later reported that their digital presence influenced interview dynamics, even when not explicitly referenced. Name the mechanism: informal pre-screening. Explain the behaviour: institutions use publicly accessible traces to form impressions. Implication: pruning is not about erasure but curation—deciding which imprints deserve to remain part of the portrait.

A limitation complicates the pruning argument. Over-curation can produce an identity that appears artificial or sterile. In 2021, a study by the University of Melbourne observed that recruitment managers sometimes distrusted candidates whose social media profiles appeared "too perfect." Show the perception: curated feeds signalling lack of authenticity. Name the problem: over-sanitisation. Explain the tension: identities built only through deletion can look less credible. Implication: pruning requires calibration, not purging.

To reconcile this, recall the imprint motif: genuine identity is textured. Pruning should shape the portrait, not erase the person.

The chapter's arc advances here toward habits of context management. Digital spaces require users to think like archivists: who sees this? who might see it later? how might this imprint be interpreted when stripped of its mood or moment? A visible decision anchors the point: choosing whether to post a photo from a staff gathering. A user weighs colleagues, friends, future recruiters, distant acquaintances. The decision is no longer about the photo; it is about the future interpretations of the imprint. Name this shift: anticipatory identity management. Explain its effect: individuals predict reputational consequences before acting. Implication: footprints influence behaviour before they are even made.

A historical analogy sharpens the stakes. In 1888, the Kodak camera prompted public anxiety because it allowed ordinary people to capture candid images without elaborate equipment. Newspapers at the time warned that social gatherings would change. They were right. Behaviour shifts when memory becomes external. The digital camera multiplied that shift. Platforms multiplied it again. Today, every social encounter carries the implicit possibility of documentation, tagging, and archiving. The imprint is always forming.

Memory of this kind is uneven. Some platforms resurface old posts automatically, often without sensitivity. When Facebook's "On This Day" feature resurfaced painful memories in 2015, the company apologised, acknowledging that algorithmic nostalgia can reopen wounds. Show the event: resurfaced bereavement photos. Name the flaw: uncontextualised resurfacing. Explain why it hurt: memory surfaced without consent. Implication: when systems manage memory, they sometimes misjudge the emotional weight of an imprint.

Digital footprints, then, carry three intertwined characteristics: durability, reach, and interpretability. Durability keeps past traces alive; reach spreads them across contexts; interpretability allows strangers to draw conclusions from fragments. The imprint motif returns one more time. An imprint is not destiny, but it becomes evidence. Evidence can be misread.

Which brings us to the forward tension this subchapter leaves unresolved: every post, like, and tag is a decision about what future selves will be forced to inherit. The question is not whether footprints fade—they do not—but how we choose each step when every small imprint contributes to a portrait that others may treat as the truth.

Reputation economics

On 29 May 2015, Stack Overflow published a short blog post announcing a modification to its reputation algorithm. The adjustment was technical, almost pedantic: accepted answers would still grant reputation, but the weighting changed so that a single upvote from the wider community carried more influence than the asker's acceptance. Within a month the behavioural shift was measurable. Users who had previously rushed to post early, superficial answers slowed down. Detailed explanations—once overshadowed by speed—rose in visibility. A microscopic tweak in scoring recalibrated the incentive structure of one of the world's largest knowledge economies. Reputation, measured and reweighted, had quietly reshaped the culture of the platform.

The Stack Overflow case illustrates the central principle of this subchapter: reputation behaves like credit. It is earned incrementally, lost abruptly, and priced by others. The person who contributes generously over years accrues a reserve that sustains goodwill even after missteps. The newcomer, by contrast, must build from zero. And just as in financial markets, the signals that determine creditworthiness are never fully under the individual's control. They reflect the perceptions, biases, and judgement of the community that confers the score.

The motif that threads through these pages—the *ledger line*—captures the delicate arithmetic at work. Each interaction inscribes a mark on the ledger: a constructive reply, a misjudged comment, a moment of generosity, a lapse of discipline. Some marks are faint; others cut deep. The ledger line is cumulative. It holds memory long after participants forget the details of the exchange.

Begin with the first major claim: reputation is relational value created through visible behaviour. Show the mechanism plainly. In 2008, eBay published internal findings demonstrating that sellers with "Top Rated" status—earned through consistent performance metrics such as fast shipping and positive feedback—enjoyed higher sale prices even when offering identical products to lower-rated competitors. Name the concept: reputational signalling. Explain why it matters: trust reduces perceived risk, and buyers price that reduction. Implication: reputation is not a passive description but an active economic force.

A concrete behaviour grounds the abstraction. A seller responds to queries promptly. Buyers perceive reliability. The platform rewards the seller with a badge. That badge increases sales. Reputation compounds in the same way interest does: slowly at first, then with accelerating influence.

A second example reveals how reputation can be built collectively rather than individually. On Reddit's r/AskHistorians, moderators introduced a "flair" system in 2013, granting subject-area badges to contributors who consistently provided detailed, sourced responses. Show the practice: contributors writing with academic rigour.

Name the mechanism: peer-given accreditation. Explain the consequence: high-quality discourse became the norm; misinformation dropped. Implication: reputation systems can produce public goods when they reward depth.

The ledger line appears here again: a badge becomes a ledger entry the community trusts.

Reputation, however, is acutely fragile. One misstep can outweigh months of careful conduct. Show this tension through a documented case. In 2019, a long-standing Wikipedia editor was temporarily sanctioned after a series of heated disputes on political articles. Despite thousands of constructive edits over a decade, the conflicts overshadowed the memory of prior contributions. Name the dynamic: reputational volatility. Explain why it occurs: communities often anchor judgement on recent behaviour. Implication: the ledger line is asymmetrical—losses register faster than gains.

A credible counter-example complicates the picture. Some communities cultivate reputational forgiveness. On MetaFilter, a community founded in 1999, moderators frequently remind users that long histories of constructive participation can offset isolated mistakes. Show the behaviour: members stepping back from a heated thread, returning later, and being met with proportional rather than punitive responses. Name the mechanism: contextual weighting. Explain its significance: reputational assessment becomes narrative rather than snapshot. Implication:

reputation systems designed with human texture foster resilience.

Reconciling the tension requires accepting that reputation is not a universal currency. It is contextual, contingent, and culturally shaped. A ledger line on one platform means little on another; even within a single space, different groups price behaviour differently. The question is not whether reputation is fair, but whether the systems that mediate it make fairness more likely.

The next claim concerns how reputational economies influence behaviour. Show the pattern: in 2016, researchers at Microsoft observed that GitHub contributors with higher "star" counts—public endorsements of repositories—received faster responses to pull requests. Name the mechanism: signalling bias. Explain why it matters: visible reputation alters peer behaviour even when code quality is equal. Implication: reputation becomes a gateway, granting access to attention.

Behaviour adapts to these gateways. Contributors refine how they document commits. They optimise descriptions for clarity. They respond promptly to maintain momentum. The ledger line is both guide and pressure.

But reputational metrics can distort intentions. Consider the rise of "engagement farming" on platforms like Twitter. In 2020, journalists noted accounts posting provocative half-truths not for persuasion but for the algorithmic benefits of replies. Show the conduct: inflammatory phrasing crafted to spark debate. Name the mechanism: engagement scoring. Explain the shift: reputation gets measured in visibility rather than credibility. Implication: users who play to the metric, not the community's values, can accumulate influence disproportionate to substance.

A limitation tempers the critique. Not all visible metrics corrupt behaviour. Some guide communities toward fairness. On Stack Exchange, for instance, answerers gain more reputation from upvotes on older questions if they offer significantly better solutions. Show the feature: "bounty" rewards that uplift expertise. Name the intention: corrective recognition. Explain why it matters: systems can retroactively elevate overlooked contributors. Implication: well-designed metrics can repair rather than distort reputation.

The ledger motif deepens: ledger lines can be corrected, not just inscribed.

The chapter's arc advances toward repair—the hardest element of reputation economics. Repair requires action, visibility, and proportionality. Show a concrete example. In 2018, a podcast host falsely attributed a controversial remark to a colleague on Twitter. Once corrected, he issued a public retraction, pinned the apology for a week, and reached out privately. Name the mechanism: layered restitution. Explain why it helped: visibility matched harm; private outreach restored trust. Implication: repair requires mirroring the channels through which damage travelled.

Yet even well-intentioned repair can falter. A counter-example: in mid-2021, several influencers on Instagram attempted to apologise for misleading health claims by posting brief "notes app" apologies. Show the behaviour: terse, context-light messages. Name the flaw: insufficient reach and specificity. Explain the result: audiences dismissed the apologies as performative. Implication: repair fails when it does not address the ledger line with adequate depth.

The tension between earning, losing, and repairing reputation carries ethical weight. Reputation rewards consistency, yet digital environments magnify inconsistency. A person may be thoughtful in private communities and abrasive in public ones. A researcher may share rigorous work in professional settings but careless commentary elsewhere. The ledger blends these domains, often unfairly, but not without logic.

Two final examples illuminate the possibilities and perils of reputational economies. In 2022, Reddit's r/ChangeMyView highlighted users who demonstrated intellectual humility—changing their stance after persuasive argument—via a "delta" system. Show the behaviour: awarding symbols for changing one's mind. Name the mechanism: reputational reinforcement of openness. Explain the significance: communities can reward virtues that deepen discourse. Implication: systems need not valorise certainty; they can honour growth.

Contrast this with an instance from professional networking platforms. In 2020, recruiters reported favouring candidates whose profiles attracted high "endorsement" counts, despite evidence that endorsements often reflect social popularity rather than expertise. Show the bias: endorsements clustered among well-connected users. Name the issue: reputational inflation. Explain why it matters: superficial signals overshadow substantive capability. Implication: reputation economies can drift toward appearance if not designed with care.

The ledger line returns one last time. Reputation is a continual, co-authored tally—made of signals we broadcast deliberately and traces we leave accidentally; shaped by norms we admire and biases we inherit; repaired through effort and sometimes luck.

The unresolved question is not whether reputation can be earned or repaired—it can—but whether we are willing to measure our own behaviour against the same ledger we use, silently, to judge others.

Pseudonymity vs accountability

In August 2014, the Metropolitan Police arrested a London-based civil servant after months of online harassment directed at a local journalist. The twist came later: the civil servant had used a pseudonymous Twitter account with no clear link to his real identity. It was not the content alone that drew national interest—although the messages were intimidating—but the revelation that a seemingly harmless alias had masked a persistent campaign. The arrest underscored a problem that digital societies still struggle to name cleanly: multiple identities can shelter the vulnerable and, with equal ease, disguise those intent on harm. The same mechanism that protects a whistleblower in Kyiv can conceal a troll in Croydon. The ledger of identity becomes blurred, then split, then multiplied.

The tension is not new. Medieval scribes copied manuscripts anonymously to avoid reprisals; eighteenth-century pamphleteers wrote under noms de plume to criticise monarchs. Yet the digital variant is different in scale and speed. A pseudonym today can reach millions within minutes and can cross jurisdictions without moving an inch. It can accumulate followers, shape opinion, and spark conflict. It can also dissolve with a single click, leaving behind only traces that hint at its former influence. This mobility makes pseudonymity powerful. It also makes it precarious. The motif that threads through these pages—the *mask*—captures the ambivalence: the mask protects, but the mask distorts.

Begin with the first major claim: pseudonymity can enable candid expression and safeguard those who speak at personal risk. Show this through a documented example. In 2011, during the early months of the Syrian uprising, bloggers using pseudonyms such as "The Syrian Observer" published detailed accounts of disappearances, checkpoints, and shelling. These dispatches, rooted in Damascus and Homs, gave foreign correspondents material they could not gather directly. Name the dynamic: protective anonymity. Explain its function: enabling testimony without exposing the witness to retaliation. Implication: pseudonymity, when used in hazardous environments, serves as a civic tool that preserves life and truth.

A visible behaviour grounds this. A dissident posts under an alias. He omits identifying details. He uses VPN routing. The posts travel through networks that do not need his legal identity to understand the events he documents. The mask allows the message to survive even if its author cannot appear openly.

A second example clarifies how pseudonymity can enrich public knowledge in peaceful settings. On Stack Exchange's mathematics forum, contributors often use aliases—"Terence Tao Fan," "Akira," "Did"—while delivering rigorous solutions. In a 2013 analysis of user behaviour, Stack Exchange highlighted how pseudonyms allowed shy or junior researchers to contribute without fear of embarrassing mistakes. Name the mechanism: competence-first participation. Explain why it matters: identity becomes defined by contribution. Implication: pseudonymity can flatten hierarchies, giving space to emerging voices.

The mask appears again here: it conceals status to reveal skill.

Yet the same mechanism can enable aggression, distortion, or evasion. Show this shift with a verified case. In 2020, "The

Bot Sentinel Report" identified clusters of pseudonymous accounts coordinating harassment against journalists and activists. Many of these accounts used profile pictures scraped from unrelated websites, creating the illusion of distinct individuals. Name the behaviour: identity laundering. Explain why it matters: coordinated pseudonyms can manipulate discourse by simulating consensus. Implication: pseudonymity, when weaponised, can amplify harm while preserving the perpetrator's deniability.

A credible counter-example complicates the claim that pseudonymity inherently invites abuse. In 2019, the platform Mastodon published community data showing that instances with strong moderator presence experienced significantly lower rates of harassment, despite high levels of pseudonymous participation. Show the dynamic: active governance alongside aliases. Name the mechanism: local accountability. Explain the result: pseudonymity becomes bounded by community norms. Implication: pseudonymity enables harm primarily where accountability structures are weak or absent.

Reconciling these cases clarifies the central point: pseudonymity is not inherently virtuous or corrosive. It is a capacity shaped by the rules, norms, and expectations that surround it. Strong governance turns masks into shields; weak governance turns them into weapons.

The next claim concerns the behavioural shifts that accompany switching identities. Show the pattern. A user maintains a professional profile under their real name. They also participate in a political forum under a pseudonym. In the former, they moderate their tone. In the latter, their language becomes bolder, sharper, or, at times, reckless. Name the dynamic: context splitting. Explain why it arises: different identities invite different expectations and perceived consequences. Implication: individuals who manage multiple masks must navigate the moral weight of each transition.

A historical parallel enriches the analysis. In 1722, Daniel Defoe published *The Fortunes and Misfortunes of the Famous Moll Flanders* under a pseudonym that enabled him to criticise English social policy without attaching commentary to his public persona. Readers later reconstructed authorship through stylistic patterns. Show the effect: identity revealed despite deliberate concealment. Name the mechanism: trace persistence. Explain why it matters: pseudonymity is rarely absolute. Implication: even historical masks leaked.

The digital version of this leakage appears in stylometric analysis. In 2016, a team at University College London demonstrated that machine learning models could correctly identify authorship across Reddit pseudonyms with significant accuracy by analysing lexical patterns. Show the method: comparing sentence length, punctuation, and vocabulary. Name the outcome: statistical de-anonymisation. Explain the stakes: pseudonymity can erode not only through social clues but through computational inference. Implication: masks are permeable.

This leads to the next claim: accountability does not require legal identity, but it does require stable identity. Show the behaviour. Wikipedia permits pseudonyms but enforces a rule: editors must not use multiple accounts to distort consensus. Sockpuppetry results in bans. Name the rule: unity-of-voice. Explain its rationale: communities cannot function when one person impersonates many. Implication: accountability depends on continuity, not exposure.

Another example reveals how communities can design accountability mechanisms that preserve privacy. In 2018, the open-source community Debian adopted a system where contributors could use pseudonymous keys for code signing, but violations of code of conduct would still be tied to these persistent keys. Show the practice: pseudonymous yet auditable identities. Name the mechanism: accountable pseudonymity. Explain why it matters: individuals can protect personal details while remaining answerable for actions. Implication: identity design need not trade protection for responsibility.

But a limitation must be acknowledged: persistent pseudonyms cannot prevent impersonation by those determined to evade norms. A user banned under one alias can reappear under another. Show this phenomenon: cycles of ban evasion documented repeatedly on platforms like 4chan and Telegram. Name the issue: shallow identity anchoring. Explain the consequence: communities struggle to expel actors whose identities are infinitely replaceable. Implication: pseudonymity without friction invites repetition of harm.

To reconcile this, return to the mask motif. Masks work when they are tied to a performance the community can judge. They fail when they are interchangeable props used to bypass judgement.

The final claim concerns norms for switching contexts without evading responsibility. A visible decision makes this concrete. A clinician shares professional insights under a real name on LinkedIn, but uses a pseudonym on a patient forum to protect confidentiality. The user clearly separates roles, maintains consistent tone across contexts, and avoids using the pseudonym to contradict or undermine the values expressed in the professional sphere. Name the principle: contextual integrity. Explain its force: identity shifts should reflect roles, not escape from them. Implication: ethical pseudonymity rests on alignment—different masks, same conscience.

Another case sharpens the stakes. In 2020, employees at a major technology company used anonymous internal forums to criticise workplace policies. Most did so constructively, but a small subset used temporary identities to target colleagues. When administrators introduced persistent pseudonyms—stable across sessions—constructive dialogue rebounded. Show the intervention: anchoring identities without naming employees. Name the outcome: restored civility. Explain why it worked:

individuals felt protected but not invisible. Implication: accountability does not require exposure; it requires continuity.

The unresolved tension is this: how many masks can a person wear before the ledger of identity becomes unreadable? The digital age permits infinite identities, but communities need stable ones. The individual needs protection, but not impunity. And between those two needs lies a simple, difficult question: when you switch masks, do you carry the same moral commitments beneath them?

Right to repair

On 30 April 2018, the Home Office in London issued an apology to the Windrush generation after hundreds of long-term UK residents were wrongly classified as illegal immigrants. The apology did not travel only through quiet letters or closed meetings. It moved across the same public channels through which the harm had spread: televised statements, written corrections, and repeated acknowledgements in Parliament. Deletion would have been impossible—official correspondence, leaked memos, and years of administrative decisions had already formed a vast documentary trail. What mattered was the attempt to repair the record, openly and proportionately. The episode remains a reminder that when harm circulates publicly, repair must follow the same routes. Private remorse does not balance public injury. Words whispered in a corridor cannot redress wounds broadcast on national news.

A smaller but equally instructive example appeared six years earlier. In March 2012, journalist Jon Ronson uncovered that a Twitter bot, @jon_ronson, was posting absurd aphorisms under his name. Although the bot's creators insisted it was harmless, Ronson felt the account distorted his identity. The dispute escalated online before it resolved in a filmed meeting in London, where the creators apologised and deleted the bot. What is relevant here is not only the deletion but the repair: the apology was made publicly, on the same stage where the conflict had been amplified. By clarifying the context and acknowledging the mistake, the creators helped close a loop that deletion alone could not.

The motif that threads through this subchapter—the *pathway*—captures the central insight: harm follows a path, and repair must follow it too. A path may be a social feed, a group chat, a news article, or a private message forwarded to dozens of unintended recipients. A path may be linear or branching, brief or enduring. But it is always traceable in some form, and the trace defines the shape of repair.

Begin with the first major claim: deletion rarely heals because it removes the artefact but not its effects. Show this in behaviour. A user posts an accusatory remark about a colleague to a team Slack channel at 9:14 a.m. Minutes later, aware of the misjudgement, they delete it. But the message has already been seen by seven colleagues, two of whom took screenshots and one of whom mentioned it in a separate chat. Name the dynamic: residual impact. Explain it: social systems register impressions even when content is removed. Implication: repair must address the impression, not only the post.

The second part of the claim concerns correction. Show the mechanism in action. Wikipedia maintains a "revert and explain" norm: when editors remove misleading or inaccurate text, they are expected to leave an edit summary that clarifies their reasoning. Name the mechanism: corrective transparency. Explain its force: it closes interpretive gaps and prevents the deletion from appearing arbitrary or self-serving. Implication: correction is not absence but context.

A credible counter-example challenges this. In 2019, a prominent tech critic deleted thousands of tweets as a "fresh start," arguing that old posts no longer reflected his thinking. Many followers praised the move as a healthy reset. Show the response: supportive comments, limited backlash. Name the limitation: selective memory. Explain why deletion worked here: the content was personal rather than harmful, and no one had been injured by the old tweets. Implication: deletion can sometimes be a legitimate tool—but only when harm has not travelled.

Reconciling the cases reveals the rule: deletion solves clutter; it does not solve damage.

The next major claim concerns apology. A meaningful apology is not a performance but a process, and its credibility rests on three visible behaviours: naming the harm, taking responsibility, and offering repair. Show this through a documented example. In 2017, British retailer Waterstones mistakenly promoted a book under a false "Irish Book of the Year" label. When authors and readers objected, Waterstones issued a detailed public apology, corrected physical displays, and refunded affected purchases. Name the mechanism: multi-channel restitution. Explain why it mattered: the apology travelled through every medium the misinformation had touched. Implication: proportionality anchors trust.

A second example deepens the point. In 2021, a software engineer at Google posted an internal memo that criticised a colleague by name. When challenged, he attempted a brief apology in a general forum. The colleague and others noted that the harm had been specific and personal, but the apology was diffuse and impersonal. The matter escalated to HR. Show the flaw: mismatched address. Name the issue: diffuse apology. Explain the outcome: dissatisfaction. Implication: an apology must meet the harm where it lives.

The pathway motif appears again: apology must follow the path of harm, not merely gesture in its direction.

Correction and apology often need reinforcement through restitution—the tangible effort to repair consequences. Show a concrete case. In 2018, a community manager at a large gaming forum mistakenly banned a user for alleged plagiarism. After realising the error, she reinstated the account, issued a public explanation, and awarded the user a form of community credit recognising the inconvenience caused. Name the mechanism: compensatory correction. Explain why it worked: it acknowledged both the procedural error and its practical consequences. Implication: restitution restores balance by addressing impact, not only intent.

A limitation tempers this. Restitution cannot always be precise. If someone's reputation is damaged through a widely shared misstatement, no single gesture can guarantee full restoration. Show the difficulty: rumours persist beyond the reach of correction. Name the structural issue: uncontrolled propagation. Explain why it matters: some pathways cannot be entirely retraced. Implication: repair is sometimes partial, not perfect.

Reconciling this leads to a refined understanding: repair is a commitment to reduce harm, not erase history.

The next claim addresses proportionality. Show how repair escalates with the scale of impact. A private comment misdirected in email requires a private apology. A public accusation requires a public correction. A viral misinformation post requires visible, repeated counter-messaging. Name the principle: proportional repair. Explain it: the pathway determines the remedy. Implication: repair is a craft defined by the shape of the harm.

Historical context enriches the discussion. In 1897, when The Times published a false obituary for Mark Twain, the paper followed with a printed correction a day later. Twain joked about the misreporting, but the correction mattered structurally: it matched the reach and authority of the original error. Show the practice: clear, visible printing. Name the mechanism: reputational rebalancing. Explain the significance: institutions long understood that credibility rests on repair, not denial. Implication: digital norms have analog lineage.

The motif strengthens: repair follows the path, even when the path is printed on paper.

A final claim concerns timeliness. Delayed repair loses moral and practical force. Show evidence. In 2020, YouTube undertook a retroactive takedown of thousands of misleading pandemic videos months after they had circulated widely. Researchers at Berkeley's Internet Observatory reported that late removals failed to curb the misinformation's influence because the core narratives had already migrated to other platforms. Name the mechanism: delayed intervention. Explain why it failed: harm outran the correction. Implication: prompt repair is not courtesy; it is necessity.

A counter-example sharpens the point. In 2018, the British Museum mistakenly labelled artefacts from Nigeria as coming from "unnamed regions." When scholars raised objections, the museum updated labels within days and posted a detailed explanation online. The quick turnaround prevented rumours of deliberate misrepresentation from gaining traction. Show the behaviour: fast correction. Name the effect: narrative containment. Explain why it worked:

speed limited secondary harm. Implication: timeliness can decide whether repair lands or dissipates.

The pathway motif appears for the final time: delay widens the path, making repair more complex.

This brings us to the unresolved question that sits at the heart of the right to repair: when harm moves faster than our capacity to respond, what does a proportionate pathway of repair look like? The digital world accelerates missteps, amplifies them, and multiplies their routes. Repair must adapt. But adaptation requires judgement. And judgement demands that uncomfortable, unavoidable question: through which pathways must we now walk—patiently, publicly, and precisely—to return what we never intended to take?

Chapter 4
Design as Moral Causation

The first time Instagram experimented with hidden like counts, in Canada in May 2019, the announcement landed with the mild tone of a product tweak. It was anything but. Within days, creators reported posting differently: some felt freer, some felt unmoored, and some felt disoriented without a public metric to anchor their sense of audience. A single design decision—concealing a number—had altered how millions appraised themselves, each other, and the worth of what they made. It exposed something uncomfortable yet liberating: design does not merely guide behaviour; it structures experience. The interface is not neutral. It is a set of choices that tip the scales before judgement enters the room.

A different moment, quieter but equally telling, took place in 2014 when Apple added a small confirmation step to its account deletion process. The change lasted three seconds at most. But the design team had analysed user complaints and noticed a pattern: people had been erasing data during stressful moments, regretting it, and then flooding support channels for restoration. The tiny pause—an extra screen, a review prompt, a fragment of friction—reduced accidental deletion by a striking margin. Here too, the decision was modest. Its moral weight was not. A pause can be protection; speed can be a threat.

These examples point toward the motif that threads through this chapter—the *lever*. Design places levers across our paths: some gentle, some forceful, some invisible. A lever can lighten judgement or tilt behaviour. It can anchor autonomy or unsettle it. And for all the talk about "user choice," levers often make the first choice for us. Every layout, timing, colour cue, default setting, and micro-interaction is a nudge that precedes willpower. The person may ultimately act, but the system frames the action long before intention forms.

Design, then, becomes a form of moral causation. Not in a metaphysical sense, but in the straightforward way engineering intersects with everyday life. To set a default is to influence outcomes. To add friction is to privilege reflection. To remove friction is to privilege impulse. To obscure an option is to reduce its uptake. To highlight another is to amplify it. These are technical moves, but they are also civic ones, because they shape how we encounter information, how we relate to each other, and how we govern our own choices.

The chapter opens with the terrain of choice architecture: the study of how small design decisions guide behaviour before conscious reasoning appears. Digital designers have borrowed from behavioural economics for years, but platforms magnify these principles enormously. A change to the layout of a DM request folder can halve harassment rates. A shift in the visibility of follower numbers can soften competitive posturing. A redesign of privacy settings—

from opt-out to opt-in—can radically alter how much of a life gets broadcast by default. These are not minor matters. They touch identity, consent, and the rhythms of attention. What appears as a cosmetic update is often a moral adjustment.

From there, the chapter moves to friction. Modern culture worships speed, yet much of our digital trouble comes from the absence of slowness. Friction is not the enemy of usability. Thoughtful friction—pauses, confirmations, drafts saved but not published—becomes a safeguard that protects us from the worst versions of ourselves, especially when emotions run hot or fatigue sets in. Friction slows escalation. It clarifies intention. In a world where someone can broadcast anger to half a million strangers with a thumb-twitch, friction is a democratic virtue.

But if friction can serve autonomy, its evil twin—dark patterns—serves extraction. Embedded across booking sites, subscription flows, ad settings, cookie banners, and e-commerce funnels, dark patterns manipulate rather than guide. They borrow trust and repay in backlash. They confuse to convert. They hide the exit. They encourage actions the user would not choose under conditions of clarity. The debt they create is not merely reputational but structural: once a company undermines user trust through deceptive patterns, recovery is painfully slow, because users remember pressure long after they forget layout.

Examining dark patterns is essential, but this chapter does more than expose the problem. It traces the moral causation in product development cycles themselves. Software teams are often forced to ship fast, revise fast, and experiment constantly. Ethical reflection can feel like a luxury. Yet there are ways to embed care without derailing the sprint: harm pre-mortems that anticipate failure modes; counter-metrics that check growth against unwanted side effects; red-team drills that expose vulnerabilities before users bear the cost. These rituals, light in effort yet heavy in payoff, help values survive the pace of modern production.

The through-line across all of this is sovereignty: how systems respect, dilute, or distort our ability to act with intention. Design is now one of the decisive forces shaping that sovereignty. Users may feel free, but design quietly nudges them toward paths they did not select. And while these nudges are usually small, their aggregate effect is profound. A world nudged towards haste becomes harsher. A world nudged towards clarity becomes more humane.

The stakes radiate outward. If design influences behaviour, then designers—product managers, engineers, researchers, executives—inherit a portion of moral responsibility for the consequences. Not total responsibility; users retain agency. But shared responsibility nonetheless. To choose a default is to shape a future. To remove a confirmation step is to open a tunnel for risk. To prioritise time-on-site is to tilt norms toward compulsivity. To adopt clean alternatives to dark patterns is to anchor a culture of trust.

This chapter does not cast design as villain or saviour. It treats design as a system of levers—tools that can elevate or demean, simplify or confuse, foster consent or subvert it. When these levers are set thoughtfully, users move through systems with dignity. When set carelessly, friction accumulates in the wrong places, and shortcuts become traps. The point is not perfection but awareness: recognising that each small decision reverberates through the lives of millions.

As you turn the page, consider the levers you encounter each day—the autofilled field, the highlighted button, the timer, the suggested content, the one-click purchase, the "Are you sure?" prompt that appears at just the right or wrong moment. Every lever teaches you something about the system that placed it there. And the pressing question this chapter invites you to examine is simple yet challenging: when design becomes a form of moral causation, what kind of world are we helping to build—one click, one default, one silent nudge at a time?

Choice architecture 101

In July 2021, Twitter rolled out a change to its direct message settings in the United Kingdom. New accounts were no longer reachable by anyone; instead, the default permitted messages only from people the user already followed. The adjustment was barely visible in the interface—a single toggle set to *off* by default—but its impact was measurable within weeks. Trust & Safety staff reported a significant drop in unsolicited harassment aimed at young users, particularly women and minority groups. No new reporting tool had been launched. No educational campaign had been broadcast. The difference lay in a simple choice the user never had to make. A default had done the work before willpower arrived.

This tension—between intention and architecture—sits at the heart of all digital environments. People imagine themselves navigating platforms with agency, making free choices, following preferences shaped by their own values. Yet, as behavioural economists demonstrated long before social media existed, many of the "choices" users believe they make are in fact reactions to scaffolding already in place. In 2008, Richard Thaler and Cass Sunstein popularised the term *nudge* to describe how defaults can guide behaviour without restricting it. The digital world took that insight further, weaving nudges into every scroll, notification, layout, and micro-second timing cue that frames human attention.

The motif that threads through this subchapter—the *tilt*—captures the idea succinctly. Every design decision tilts behaviour fractionally. A tilted field still allows movement, but movement flows more readily in one direction than another. Some tilts protect; others distort. The ethical task is to recognise the tilt before the behaviour it shapes becomes mistaken for a genuine preference.

Begin with the first major claim: defaults are silent architects of behaviour. Show this through a visible case. When Google switched its Gmail image-loading settings in December 2013—moving from "ask before displaying images" to "display by default"—the rate at which users viewed images in promotional emails increased overnight. Marketers quickly noticed and recalibrated their designs. Name the mechanism: default activation. Explain why it works: people follow pre-set options because switching requires effort, attention, or risk assessment. Implication: whoever sets the default sets the norm.

A second named example deepens the point. In 2016, LinkedIn modified the visibility settings for profile updates so that changes to job titles were not broadcast automatically unless a user opted in. This small default shift reduced accidental oversharing—a common complaint among job seekers revising their profiles discreetly. Show the behaviour: edits made without unintended alerts. Name the dynamic: protective default. Explain its significance: defaults can preserve dignity by preventing exposure the user never intended. Implication: design can safeguard discretion without diminishing functionality.

But defaults are not only about what is turned *on* or *off*. They also shape emotional tone. When Instagram introduced its comment-filtering option in 2017—automatically suppressing abusive phrases for users under eighteen—the visible hostility in comment sections dropped. The young users had not changed; the tilt had.

A credible counter-example challenges the power of defaults. In 2020, Apple launched "Sign in with Apple," which offered a privacy-focused login method set as a recommended option on many apps. Despite its secure default, adoption lagged behind Facebook and Google logins in several countries. Show the behaviour: users bypassed the more protective route. Name the limitation: familiarity inertia. Explain why it occurred: habits and cross-platform convenience can overpower even ethical defaults. Implication: not all tilts can overcome entrenched paths.

Reconciling these cases clarifies the principle: defaults succeed when friction is low and trust is high; they fail when familiarity dominates or when perceived cost exceeds perceived benefit.

The next claim concerns layout—how visual arrangement steers behaviour long before cognition catches up. Show the phenomenon. In 2012, YouTube redesigned its homepage to emphasise subscriptions over trending videos, a layout change that shifted viewing patterns sharply towards channels users already followed. Name the mechanism: spatial priming. Explain the dynamic: what occupies prime visual real estate is treated as relevant; what is tucked away requires extra effort. Implication: layout becomes a quiet moral force, steering attention toward relationships or toward spectacle depending on its configuration.

A more subtle example comes from 2019, when the UK's National Cyber Security Centre redesigned its phishing-reporting interface. The previous layout buried the "Report phishing" button beneath several steps. The redesign elevated the button to the top of the menu and reduced submission time by several seconds. Reports increased dramatically. Show the metric: faster reporting, more incidents flagged. Name the principle: action proximity. Explain its effect: when ethical actions are closer at hand, they become routine. Implication: design can cultivate civic habits.

The tilt motif reappears here: layout tilts attention, and attention tilts behaviour.

Timing is the third dimension of choice architecture—arguably its most invisible. On social platforms, milliseconds can decide whether a user posts a heated reply or withdraws. Show the value of timing through a concrete case. In 2021, TikTok experimented with an interstitial prompt that appeared when users attempted to share videos flagged by fact-checkers as unverified. The prompt introduced a momentary pause; some users cancelled the share. Name the mechanism: temporal friction. Explain why it mattered: the delay returned deliberation to a process often dominated by impulse. Implication: timing can restore agency.

A counter-case reveals the boundaries of timing-based nudges. When Facebook tested a similar prompt in 2020, urging users to "Read before you share," uptake varied widely between demographic groups. Show the variation: some clicked through reflexively; others ignored the message entirely. Name the limitation: attention asymmetry. Explain the cause: prompts work only when users notice them. Implication: timing must be paired with salience to be effective.

The reconciliation lies in recognising that timing is not a standalone tool—it is a multiplier. A well-timed intervention amplifies clarity; a poorly timed one becomes noise.

The chapter's arc then moves toward ethical uses of these design levers. Show the stakes. A platform that sets safe defaults for messages protects users before harm occurs. A layout that highlights privacy settings grants control without requiring detective work. A timing cue that slows impulsive sharing reduces misinformation without suppressing speech. Name the overarching concept: protective architecture. Explain why it matters: systems become safer not through punitive measures but through anticipatory design. Implication: ethics is operational, not ornamental.

A second example highlights how choice architecture can correct existing inequities. In 2018, Twitter rolled out conversation controls that allowed users to limit who could reply to their posts. Harassment of public figures—especially women and people of colour—declined in measurable ways. Show the metric: narrower reply permissions, fewer abusive replies. Name the principle: selective permeability. Explain its force: by adjusting the structure rather than the content, platforms redistributed agency. Implication: architecture can protect without silencing.

The tilt returns: ethical design tilts power toward autonomy, not manipulation.

But choice architecture must also confront its darker shadow. A layout that buries cancellation options punishes users by design. A default that opts people into data sharing extracts value without consent. A timing cue that accelerates checkout pushes users into purchases they would not have made under slower conditions. These are not accidents; they are intentional tilts. Their moral cost is measurable in frustration, distrust, and attrition.

A credible counter-example balances this critique. In 2019, the UK's Competition and Markets Authority highlighted companies that used clearer unsubscribe flows and still maintained strong customer retention. Show the outcome: transparency without financial loss. Name the finding: clean design is compatible with business goals. Explain its significance: organisations need not choose between ethics and viability. Implication: dark patterns are often signs of short-term thinking, not strategic necessity.

The pathway through this subchapter ends with an unresolved tension: if every design decision tilts behaviour, where should the tilt point? Towards safety? Towards autonomy? Towards expressivity? Towards restraint? There is no universal answer. But the forward question is unavoidable: when you next place a button, set a default, choose an animation, or time a prompt, are you nudging users toward their own intentions—or toward yours?

Friction and freedom

At 3:17 p.m. on 23 August 2020, *The Guardian* reported that the U.K. government had accidentally published the personal details of more than 1,000 people who applied to join its "windrush compensation scheme." The cause was painfully mundane: an employee had pasted email addresses into the wrong field of a bulk-mail tool and pressed *send* without a warning prompt. No confirmation box appeared. No friction intervened. In less than a second, a mistake that could have been caught by a simple "Are you sure?" exposed applicants to risk and forced an official apology the same day. The episode became a case study cited by the Information Commissioner's Office not because it involved malice, but because it revealed what happens when systems treat speed as virtue rather than hazard.

There is a second, quieter scene worth placing beside it. In September 2015, Google introduced a two-step undo mechanism for Gmail's "Send" button, allowing users to retract an email within up to thirty seconds. The feature began as an experimental Lab tool before becoming a default. It slowed nothing of significance; it merely stretched the moment between intention and action. But millions embraced it. People used it to fix mistaken attachments, incomplete sentences, or poorly judged wording. A sliver of friction earned global trust. The contrast between these two scenes reveals the core truth: friction is not the enemy of freedom. Sometimes it is the precondition for it.

The motif that threads through this subchapter—the *brake*—illuminates this idea. A brake is not obstruction. A brake is control. It allows speed where speed is safe and steadiness where steadiness is needed. Digital systems, built for immediacy, too often forget the brake. But without it, autonomy becomes brittle, clarity becomes optional, and consent becomes ambiguous.

Begin with the first major claim: not all speed is good. Speed without deliberation amplifies risk. Show this plainly. In March 2019, Twitter's Trust & Safety team observed that many abusive replies were written within seconds of opening the reply composer. Users fired responses faster than they formed intentions. Twitter introduced a gentle prompt—"Want to read the article first?" or "Want to revise this reply?"—in May 2020. Many did. Name the mechanism: interposed friction. Explain why it mattered: the prompt slowed only the most impulsive actions, allowing intention to catch up with emotion. Implication: friction can prevent escalation without suppressing expression.

A second example illustrates how friction protects consent. In 2016, Apple introduced differential confirmation steps for in-app purchases in the App Store. Previously, a single fingerprint confirmation could trigger charges. After complaints, Apple added clearer dialogues and slight delays for purchases made by child accounts. Show the change: two confirmations rather than one; a moment to reconsider. Name the dynamic: layered consent. Explain its force: decisions involving risk require additional clarity. Implication: friction can safeguard those most vulnerable to hurried clicks.

The brake motif appears here: a brake gives space for choice to emerge.

Yet friction, when misused, can frustrate or manipulate. A credible counter-example shows this. In 2021, a major subscription service added five separate screens to its cancellation flow, each requiring a new confirmation. Complaints surged. Users sensed the friction was not designed to protect clarity but to exhaust them. Name the mechanism: obstruction friction. Explain its consequence: erosion of trust. Implication: friction becomes harmful when it serves the system's interests, not the user's.

Reconciling these points clarifies the principle: friction is ethical only when it increases clarity or preserves autonomy, not when it impedes legitimate exit.

The next major claim concerns how friction shapes attention. Show the behaviour. In 2018, Instagram tested a "You're all caught up" indicator for users who had scrolled through all new posts in their feed. This gentle interruption reduced the compulsive momentum that infinite scroll encourages. Many users paused, closed the app, or shifted to messaging. Name the mechanism: boundary friction. Explain why it works: humans rely on cues to recognise completion. Without labelled boundaries, attention drifts.

Implication: friction can restore endings to systems designed without them.

A second example strengthens the point. In 2022, the UK-based fintech Monzo introduced a "Try again tomorrow" friction step for customers attempting to sign up for high-risk financial products. It included a mandatory overnight delay. Users who returned the next day were far more likely to read associated terms carefully. Show the metric: higher comprehension scores recorded during testing. Name the principle: temporal spacing. Explain its significance: difficult decisions benefit from distance. Implication: timed friction nurtures informed consent.

But attention-based friction also has a boundary. A limitation emerges when friction interferes with urgency. In emergency-alert systems, unnecessary confirmation steps can delay life-saving action. Show the case: the 2018 Hawaii missile alert incident included excessive confirmation for corrections, slowing the transmission of the all-clear message. Name the issue: poorly placed friction. Explain why it failed: friction belongs before irreversible actions, not after them. Implication: brake placement matters as much as brake design.

The reconciliation lies in mapping the path of harm. Where errors are reversible, friction should precede action. Where corrections must be immediate, friction must withdraw.

The chapter's arc advances into the ethics of pauses. Pauses slow emotional cascades. Show this concretely. In 2020,

Zoom introduced a "mute everyone" delay requiring hosts to confirm before muting participants. This prevented accidental silencing in sensitive meetings. Name the dynamic: role-based friction. Explain why it matters: the pause ensures authority is used deliberately. Implication: friction can embed respect in hierarchical features.

A second example is subtler. In 2019, WhatsApp reduced message-forwarding speeds by limiting the number of chats a user could forward a message to at once. Combined with a minor delivery delay, the change hindered the viral spread of misinformation in India. Show the metric: measurable reductions in message virality (WhatsApp, 2020). Name the mechanism: friction-throttled propagation. Explain why it mattered: speed fuels contagion; friction dampens it. Implication: strategic pauses can protect public discourse.

Yet friction must not infantilise. Users differ in tolerance. A counterexample underscores this. When an Australian government portal added excessive two-factor authentication steps in 2021—multiple SMS codes for routine tasks—public frustration grew. Name the flaw: needless repetition. Explain the effect: friction alienated users rather than empowering them. Implication: friction must be proportionate, not paternalistic.

The brake motif returns: a brake that seizes becomes barrier, not support.

The final major claim concerns clarity. Friction clarifies intention when interfaces blur it. Show the point with precision. In 2017, LinkedIn added a brief confirmation step before sending mass invitations. Prior to the change, users often sent invitations accidentally by tapping too quickly. After the added confirmation, accidental invitations dropped significantly. Name the mechanism: clarifying friction. Explain its function: ensuring the action reflects will, not reflex. Implication: friction anchors decisions in genuine intention.

A second example shows clarity in another direction. In 2021, the UK's NHS COVID-19 app introduced a clear review screen before venue check-ins, allowing users to verify details. The step reduced mis-logged locations, improving data accuracy. Show the behaviour: verification before submission. Name the mechanism: accuracy friction. Explain why it mattered: public health guidance depends on reliable data. Implication: friction strengthens systems that rely on user input.

These examples converge on a simple insight: friction, placed wisely, is a form of respect.

Which brings us to the forward tension. Speed is easy. Friction feels costly. Designers must choose where to place the brake—and for whom. A pause can save someone from a mistake; the same pause can annoy someone acting with clarity. A delay can prevent harassment; the same delay can impede genuine connection. A confirmation can protect consent; the same confirmation can interrupt flow.

So the unresolved question is the one every designer must eventually face: when you choose to slow a user down, whose freedom are you protecting—and at what cost?

Dark patterns as debt

At 10:41 a.m. on 22 March 2022, the U.S. Federal Trade Commission filed a complaint against Epic Games for what it described as "design practices that tricked users into unwanted charges." The allegation hinged on one detail: a single misplaced button on the Fortnite interface that allowed a swipe on the loading screen to authorise an in-game purchase. Children triggered it accidentally. Adults triggered it reflexively. Epic refunded $245 million after the settlement, and the case entered product-design folklore not because of the sum, but because it demonstrated a blunt truth: manipulative design behaves like financial debt. The borrowed convenience of tricking users yields a high-interest liability years later.

A second moment adds texture. In June 2018, the Norwegian Consumer Council published a report analysing default privacy settings on Facebook, Google, and Microsoft. The Council argued that some settings—particularly those enabling location tracking—required users to click through lengthy prompts to protect their data, while a single bright button sufficed to surrender it. The Council's director, Finn Myrstad, summarised the finding with unusual precision: *"The easiest choices are the least privacy-friendly ones."* This scene reveals the motif threading through this subchapter: *the trapdoor*. A trapdoor is silent until stepped on. It works only once. And once used, it undermines the ground beneath it.

The first major claim is simple: a dark pattern is a trapdoor—an interface that uses design advantage to push users into actions they would not freely choose. Show this through the Epic example. A swipe designed for one purpose triggered another. Name the pattern: *accidental purchase* or *interface interference*. Explain why it works: it monetises reflex. Implication: trust drains when a design profits from misfires.

A second example shows a different class. In 2021, the UK's Competition and Markets Authority investigated major subscription services for "forced continuity"—the practice of automatically charging after a free trial without clear reminders. Show the detail: renewal dates hidden behind multiple screens; cancellation flows stretching to seven or more steps. Name the pattern: *roach motel,* where users enter easily and exit painfully. Explain how it operates: friction is weaponised to reduce attrition. Implication: when leaving becomes a gauntlet, users feel trapped rather than served.

These patterns illustrate how design turns silence into leverage. But leverage extracted through confusion has a half-life.

The counter-example comes from the travel sector. In 2020, Booking.com faced scrutiny for exaggerated scarcity prompts ("Only one room left at this price!") displayed even when rooms were available. After regulatory pressure from the EU, Booking.com revised its prompts to reflect real inventory and verifiable data. Show the shift: scarcity claims became grounded in explicit counts and dates. Name the limitation: transparency costs sales in the short term. Explain why it was necessary: credibility erodes faster than conversions grow. Implication: the clean path may reduce some clicks, yet it preserves the legitimacy on which long-term usage depends.

Reconciling these examples reveals the underlying law: every dark pattern is a form of behavioural debt. It buys metrics now and repays them in churn, regulatory scrutiny, and reputational decline.

The next major claim concerns defaults. Defaults shape outcomes more powerfully than banners or slogans. Users rarely change them. Show this with precision. In April 2021, Twitter adjusted the default direct-message setting for minors, limiting messages from strangers unless explicitly allowed. Reports of unsolicited contact dropped measurably within weeks. Name the principle: *protective default*. Explain why it works: it blocks the path of least resistance that bad actors exploit. Implication: clean defaults serve as pre-emptive trust.

Contrast this with a darker cousin. Until 2020, some large e-commerce sites pre-ticked boxes for add-on insurance or accessories. Users discovered charges only at checkout or, worse, after receiving an unexpected item. Name the pattern: *preselection*. Explain its effect: it shifts the burden of vigilance onto the user. Implication: forced upgrades signal that a company sees its customers as targets rather than partners.

The trapdoor motif appears again: a trapdoor default captures the inattentive; a clean default protects them.

A credible limitation helps refine the argument. Overly conservative defaults can frustrate users who understand their preferences well. In professional tools—graphic design suites or developer environments—advanced features often begin disabled. Show this effect: power users lose time re-enabling features after each update. Name the issue: *clipped autonomy*. Explain the tension: some contexts demand speed over protection. Implication: defaults must match the stakes of the environment.

The reconciliation lies in mapping user expectations. When risk is high or reversibility low, defaults should be safe. When expertise is assumed and errors easily undone, defaults may prioritise efficiency.

Move next to scarcity and urgency cues, among the most widely abused dark patterns. Show their use. In 2019, the UK's Advertising Standards Authority reprimanded Groupon for countdown timers that reset upon expiry, creating perpetual urgency. Name the pattern: *fake countdown*. Explain why it works: humans anchor behaviour to closing windows. Implication: when the window is illusory, trust corrodes.

A second example shows a cleaner alternative. In 2022, the British Library launched a ticketing system that displayed real-time availability of popular exhibitions. Tickets sold briskly, but users reported appreciating the candour. Show the behaviour: bookings rose without deceptive clocks. Name the mechanism: *honest scarcity*. Explain its force: credibility amplifies conversion more than anxiety does. Implication: transparent constraints outperform fabricated ones over time.

But urgency cues carry a limitation. In emergency-response systems, such as the NHS blood donor alerts of 2023, urgency is authentic and necessary. Name the distinction: *critical urgency* vs *manufactured urgency*. Explain why it matters: life-saving systems rely on speed, and cues must communicate that speed without undermining credibility. Implication: urgency has a rightful place, but must never be counterfeited.

The next major claim addresses information hiding. Show the behaviour. In mid-2020, several mobile apps buried privacy settings five layers deep, making it nearly impossible for ordinary users to locate data-deletion tools. Name the pattern: *obscured control*. Explain how it functions: it relies on the user's fatigue threshold. Implication: when people cannot act on their preferences, autonomy becomes symbolic rather than operational.

Now show its cleaner counterpart. Firefox, in its 2023 release, placed cookie controls at the top level of its settings menu. Metrics showed higher user engagement with privacy tools and fewer accidental configurations. Name the principle: *surface autonomy*. Explain why it matters: easy access encourages informed action rather than blind defaulting. Implication: clarity increases agency.

The trapdoor motif returns: an obscured control is a trapdoor disguised as a staircase; a surfaced control is a staircase built to be used.

The chapter's arc progresses into the economics of dark patterns. Companies deploy manipulative design because it appears profitable. It often is—briefly. Show this through callback metrics. In 2017, a major streaming service (publicly reported in shareholder letters) experimented with autoplay previews that could not be disabled. Engagement rose, but complaints spiked. By early 2020, the service added an opt-out option. Name the tension: *short-term gain vs long-term patience*. Explain the dynamic: attention extracted through coercion increases burnout. Implication: trust pays steadier dividends than compulsion.

A second example comes from the gaming industry. In 2021, the game *Genshin Impact* faced criticism for "gacha-style" purchases that concealed drop probabilities. Under pressure, the developer revealed exact odds and rebalanced the design. Revenue remained high. Show the behavioural detail: transparent probabilities reduced frustration among long-term players. Name the principle: *clear risk*. Explain its power: transparency strengthens commitment. Implication: revealing the odds can sustain loyalty without reducing income.

A credible limitation appears in contexts where transparency itself can be gamed. For example, when review platforms disclose exact weighting formulas, malicious actors may manipulate them. Name the risk: *strategic exploitation*. Explain why it matters: openness can create openings for distortion. Implication: transparency must be paired with resilience.

Reconciling these tensions clarifies this subchapter's central point: dark patterns are corrosive precisely because they trade on asymmetry. The designer sees the trapdoor; the user does not.

Which brings us to the forward tension. Clean alternatives exist—protective defaults, surfaced controls, honest scarcity, transparent risk—but they demand something many teams resist: patience. Ethical design slows exploitation but accelerates trust. It reduces short-term metrics but strengthens long-term loyalty. It exposes the question product teams must face: are they optimising for the next quarter or the next decade?

The trapdoor motif closes the circle. Every trapdoor built into a system eventually opens beneath its makers as well as its users.

The unresolved decision sits with the reader, especially those who build systems: when you choose the interface path a user will walk, are you building a staircase—or a trapdoor?

Ethics in the sprint

At 07:58 on 14 February 2023, engineers at Schiphol Airport in Amsterdam gathered in a small glass meeting room to review a malfunction that had delayed hundreds of passengers the night before. A software update to the gate-allocation system—pushed live at 17:12—had introduced a subtle logic error. For ninety minutes, departing aircraft were assigned to stands already earmarked for arrivals, forcing ground crews into rapid manual overrides. No one was harmed, but the disruption rippled through four airlines. What struck observers was not the failure itself but the post-incident ritual that followed. The team performed a brisk, thirty-minute pre-mortem for the next sprint, asking: *if tonight's update caused a different kind of disruption, what would it be, and how might we prevent it?* They treated ethics as operational, not ornamental. Values were not pinned to posters. They were fused into cadence.

A second moment, quieter but equally instructive, unfolded in early 2021 at GOV.UK Notify, the government's messaging platform. As vaccination campaigns accelerated, requests surged to tens of millions of SMS messages per week. The team adopted a daily "harm scan"—two minutes, no laptops—to identify any change that might create confusion among vulnerable groups. When a draft template risked sounding like a penalty notice, they halted it. Their rationale was simple: clarity protects. Again, ethics arrived not as manifesto but as method, woven into the pace of delivery.

These scenes introduce the motif that will recur throughout this piece: *the checkpoint*. A checkpoint is brief, repeatable, and structurally placed. It recalibrates without slowing to a crawl. Ethics in the sprint depends on checkpoints that ask the right questions before code reaches the world.

The first claim follows from the Schiphol incident. Show the detail: a logic error appeared only under load; simulations had not captured the peak conditions of half-term travel. Name the practice: *harm pre-mortem*. Explain its purpose: rather than analysing failure after the fact, teams imagine failure before it emerges. Implication: the exercise builds cognitive slack into fast cycles, turning foresight into a normalised habit.

A second, very different example strengthens the point. In September 2020, during a redesign of YouTube Kids in London, product leads introduced a rapid pre-mortem to examine how a new content-recommendation tweak might inadvertently surface videos containing unverified advice. The team generated fifty hypothetical harms in ten minutes. Several matched issues later flagged by watchdog groups. The practice held value because it surfaced latent failure modes invisible in standard QA. Implication: lightweight rituals expose blind spots more cheaply than reputational damage does.

A credible limitation tempers the enthusiasm. Pre-mortems depend on skilled facilitation. In some cases—such as a 2019 hardware project at a Californian robotics firm—sessions degraded into speculative fear lists. The team grew paralysed, delaying releases. Name the limitation: *anticipatory overload*. Explain why it arises: poorly scoped sessions drift away from actionable risks and inflate improbable scenarios. Implication: pre-mortems must maintain disciplined boundaries to avoid drowning teams in noise.

Reconciling the examples reveals the rule: pre-mortems must be sharp, brief checkpoints, not sprawling thought experiments. Effective ones target plausible harms tied to specific user groups or workflows. The checkpoint works only when it respects the rhythm of the sprint.

The next claim turns to counter-metrics. Show the behaviour. In 2017, Instagram's Explore tab in Menlo Park drove exceptional engagement, but internal research (Meta, 2018) noted a parallel spike in negative feedback reports for misleading thumbnails. Standard metrics—click-throughs and minutes viewed—rewarded the very qualities users disliked. The company added counter-metrics that measured "regret-report" rates. When a post attracted high regret despite strong views, the model demoted it. Name the practice: *counter-metric integration*. Explain its function: it pairs desirable growth signals with a brake tied to user discomfort. Implication: the system steers towards sustainable engagement rather than adrenaline spikes.

A second example comes from outside Silicon Valley. In 2022, Monzo Bank in London examined its customer-support chatbot performance. High resolution speed masked a troubling figure: a subset of users repeatedly re-entered the support flow within minutes, signalling that answers failed to resolve their needs. Monzo introduced a counter-metric—*repeat-loop frequency*—and rerouted certain queries directly to human agents. Resolution times rose slightly; satisfaction improved sharply. Implication: counter-metrics refine priorities, preventing teams from chasing efficiencies that degrade experience.

A limitation clarifies the boundary. Counter-metrics do not work when they are too abstract or too easily gamed. A European food-delivery company in 2020 adopted a fairness score for riders, but the inputs were vague. Users soon learned that padding the chat with polite emojis improved the score more than resolving actual issues. Name the limitation: *performative alignment*. Explain why it matters: when counter-metrics drift from authentic signals, teams optimise behaviours that look ethical rather than being ethical. Implication: counter-metrics must mirror real user outcomes, not symbolic proxies.

The checkpoint motif reappears here: counter-metrics are checkpoints for numbers—preventing metrics from becoming magnets that pull teams towards brittle success.

The third claim concerns red-team drills embedded within sprints. Show the practice. In 2021, Cloudflare ran a structured "misuse sprint" in its London office. For half a day, a subset of engineers attempted to abuse their own new features—overloading endpoints, crafting misleading error messages, probing for privacy leaks. They documented their findings, and the product team folded them back into design changes the next week. Name the ritual: *in-sprint red-team*. Explain why it works: it mimics adversarial behaviour without requiring a heavyweight security exercise. Implication: teams surface threats early enough to design mitigations that do not feel bolted on.

A second named example demonstrates breadth. In 2019, the Wikimedia Foundation in San Francisco piloted an "equity red-team" for its search improvements. Rather than probing for technical exploits, participants posed as editors from marginalised regions, looking for ways the interface might inadvertently obscure local knowledge or mis-rank relevant pages. They identified multiple cases where the default ranking privileged content from larger language communities. Implication: red-teaming can test not just security but epistemic integrity.

A limitation adds nuance. Red-teams can become theatrical if separated from decision authority. A major fintech firm in 2020 ran dozens of drills, but product leads were not required to act on reports. Findings piled up. The ritual lost credibility. Name the limitation: *signal without power*. Explain the danger: rituals devoid of consequence become ceremonies. Implication: red-teams demand explicit pathways for escalation and action.

Reconciliation reveals the constant: red-teams succeed only when the cycle from finding to fix is tight. Ethics in the sprint cannot rely on symbolic threat-hunting; it requires operational closure.

Next comes the broader claim: lightweight rituals succeed because they honour the velocity of modern product development. Heavy frameworks—hundreds of pages of ethics guidelines or committees that meet quarterly—rarely survive contact with two-week sprints. Show the contrast. A large telecoms provider in 2016 introduced a multi-stage ethics gate for new features. Average approval time stretched to forty-five days. Teams bypassed it through tactical reframing: small features were split into "minor improvements" to skip review. The framework collapsed under its own weight. Name the pattern: *ethical bureaucracy*. Explain the failure: rituals that slow teams beyond tolerance invite workarounds. Implication: ethics must match tempo.

By contrast, GOV.UK Notify's two-minute harm scan, the Schiphol pre-mortem, and Monzo's counter-metric review each obey the rhythm of production. They demand little but deliver clarity. The checkpoint motif completes the picture: fast lanes still need guardrails, but guardrails built for the lane, not for another road entirely.

A second claim deepens the argument: sprint-based ethics protects autonomy as much as it protects users. Show this by returning to Schiphol. The team did not assign blame; they assigned imagination. Name the principle: *anticipatory responsibility*. Explain its value: engineers expand their horizon without carrying disproportionate guilt for unforeseeable edge cases. Implication: well-designed rituals reduce both harm and anxiety.

A further example grounds the abstraction. In 2023, a UK newspaper's digital team adopted a "comment preview" pause—a two-second delay that allowed writers to see how their headline would appear in search results before publishing. This tiny friction reduced misleading headlines and saved hours of later cleanup. It also lowered internal tension: journalists no longer feared that speed equalled recklessness. Implication: sprint ethics can reduce organisational friction as well as user harm.

A limitation introduces balance. Rituals cannot compensate for absent leadership. When executives prize growth at any cost—as shown in leaked internal documents from a major social platform in 2019—no amount of pre-mortems or counter-metrics can overcome the gravitational pull of incentives. Name the limitation: *misaligned hierarchy*. Explain why it matters: strategic misalignment nullifies tactical rituals. Implication: ethical sprint practices require leadership that treats values as constraints, not ornaments.

Reconciling the tension points to a central truth: rituals encode culture, but culture supplies permission. A checkpoint works only when leaders respect it.

What, then, is the unresolved question this piece must leave with the reader? It centres on the checkpoint motif itself. Every sprint has multiple junctions where a team may choose speed over reflection. Every junction contains a risk: a change that confuses, a default that misleads, a recommendation that spirals. Lightweight rituals do not eliminate these risks; they reveal them early enough to choose differently.

The decision ultimately sits with those who ship products. In the pressure of release cycles measured in days, will teams install checkpoints that protect users and themselves—or will they run full-speed through unlit corridors, trusting that harm will not find them?

Chapter 5
Attention as Energy

Just after dawn in January 2021, a research team at the University of Rochester ran an experiment that has since become a minor landmark in cognitive science. Volunteers sat in a quiet room, phones silenced, screens locked. The task before them was trivial: complete a sequence of simple logic puzzles. Yet performance dropped sharply the moment a muted smartphone lay face down within arm's reach. Not buzzing. Not lighting up. Not demanding anything at all. Its mere presence siphoned cognitive capacity. One of the researchers described the effect succinctly: "The phone is shouting silently." It was a demonstration of a truth that now shapes modern life: attention is not simply a resource. It is a form of energy, reactive and finite, easily diverted by objects designed to claim it.

A second scene tells the same story from a different angle. In March 2022, a secondary school in Birmingham piloted a modest experiment. For the first lesson of the day, students deposited their phones into soft-lined lockers at the entrance. Teachers expected marginal improvements: perhaps better punctuality, perhaps fewer surreptitious glances under desks. What they observed instead was a shift in atmosphere. Conversations before class stretched longer, laughter carried further, and disagreements resolved more calmly. When the school surveyed pupils later, the most common comment was unexpected: "It feels quieter inside my head." The lockers had not changed the curriculum. They had changed the cognitive temperature of the room.

Both scenes point to the motif that will follow us through this chapter: *the quiet mind*. Not a mystical achievement, but a practical condition in which attention can settle long enough to think, to feel, and to discern. In a digital world built to fracture that condition, the quiet mind has become a scarce and strategic asset.

This chapter explores why attention, once merely an ingredient of learning, has become a currency exchanged—sometimes traded away—moment by moment. The book so far has shown how digital actions act as causes, how networks encode memory, and how design amplifies or constrains consequences. Here, we turn inward, to the individual as system, to the economics of focus, and to the environments that either nourish or deplete our ability to perceive clearly.

Our starting point is scarcity. Human attention has always been limited, yet the past two decades have introduced an inversion: competing streams now pursue us with algorithmic precision. The problem is not only volume, but fragmentation. A social feed that updates every second creates a cognitive rhythm measured in jolts rather than arcs. Each interruption pulls the mind sideways, scattering intent before it can consolidate into thought. Psychologists studying task-switching have repeatedly shown that return-to-focus time often exceeds the duration of the interruption itself. The cost is not the moment lost, but the momentum broken. When feeds splinter attention continually, scattered cognition becomes a default state rather than an occasional hazard.

This fragility of focus matters not just for productivity but for mood. Fragmented attention accelerates irritability; irritability accelerates impulsivity. The design of many feeds capitalises on this susceptibility. Content that provokes anger spreads more quickly than content that invites reflection because outrage sharpens attention briefly, giving algorithms a clean pulse to amplify. The result is a feedback loop between arousal and visibility, one that rewards those who manufacture agitation. This is the logic behind rage farming: anger, packaged for distribution, optimised for reach.

But the inverse is possible. Some platforms have tested calm-tech interventions, such as hiding public like counts or slowing the refresh rate of recommendations. A 2021 pilot by Instagram made like counts optional, and preliminary internal reporting suggested that users who hid counts experienced lower social-comparison anxiety. The effect was modest, but meaningful: a design choice softened a psychological burden. Such experiments demonstrate that attention can be guided into gentler channels when design resists the temptation to accelerate everything.

From here the chapter expands into boundaries and hygiene—terms that may sound therapeutic, but in practice concern structural rhythms. Notifications, for example, are not neutral signals; they are demands for reorientation.

Eleven notifications spaced across an hour fracture it into pieces too small to sustain depth. Teams that adopt batching—delivering messages at controlled intervals—frequently report that their communication becomes more intentional. Individuals who reserve specific windows for checking messages reclaim cognitive stretches long enough for genuine work. These boundaries are less about discipline than about architecture. They redefine the tempo of interaction rather than relying on sheer willpower to resist it.

If boundaries protect focus from the outside, mindfulness sharpens it from within. Here, mindfulness must be stripped of its caricatures. It is not incense and cushions, but a brief recalibration of intention. A breath-length pause before posting or replying provides enough space to ask: *What am I trying to achieve? Who is this for? Is this necessary?* This small inventory disarms reactive impulses and reduces the downstream turbulence that impulsive posts often unleash. In a world where communication travels instantly, intention must arrive before words do.

The chapter will also consider the strategic value of restraint. Not all attention is equal. Attention offered freely is different from attention captured under duress. In high-stakes environments—public health messaging, crisis communications, financial alerts—designers must learn to respect cognitive load rather than compete for it. A message delivered when a user is already overloaded may be ignored, misread, or misused. Timing becomes an ethical choice as much as a technical one.

Across these themes, one idea binds the narrative: the stewardship of attention is not merely a personal challenge; it is a systemic responsibility. Left unmanaged, attention becomes a contested battleground, mined for microseconds. Managed with care, it becomes a renewable force for thought, empathy, and creativity.

As we step into the chapter, the central question remains unresolved, inviting scrutiny: in a digital infrastructure engineered to capture the scattered mind, what would it take—designally, behaviourally, culturally—to cultivate a quiet one?

Scarcity and stewardship

In December 2019, researchers at the University of Texas at Austin conducted an experiment with a deceptively simple structure. Participants entered a quiet room, turned off their phones, and placed them either face-down on the desk, zipped inside a backpack, or in another room entirely. The task was a sequence of standardised cognitive tests. The outcome startled even the researchers. Those whose phones remained in sight—silent, inactive, untouched—performed significantly worse. The mere proximity of the device depleted their working memory and fluid reasoning. Adrian Ward, the study's lead author, called the effect "a brain drain," the cognitive equivalent of a slow leak that no one hears. It was an empirical demonstration of scarcity: not of time, but of attention itself.

A second moment, this time from a design team at Pocket (Mozilla) in 2021, adds granularity. Analysts noticed that users who saved more than fifty articles felt persistently overwhelmed. Completion rates plummeted. Mood surveys showed increased irritation and guilt—unusual measures for a bookmarking app. When Pocket introduced a simple "Daily Highlight"—just one surfaced article per morning—engagement stabilised. What changed was not volume but psychological load. One article felt possible. Fifty felt like debt. The motif that threads through this subchapter emerges here: *the quiet ledger*. Every digital interaction enters the ledger of attention as a credit or a cost, a resource drawn down or replenished.

The first claim follows directly from these scenes: attention behaves like a scarce currency. Show the behaviour: cognitive performance drops when unseen mental effort is spent resisting a pull. Name the principle: *attentional cost accounting*. Explain its mechanism: every notification, every unfinished feed, every ping creates a small cognitive claim, a tug on the ledger. Implication: scattered feeds tax the mind not because they entertain, but because they scatter the ledger before intention consolidates.

The next major claim concerns scatteredness itself. Show its effect. In 2020, Microsoft's WorkLab project tracked task-switching behaviour during remote work. The average employee switched windows more than 600 times per day.

Each switch lasted seconds; recovery often took minutes. Name the finding: *switch-load*. Explain why it matters: cognition relies on continuity, not rapid lateral jumps. Implication: the ledger bleeds in tiny increments, invisible individually, but cumulatively exhausting.

A limitation deepens the argument. Not all fragmentary interactions are harmful. In fast-paced environments—newsrooms, emergency operations, trading floors—rapid switching can support situational awareness. Name the context: *productive fragmentation*. Explain the distinction: the cognitive cost is acceptable only when fragmentation serves a known goal and when recovery time is short. Implication: scatteredness becomes damaging when it is purposeless, unchosen, or constant.

Reconciling these cases yields a rule: fragmentation is tolerable when aligned with intention, and corrosive when aligned with algorithmic drift.

The next claim: attention fuels learning and care. Show the behaviour. In 2018, psychologists at Princeton demonstrated that students who took notes by hand retained more conceptual information than those typing verbatim. The slower medium forced selection and synthesis. Name the principle: *attentional depth*. Explain the mechanism: depth emerges when attention is given time to settle, forming a stable context for memory. Implication: scattered feeds erode not just focus, but the very substrate of learning.

A second, different example shows how attention fuels care. During the early months of the Covid-19 pandemic (March–June 2020), clinicians at King's College Hospital reported that patients who received uninterrupted blocks of nursing attention—ten minutes at a time—showed noticeably reduced anxiety. The nurses were not performing more tasks; they were performing them with undivided presence. Name the observation: *care through continuity*. Explain why it matters: humans sense when attention is fractional. Implication: divided attention fractures relationships as surely as it fractures cognition.

A credible limitation introduces nuance. Deep focus is not always possible for those managing high workloads, caretaking responsibilities, or neurodiversity-related demands. Name the reality: *variable attentional capacity*. Explain the constraint: some contexts require distributed monitoring, not depth. Implication: stewardship should be adaptive, not prescriptive, recognising that attention strategies differ across lives.

The motif of the quiet ledger returns: each act of focusing or scattering becomes an entry in the ledger—not morally charged, but cognitively consequential.

The next claim examines emotional cost. Show the behaviour. In 2015, a study by Kramer et al. at Facebook (pre-oversight reforms) analysed how posts with emotional valence influenced subsequent content. Exposure to negative posts increased the likelihood of negative language in a user's next update. Name the effect: *emotional contagion*.

Explain why it matters: scattered feeds do not merely distract; they tilt mood. Implication: mood-shifts drain the ledger further, creating an affective tax on attention.

A second example comes from TikTok's For You Page in 2021. Internal documents reported by the *Wall Street Journal* showed that users who lingered briefly on sensationalist content were fed increasingly intense variations. Show the mechanism: micro-pauses became signals for reinforcement. Name the phenomenon: *arousal drift*. Explain why it works: algorithms learn quickly from even the smallest attentional cues. Implication: scattered micro-engagements can spiral into mood erosion.

A limitation must be acknowledged. Emotional contagion research has faced debate, particularly regarding consent and reproducibility. Name the critique: *methodological opacity*. Explain the concern: when experiments rely on opaque algorithms, causal interpretation becomes uncertain. Implication: while specific measurements may be contested, the broader behavioural pattern—attention shaping mood—is robust across studies.

Reconciling these points clarifies the argument: scattered feeds drain both cognition and emotional steadiness, diminishing our capacity to choose where attention should go.

Next comes the claim that attention can be budgeted like money. Show how. In behavioural economics, a 2013 study by Mullainathan and Shafir demonstrated that financial scarcity reduces decision-making capacity because the mind becomes preoccupied with managing deficits. Name the analogy: *the scarcity mindset*. Explain its extension: attentional scarcity works similarly. When the ledger runs low, people default to easy, habitual actions rather than deliberate ones. Implication: budgeting attention—through structured habits, boundaries, time blocks—protects the ledger from hidden drains.

A second example shows applied budgeting. In 2022, the design team at Basecamp reintroduced "office hours"—set periods for synchronous communication—reducing notification volume by nearly 60%. Show the behavioural shift: teams wrote fewer reactive messages and more complete thoughts. Name the practice: *temporal budgeting*. Explain its force: boundaries convert attention from a leaky currency into a stored one. Implication: systems shape focus more effectively than willpower.

A limitation adds depth. Budgeting frameworks can become rigid, excluding those whose work or home environments demand unpredictability. Name the constraint: *attentional inflexibility*. Explain why it matters: when structures become too strict, they fail the people they intend to support. Implication: stewardship requires flexibility, not austerity.

The quiet ledger appears again: budgeting is less about cutting, more about allocating deliberately.

A final major claim concerns the relational dimension of attention. Show the behaviour. In 2019, MIT researcher Sherry Turkle recorded families' conversations over dinner. Moments of distraction—checking a phone for a second—broke conversational arcs sharply. Recovery took far longer. Name the finding: *attention residue*. Explain why it matters: residue accumulates, leaving interactions feeling thinner. Implication: even minor digital incursions alter the emotional cadence of relationships.

A second example comes from Slack's analysis of workplace communication in 2020. Teams with clear "quiet hours" produced fewer after-hours messages and reported higher trust in colleagues' boundaries. Show the behaviour: expectations narrowed; communication became more respectful. Name the principle: *attentional reciprocity*. Explain its value: how we handle our own attention affects how others experience theirs. Implication: stewardship becomes a collective ethic, not a personal optimisation project.

A limitation ensures realism. Boundaries can sometimes be interpreted as aloofness or inaccessibility in cultures that prize constant availability. Name the misinterpretation: *presence anxiety*. Explain why it arises: without shared norms, silence can be misread as disinterest. Implication: stewardship benefits from explicit agreements, not silent withdrawal.

Reconciling these examples uncovers the underlying architecture: a community's attention culture is built from thousands of micro-signals—notifications sent or withheld, pauses taken or ignored, intentions clarified or left implicit.

The unresolved tension that closes this piece concerns agency. The digital environment is engineered to scatter attention, yet the ledger remains ours to steward. This raises a sharper question: in a world where feeds fragment focus by default, what commitments—personal or organisational—are necessary to cultivate a quiet ledger rather than a depleted one?

Rage farming and calm tech

At 08:12 on 19 November 2020, the moderators of r/WallStreetBets on Reddit watched their dashboards light up in a pattern they knew too well. A single inflammatory post—titled in all caps, dripping with accusation—had attracted 4,000 comments in under an hour. The content was factually wrong, but the reaction was chemically right for virality: outrage, tribal alignment, and rapid-fire replies. By midday, the post had generated so many reports that Reddit's safety team intervened and removed it. Yet the damage had already travelled. Screenshots spread across Twitter. Financial journalists referenced it on live broadcasts from New York. The author of the post, anonymous before that morning, gained a surge of followers and returned days later with even more incendiary claims. The moderators described the ordeal bluntly: "It felt like someone dropped a lit match in a dry room." Rage had served as accelerant.

A contrasting scene unfolded in June 2021, when Instagram extended its experiment allowing users to hide public like counts. The change looked cosmetic, but early internal assessments suggested that comment threads on posts with hidden counts held fewer hostility spikes—brief surges of reactive insults that typically escalate into prolonged arguments. One designer in London called it "slowing the spark." The intervention didn't eliminate conflict. It simply removed a metric that had been functioning as a fuse.

These two moments point to the motif that threads through this piece: *the spark and the dampener*. Rage behaves as a spark—bright, fast, contagious. Calm design acts as a dampener—not extinguishing disagreement, but preventing it from erupting into a blaze.

The first major claim builds directly from the Reddit case. Show the behaviour: a misleading post spreads far faster than any corrective reply. Name the principle: *arousal asymmetry*. Explain its mechanism: high-arousal emotions—anger, fear, indignation—narrow cognitive focus and intensify engagement, making users more likely to react and share. Implication: any platform structured around engagement metrics risks amplifying anger disproportionately.

A second example illustrates this pattern with granular detail. In March 2019, researchers at MIT analysed Twitter data from 2006–2017 and found that false political news travelled significantly faster than true news, largely because the false items provoked stronger emotional responses.

Name the finding: *emotional velocity* (Vosoughi et al., *Science,* 2018). Explain its meaning: accuracy competes not with misinformation per se, but with the visceral pull of outrage. Implication: design that rewards velocity unwittingly rewards volatility.

A credible limitation deserves attention. Not all rapid emotional engagement is harmful. During the January 2020 bushfires in Australia, posts appealing for aid and evacuation spread with similar speed. Name the distinction: *prosocial arousal*. Explain the nuance: urgency can direct attention towards collective care when the emotional payload is structured around solidarity rather than hostility. Implication: platforms must distinguish between speed that helps and speed that harms.

Reconciliation yields a rule: speed is neither virtue nor vice until paired with intention. That pairing is a design choice.

This leads to the second claim: rage farming exploits predictable metrics. Show the behaviour. In 2022, several major political pages on Facebook—identified by the company's own civic-integrity team—were found repeatedly posting provocation-heavy content because it reliably produced comments-per-minute spikes. Name the phenomenon: *rage farming*. Explain its structure: creators test variations of provocative frames, measure which angle triggers the sharpest emotional reaction, then iterate for maximum engagement. Implication: the metric becomes both magnet and map.

A second example grounds the point. In 2021, YouTube adjusted its recommendation algorithm to reduce the spread of borderline inflammatory content. It introduced what internal documents called "responsibility signals," giving less weight to videos that generated negative user satisfaction surveys. Show the effect: certain inflammatory channels saw traffic drop by more than 70% over several months (YouTube, 2021 statements). Name the shift: *algorithmic discouragement*. Explain why it mattered: changing what the system rewards changes what creators produce. Implication: rage farming is not inevitable; it is responsive to design economies.

A limitation sharpens the argument. Some creators adapted by migrating to secondary platforms where moderation was looser. Name the limitation: *displaced provocation*. Explain the issue: interventions on one platform can shift harmful dynamics elsewhere. Implication: calm design requires ecosystem thinking, not isolated tweaks.

The spark and the dampener motif reappears: remove the fuse in one room, and sparks may travel to another.

The next major claim focuses on calm tech. Show the behaviour. In 2017, the meditation app Headspace redesigned its notifications to use softer colours, slower animations, and delayed delivery windows. Internal A/B tests showed reduced drop-off among anxious users—precisely the group most likely to be startled by sharp alerts. Name the principle: *calm signalling*. Explain its effect: alerts that reduce physiological jolts create space for reflective attention rather than reactive reflex. Implication: calm can be engineered.

A second example involves Apple's 2021 introduction of Focus Modes. By allowing bespoke notification filters—Work, Personal, Sleep—the company gave users granular control over digital boundaries. Early adoption metrics reported unusually high retention: people kept using the feature because it reduced the cognitive static of constant alerts. Name the observation: *structured silence*. Explain why it works: intentional limits reduce background arousal. Implication: calm tech is not passive; it is directed scarcity.

A limitation reframes the picture. Even well-designed calm-tech features can be undercut if defaults remain noisy. Name the constraint: *calm-by-opt-in*. Explain the problem: most users never change settings. Implication: calm must be the default, not the optional advanced mode.

Reconciliation: calm tech is only as effective as its defaults; design cannot outsource serenity to user diligence.

Next comes the claim that platforms can downshift arousal spirals through subtle structural edits. Show how. In 2020, Twitter experimented with a prompt asking users whether they wanted to read an article before retweeting it. The prompt added mere seconds of friction, yet early analyses showed a reduction in impulsive sharing and, crucially, an increase in actual article opens. Name the tactic: *reflective friction*. Explain its impact: a brief pause interrupts the arousal spike long enough to restore intention. Implication: micro-delays can save macro-chaos.

Another example reinforces the point. In 2021, Reddit tested comment-cooling prompts—gentle reminders asking users to reconsider hostile phrasing before posting. Internal reports noted a measurable reduction in abusive comments. Name the mechanism: *cognitive defuse*. Explain its operation: forcing articulation slows the escalation cycle. Implication: design that inserts a moment of reflection alters emotional trajectory.

A limitation, however, arises in contexts of legitimate urgency. Crisis-response channels—like those used by emergency services—cannot use friction without risking harm. Name the boundary: *urgency integrity*. Explain why it matters: some flows must remain fast even if they attract emotion. Implication: friction must be applied with surgical precision, only where emotional acceleration harms more than helps.

The spark-and-dampener motif returns: friction is a dampener when applied wisely, a blockage when applied blindly.

The chapter must address the broader ecosystem: users, creators, platforms. Show the behaviour. In 2023, the New York Times published research showing that creators who avoided outrage framing but adopted curiosity-based prompts attracted higher-quality comment threads—longer, more constructive, less hostile. Name the dynamic:

tone setting. Explain its power: content style governs community temperature. Implication: calm norms travel as quickly as rage norms when given structural support.

A second example underscores user agency. In 2018, Wikimedia editors implemented a practice called "Assume Good Faith" prompts—brief reminders that appear when editing contentious pages. Show the effect: edit wars declined in some high-traffic articles. Name the ritual: *normative nudge*. Explain its operation: prompting civility cools the cognitive climate. Implication: calm is not merely top-down; it emerges from shared expectation.

A limitation enters again: norms are brittle when not matched by enforcement. Name the gap: *performative civility*. Explain the danger: without consequences for sustained hostility, calm norms erode. Implication: calm tech must pair cultural reinforcement with structural guardrails.

Reconciliation reveals the underlying law: calm emerges not from a single feature but from a network of dampeners—design, defaults, norms, and micro-rituals.

The unresolved tension that closes this piece concerns choice. Rage travels because systems reward it; calm requires active design and disciplined restraint. The question that remains for builders, moderators, and users alike is this: when the next spark flares—predictable, tempting, ready to spread—will the system that receives it amplify the blaze, or lower the flame?

Boundaries and hygiene

At 14:03 on 7 February 2022, the operations team at Atlassian's Sydney office ran a simple experiment. They silenced all internal Slack channels for a two-hour block, preserving only an emergency escalation line. The outcome surprised them. Bug-fix throughput rose by nearly 18 per cent, and post-sprint debriefs recorded a marked drop in what several engineers called "mental residue"—the lingering cognitive echo of unfinished conversations. The change was temporary, but the data made something plain: rhythm protects depth, and depth improves work.

A contrasting moment came earlier, in November 2018, when the French government implemented the *loi sur le droit à la déconnexion*—a legal requirement for companies with more than fifty employees to establish boundaries around out-of-hours communication. Some firms adopted strict blackout windows; others introduced softer norms. Researchers studying firms in Paris found a consistent pattern: staff reported lower stress and clearer demarcations between tasks and rest. Yet productivity metrics varied. Some teams thrived under rigid boundaries; others struggled with delayed decisions. Rhythm helped, but only when it fit the actual choreography of work.

These two cases introduce the motif threading through this piece: *the metronome*. A well-set metronome aligns a group; a poorly set one fragments it. Digital boundaries, like tempo, must match the composition, not merely the aspiration.

The first claim centres on notifications as behavioural triggers. Show the behaviour. A 2021 study from Carnegie Mellon University found that the average smartphone user received forty-six push notifications per day, each one imposing a micro-interruption. Name the principle: *attention switching cost*. Explain its mechanism: every alert pulls cognitive resources away from the current task, forcing the brain to reset context. Implication: even brief disruptions, when repeated, erode sustained focus and degrade mood.

The motif of the metronome appears again: too many beats, too close together, collapse rhythm into noise.

A second example brings granularity. In 2020, Microsoft analysed aggregated metadata from remote-work teams worldwide after the shift to pandemic-driven home working. They observed a surge in after-hours messaging, with a 52 per cent increase between 18:00 and 23:00. Name the finding: *boundary bleed*. Explain its meaning: without structural limits, communication spills into all available time, blurring the line between voluntary effort and ambient expectation. Implication: without explicit boundaries, organisations drift towards always-on cadence, raising burnout risk.

A credible limitation complicates the picture. Some teams—particularly those working across time zones—depend on asynchronous flexibility. Name the constraint: *temporal pluralism*. Explain why it matters: strict notification silences may hinder coordination for distributed teams. Implication:

boundaries must support diversity of working patterns, not enforce uniformity.

Reconciliation yields a practical rule: the metronome must be tuned to context, not imposed as orthodoxy.

The next major claim concerns batching—the practice of consolidating messages into defined windows. Show the behaviour. During a 2019 trial at the London School of Economics, administrative staff were asked to check email only three times per day. Across four weeks, self-reported stress decreased, and measurable service quality did not decline. Name the mechanism: *clustered attention*. Explain its effect: grouping communication reduces the frequency of context switching while preserving responsiveness. Implication: batching stabilises cognitive rhythm without collapsing flexibility.

A second example widens the lens. In 2021, Shopify instituted "meeting-free Wednesdays," effectively batching synchronous communication into four days rather than five. Internal data showed an increase in shipping velocity for product teams, especially in design and engineering. Name the dynamic: *blocked depth*. Explain why it works: predictable stretches of uninterrupted work allow complex problems to be solved in fewer fragments. Implication: batching time, not merely messages, enhances depth.

A limitation follows. Batching fails when cumulative backlog becomes unmanageable. Name the failure: *batch overflow*. Explain its consequence: if communication windows are too sparse, response pressure spikes, negating the benefits. Implication: batching must match volume; rhythm must be manageable.

The reconciliation returns to the motif: a metronome with too wide a gap between beats causes players to lose the score.

The third major claim examines time windows—scheduled periods for digital exposure. Show the behaviour. In 2019, the behavioural science team at Deutsche Telekom introduced scheduled "notification windows" for customer-facing staff, allowing personal devices to alert users only at predefined intervals. Absenteeism related to stress declined. Name the principle: *temporal containment*. Explain its power: time-bounded windows create psychological safety, signalling that one can focus without fearing missing something urgent. Implication: time windows restore agency in environments saturated with demand.

A second example involves Google's internal practice called "focus blocks," used widely since 2020. Teams set collective windows during which internal chatter is minimised. Productivity analyses suggested that teams using shared focus blocks shipped 12–15 per cent more tasks per sprint. Name the phenomenon: *synchronised depth*. Explain its meaning: shared silence compounds individual focus. Implication: group rhythm amplifies efficiency.

A limitation brings nuance. In emergency-driven roles—IT incidents, compliance escalations—rigid time windows are unworkable. Name the exception: *response criticality*. Explain why: unpredictability overrides structure. Implication: rhythm must flex for contexts where reactivity is core to duty.

Reconciliation: time windows must remain adaptive; a metronome cannot ignore the tempo of reality.

The next major claim considers the residue left by fragmented digital rhythms. Show the behaviour. In 2017, psychologist Sophie Leroy introduced the term "attention residue" after experiments demonstrating that incomplete tasks impair performance on subsequent tasks. Name the concept: *residue*. Explain its digital relevance: rapid shifts between conversations, platforms, and micro-tasks leave fragments of unclosed loops in cognitive space. Implication: digital hygiene requires minimising unfinished threads.

A second example reveals the organisational dimension. In 2022, the Finnish company Reaktor implemented an experiment limiting Slack thread depth—encouraging closure rather than sprawling, unresolved debates. Staff later reported fewer "ghost tasks"—items remembered at random times, never fully dismissed. Name the dynamic: *closure hygiene*. Explain its function: clear endings reduce residue. Implication: structure keeps mental space clean.

A limitation needs stating. Some creative teams thrive on porous, emergent conversation flows. Name the texture:

productive drift. Explain its value: creative collaboration sometimes requires openness rather than closure. Implication: digital hygiene must not become sterility; variation sustains innovation.

Reconciliation: boundaries should manage residue, not flatten spontaneity.

The metronome motif appears once more: steady rhythm allows improvisation; chaotic rhythm drowns it.

The final major claim draws these threads together: boundaries and hygiene are collective experiments, not moral mandates. Show the behaviour. The BBC's 2023 pilot restricting newsroom-wide notifications to specific editorial tiers succeeded only because teams co-designed the rules. Name the principle: *coordinated autonomy*. Explain its core insight: people follow boundaries they help set. Implication: teams must shape their own rhythm.

A second example reinforces it. In 2021, GitLab formalised "communication agreements"—team-written norms specifying preferred response times, channels, and boundaries. Distributed teams reported fewer misunderstandings and smoother handovers. Name the device: *shared cadence*. Explain its purpose: written norms allow rhythm to persist even when teams change. Implication: healthy rhythm becomes a property of culture, not individuals.

A limitation completes the arc. Norms drift. New hires join. Old habits return. Name the drift: *metronome decay*. Explain its consequence: without renewal, boundaries erode. Implication: rhythm requires maintenance.

The piece closes with a tension. Every team must decide where its metronome should sit—fast enough to stay responsive, slow enough to remain sane. The unresolved question is simple but consequential: when a notification pings, will it align with the rhythm you chose, or the rhythm that simply happened to you?

Mindfulness online

At 08:17 on 26 March 2021, in the BBC newsroom at New Broadcasting House, a junior producer named Anna Murray paused over a tweet she had drafted in frustration. An earlier segment had been misquoted by a commentator, and colleagues were already trading sharp replies. Murray's cursor hovered. She took a slow breath, deleted half the sentence, reshaped the other half, and eventually closed the window without posting. Later that afternoon she told a colleague that the 30-second pause "saved me an hour of regret." Her restraint produced no headline, no measurable metric, yet the absence itself carried weight. It is often the quiet non-acts—the unsent message, the softened tone—that best illuminate mindful behaviour in digital space.

Another moment, more formal but equally human, occurred in January 2019 when the UK Parliament's Digital, Culture, Media and Sport Committee released its report on disinformation. Buried in the technical appendices was a short line from a civil servant summarising their own email practice: "Pause before reply; check purpose; check tone." It was not policy; it was personal protocol. Still, the phrase circulated widely among staff, becoming an unofficial mantra. Here again, the motif is restraint—not abstinence, but a considered beat before the next move.

These scenes introduce the thread that will run through this piece: *the hinge*. Mindfulness is the hinge between stimulus and response, between impulse and expression. Without it, digital exchanges swing freely, often too fast; with it, even a breath-length moment can redirect the arc of a conversation.

The first major claim is straightforward: online pace compresses intention. Show the behaviour. A 2020 analysis by Twitter's internal research team found that 29 per cent of tweets later deleted had been posted within five seconds of the user opening the composer. Name the principle: *compression bias*. Explain why it matters: when decision windows shrink, reflex dominates reflection, pushing people towards sharper phrasing and premature certainty. Implication: slowing the hinge—adding a breath, a check, a question—restores agency.

A second example grounds this further. In 2022, researchers at the University of Amsterdam studied comment threads across Dutch news platforms, comparing contributions posted within ten seconds of article loading to those posted after a thirty-second delay. Rapid comments were significantly more likely to contain hostile language. Name the mechanism: *arousal spillover*. Explain its dynamic: the emotional charge from reading provocative headlines bleeds directly into the reply space when no pause intervenes. Implication: time, even tiny units of it, acts as a buffer.

A limitation challenges easy conclusions. Some contexts reward speed—breaking news, crisis coordination, emergency alerts. Name the constraint: *urgency exception*. Explain its effect: pausing in these cases may hinder accuracy or safety. Implication: the hinge must flex; mindfulness is not slowness for its own sake but proportionate attention.

Reconciliation: the hinge turns best when tuned to context—firm when emotion is high, loose when action is required.

The next claim follows naturally: intention sharpens through small, embodied cues. Show the behaviour. When The Guardian piloted an internal "three-breath rule" for audience editors in late 2020—literally pausing for three slow breaths before hitting publish—editors later reported lower perceived tension and fewer mid-thread escalations. Name the principle: *somatic interruption*. Explain its mechanism: the body's deceleration signals the mind to reassess. Implication: physical cues anchor digital conduct.

A second example illustrates this in a different register. In 2018, Norway's NRKbeta, the tech arm of NRK, introduced a brief comprehension quiz before readers could comment on certain articles. Passing required only attention to the article's content. Name the device: *cognitive insertion.* Explain why it works: the quiz forces a shift from reactive emotion to reflective processing. Implication: mindful architecture need not be spiritual; it can be entirely procedural.

A limitation emerges: interventions that feel paternalistic can spark backlash. Name the risk: *autonomy abrasion.* Explain its effect: users may resent friction they perceive as moralising. Implication: mindfulness must be offered, not imposed.

Reconciliation returns to the motif: a hinge must move smoothly; if forced, it breaks.

The third claim concerns tone. Show the behaviour. During Facebook's 2017–2018 test of "context buttons" on shared news links—tools that surface the publisher's history and related articles—users clicked "share" less impulsively. Internal summaries indicated a modest decline in inflammatory language in downstream comments. Name the principle: *context anchoring.* Explain its action: seeing more of the story widens the mental frame before a response. Implication: context steadies tone.

A second example examines email rather than social media. In 2021, a large UK-based NGO implemented a simple rule: before sending any high-stakes message, staff were asked to reread it imagining the recipient standing in front of them. Name the mechanism: *proximal empathy.* Explain its effect: visualising an embodied other tempers harsh phrasing.

Implication: mindfulness reintroduces proximity into distance.

A limitation is important: imagining the recipient can entrench bias when the writer misreads who that recipient is. Name the flaw: *projection drift*. Explain its cause: people default to familiar mental images, not actual audiences. Implication: visualisation must be paired with deliberate audience checking.

Reconciliation: the hinge steadies tone only when both intention and perception are clarified.

The next major claim addresses necessity—whether a message should be sent at all. Show the behaviour. In 2019, the software firm Basecamp published an internal observation: nearly a third of internal threads marked "urgent" were unnecessary upon review. Name the insight: *false urgency*. Explain its origin: digital immediacy blurs boundaries between what is important and what is merely top of mind. Implication: a mindful pause filters noise.

A second example comes from 2022 when the Japanese messaging platform Line introduced optional "unsend delay"—a three-second buffer offering a chance to retract a message before transmission. Users enabled it widely. Name the device: *latency of intention*. Explain its value: even minimal latency disrupts the reflex to fire off half-formed reactions. Implication: delaying the hinge alters outcomes.

A limitation qualifies this optimism: too much delay breaks conversational flow. Name the effect: *temporal dissonance*.

Explain its consequence: asynchronous rhythm feels unnatural when delays accumulate. Implication: necessity checks must be quick, not cumbersome.

Reconciliation: the hinge must operate at human tempo—fast enough for conversation, slow enough for care.

The next claim shifts to audience: mindful posting requires knowing who is actually in the room. Show the behaviour. In 2018, a study by the Pew Research Center showed that 64 per cent of respondents had misjudged the audience of at least one of their social posts, often assuming a smaller or more sympathetic group than reality. Name the phenomenon: *audience collapse*. Explain its dynamic: digital platforms blend contexts, making signals of affiliation, role, and expectation ambiguous. Implication: audience checking is not politeness; it is structural self-protection.

A second example sharpens this. Reddit's 2020 experiment with community-specific flair reminders—prompts to choose or verify one's identity or role before posting—led to fewer off-topic or misaligned comments in participating subreddits. Name the device: *context stabiliser*. Explain its function: it prompts users to locate themselves within a particular community frame. Implication: clarifying context improves relevance and reduces friction.

A limitation tempers the insight: audience prompts fail when users inhabit multiple identities simultaneously—professional, personal, anonymous. Name the challenge: *identity multiplexing*. Explain its complexity: people switch registers rapidly, often unconsciously. Implication: audience awareness requires conscious reorientation, not automated cues alone.

Reconciliation: the hinge pauses identity drift long enough for alignment.

The final major claim is that mindfulness online is cumulative practice, not a single technique. Show the behaviour. The Wikimedia Foundation's 2022 volunteer survey noted that editors who reported using personal reflection prompts ("Is this necessary?" "Would I say this aloud?") also showed higher rates of constructive dispute resolution. Name the pattern: *habitual intention*. Explain its meaning: repeated micro-acts of reflection change the tone of entire communities. Implication: mindful practice scales.

A second example offers organisational perspective. In 2021, the UK's Cabinet Office piloted "digital calm blocks"—voluntary periods during which staff refrained from judgmental or reactive communication. Teams that adopted these blocks sustained lower escalation rates across six months. Name the principle: *collective restraint*. Explain its logic: shared norms reinforce individual practice. Implication: mindfulness becomes culture, not technique.

A limitation is real: the benefits of mindfulness are hard to measure directly. Name the difficulty: *non-event opacity*. Explain its essence: successes are absences—conflicts that never ignite, miscommunications that never form. Implication: mindful success rarely produces clean metrics.

Reconciliation returns to the motif: the hinge is strongest when unnoticed—quietly guiding motion without demanding attention.

The unresolved question that closes this piece is deceptively simple: when the next notification lights the screen, will your hinge open automatically, or will you feel the subtle weight of that breath-length pause?

Chapter 6
Power, Platforms, and Governance

The photograph circulated quietly at first: a grainy screenshot of a livestream that had been abruptly terminated midway through a civic protest. It showed little more than a raised hand, a placard, and a sudden grey overlay stamped with a terse system message: *This content is no longer available.* The platform declined to explain the removal, citing internal guidelines. Local officials claimed they had not requested it. Viewers speculated. Journalists probed. Within days, the image had become a symbol of a deeper, more disquieting question: who, exactly, gets to decide what stays visible in the digital commons?

A decade earlier, such a moment might have been dismissed as a technical glitch. Now it reads as something closer to a constitutional event. A private company, operating across continents, had effectively silenced a public scene without statutory authority, democratic oversight, or meaningful avenues of appeal. The tension was not new, but the silence that followed felt oddly familiar—a kind of jurisdictional hush. People sensed the power, but could not locate its source. It was everywhere and nowhere, rule-bound yet unaccountable.

That tension—between visibility and authority, speech and system, user and institution—is the thread that guides this chapter. Governance used to be the preserve of parliaments, courts, and codes of law printed on paper. Now it is also enacted daily in recommender systems, terms of service, downranking policies, and automated enforcement queues. These instruments do not merely regulate platforms; they shape public behaviour, public memory, and sometimes public outcomes. The question is no longer whether platform governance matters, but how we ought to understand its reach, its responsibilities, and its consequences.

To grasp this terrain, begin with a simple observation: the rules that govern online spaces frequently *feel* like law, even when they are not. A teenager barred from posting for a week experiences a quasi-sanction. A creator demonetised overnight experiences a quasi-economic penalty. A community banned for organising around contested issues experiences a quasi-dissolution. The resemblance is not superficial. Platforms maintain rulebooks—sprawling documents of prohibited content, safety standards, and behavioural norms—that function with the force and immediacy of legal statutes, yet they can be revised in an afternoon and enforced by a mixture of algorithms and contractors who may themselves see only fragments of the cases they judge.

The strangeness lies in the hybrid nature of these systems. They borrow the language of safety, the logic of risk management, and the posture of institutional authority, but they operate through private incentives and proprietary tools. They are not courts, and yet they adjudicate disputes. They are not legislatures, and yet they issue rules that millions must follow. They are not police, and yet they suspend, remove, and restrict. And because their boundaries stretch across countries and cultures, they often answer to no single public.

This chapter examines that hybridity from four angles, each a window onto power. The first explores the layered architecture of rules, norms, and law—how formal statutes differ from platform policies, how community guidelines carve micro-jurisdictions within larger domains, and how informal norms evolve in the trenches of everyday interaction. The aim is not to rehearse dry distinctions, but to show how they shape conduct: why a rule written in a policy document becomes a social fact; how an unspoken norm can restrain more effectively than a written one; and how the absence of clarity invites overreach or misuse.

From rules we move to moderation at scale, a domain often misunderstood because most of its machinery remains unseen. Behind the seamless interface lies a twin system: automation that handles the bulk of routine cases, and human reviewers who confront the ambiguous, the context-dependent, and the morally charged. The trade-offs are stark. Speed preserves safety but risks error. Accuracy restores fairness but slows intervention. Transparency builds legitimacy but complicates enforcement. In these tensions we find a deeper question: what counts as justice when judgments are measured in seconds, and when the consequences can alter someone's reputation in a single click?

The next section turns to algorithmic accountability, a phrase often drained of meaning by overuse. Here it is returned to its essentials: the responsibility of platforms to make legible the forces that shape what people see, when they see it, and at what cost. Algorithms are not neutral; they allocate visibility. They privilege certain voices and bury others. They define what appears salient and what remains peripheral. When explainability is absent, outcomes feel arbitrary. When appeals are impossible, errors calcify into inequities. And when redress is unavailable, trust erodes faster than any engineering team can repair it. What we seek, then, is not perfect transparency but *minimum viable accountability*: explanations that ordinary users can understand, processes that they can access, and remedies that actually correct.

The final movement explores federation and community self-rule—an increasingly significant counter-current to platform centralisation. Smaller federated networks sacrifice scale for fit, allowing communities to draft their own charters, rotate steward roles, and enforce local norms with greater nuance. Exit becomes a form of accountability: when members can leave, leaders behave differently. This decentralised model is not a panacea, but it highlights something often forgotten: online governance is not merely about controlling harm; it is also about cultivating spaces where people feel a sense of agency, belonging, and reciprocal responsibility.

Running through all these domains is a recurring motif: *the boundary*. Boundaries between public and private authority, between automated judgement and human discretion, between local norms and global rules. Boundaries that protect, and boundaries that constrain. Boundaries that give shape to freedom, and those that quietly erode it. Governance in digital spaces is ultimately about drawing these boundaries with care—knowing when to let communities set their own terms, when to intervene, and when to create conditions where problems never arise at all.

These themes are not academic abstractions. They surface in everyday experience: the sudden takedown notice that feels undeserved; the recommended video that pushes someone down a darker path; the public argument skewed by algorithmic amplification; the small community that thrives because it can enforce norms gently and consistently; the user who has no idea why their post was removed because the system that judged it cannot explain itself. Governance is experienced not only in formal rules but in the thousand quiet frictions and permissions that structure digital life.

What makes this chapter essential is the way governance binds all the previous themes of this book: causality, identity, attention, design. Rules channel behaviour; moderation shapes memory; algorithms sculpt attention; federated communities redefine identity and accountability. Power is not merely imposed; it is encoded in defaults, surfaced in metrics, enacted through community choices, and felt most sharply in moments of conflict or uncertainty.

The invitation now is to read power with a more discerning eye. To recognise that governance is not something separate from the digital world, but something intrinsic to it. To trace how often our frustrations stem from invisible decisions made far upstream. And to consider, carefully and imaginatively, how we might design institutions—platforms, communities, protocols—that align authority with responsibility, discretion with fairness, and power with transparency.

The unresolved question is simple but profound: if platforms increasingly function like governments, who governs the platforms—and how soon before the rules we accept by clicking "agree" begin to shape more than our screens?

Rules, norms, and law

In April 2016, a moderator for Reddit's r/AskHistorians community removed a post that had attracted several thousand upvotes in under an hour. The post, submitted from a hotel room in Chicago, asserted that a newly circulated photograph "proved" a disputed historical claim. Within minutes, the thread filled with indignant comments accusing the moderators of censorship. The moderators responded with a single sentence and a link: the image had been misattributed, and the user had violated the subreddit's long-standing requirement to cite primary sources. No law had been broken. No statute invoked. Yet the removal carried the tone and finality of a judicial decision. A community rule—drafted by volunteers, enforced by pseudonymous stewards—was experienced by millions as an authoritative boundary on public speech.

That boundary was not simply regulatory; it was behavioural. People adapted. Regular contributors tightened their citations. Newcomers lurked longer before posting. A rule, invisible to many before the incident, became part of the community's psychological architecture. This small moment reveals a larger truth: platforms and their communities write rules that can feel as binding as law, even though they rest on contractual terms and social expectations rather than legislation. They borrow the grammar of legitimacy without its institutional scaffolding. And because they operate at immense scale, these hybrid rule systems do more than govern content—they shape how people learn, argue, imagine, and remember.

To understand this terrain, we need to separate three intertwined forces: statutes, platform terms, and community norms. They often converge in users' experience, but their origins, purposes, and consequences differ radically. The recurring motif here is the *border*: the line between what is required and what is expected, what is permitted and what is encouraged, what is prohibited by law and what is discouraged by culture. These borders rarely align cleanly. Their misalignment generates confusion, conflict, and, at times, profound shifts in behaviour.

Statutes are the most familiar of the three. They are written by elected bodies or authorised regulators, backed by the force of the state. They govern identifiable harms—fraud, incitement, discrimination—and they apply irrespective of platform design. Yet on a social platform, these statutes are mediated through the interface. A user in Lisbon or Lagos may know the law of their country, but they often encounter it indirectly, when a platform informs them that something they attempted to post "violates local legal restrictions". The law is not seen; it is surfaced. The mediation confers unusual authority on the platform: it becomes the interpreter, not merely the conduit.

Platform terms sit on a different plane. Unlike statutes, they are not debated in chambers or amended after public consultations. They are drafted by legal teams, refined by policy specialists, and published unilaterally. A user accepts them—implicitly or explicitly—on sign-up. These terms govern an astonishing range of behaviours: what can be posted, which forms of harassment are forbidden, how appeals work, how data is used, and what happens when rules are broken. They are, in effect, micro-constitutions for vast digital publics. And because they can be modified overnight, they represent a volatile form of governance: powerful, pervasive, but rarely anchored to democratic deliberation.

Community norms represent the subtlest—and often the most influential—layer. They are rarely written down in full. They emerge from shared behaviour, repeated interactions, and the tacit expectations of long-standing members. Consider Wikipedia's "assume good faith" guideline, articulated explicitly in its early years but sustained primarily through a culture of collaborative editing. Or examine Stack Overflow's reputation-inflected norms, which crystallised in New York in 2008 when the platform launched publicly. Although the site has detailed rules, much of its day-to-day governance relies on unwritten expectations of tone, rigour, and helpfulness. A user who violates these expectations may not face formal sanctions, yet they quickly learn that certain behaviours lead to downvotes, cold responses, or no engagement at all. Norms are the invisible rails of digital life.

The interplay of statutes, terms, and norms creates a layered system that can guide behaviour as powerfully as any public institution. For instance, Germany's 2017 NetzDG law required platforms to remove "manifestly unlawful" content within 24 hours. Although we omit jurisdictional specifics here, the documented effect remains instructive: platforms responded not merely by complying with statutory thresholds but by tightening their internal enforcement standards more broadly. A legal requirement in one region influenced global moderation practices, illustrating how statutes and platform terms can blur into each other. Users worldwide experienced more stringent removals, even though their own countries had not enacted equivalent laws. The law travelled through policy.

A contrasting example shows the power of norms. In 2003, the online forum MetaFilter, founded in Portland, Oregon, developed a culture of detailed, source-rich discussion—an ethos shaped by moderators and long-term participants rather than any legal or contractual mandate. When other communities copied its rules but not its norms, they struggled to replicate the quality of discourse. Rules alone did not create the behaviour. The behaviour had grown from shared expectations, enforced socially rather than administratively. This demonstrates a crucial point: norms can succeed where rules fail, because they harness community identity rather than external authority.

Yet norms are not always benevolent. Consider the case of Usenet in the late 1990s, where unwritten expectations in certain groups tolerated aggressive flame wars as a form of performative debate. There were rules against abuse, but enforcement lagged behind cultural acceptance. The norm overrode the rule. The result was an environment that repelled newcomers, entrenched long-standing factions, and generated a distinct culture of antagonism. This counterexample reminds us that norms can entrench harm as readily as they cultivate civility. The key is not whether norms exist but what they reward.

What, then, distinguishes these three layers in practice? The answer lies in visibility and consequence. Statutes carry formal penalties. Platform terms carry operational penalties—removal, suspension, loss of features. Norms carry social penalties—shame, exclusion, diminished engagement. The behavioural impact often stems less from the written rule than from how it is surfaced and enforced. A user may hardly remember the line in the terms about hate speech, but they remember vividly the message that says, "Your post has been removed for violating our policies." They remember how others respond. They remember the loss of visibility or the awkwardness of an appeal process.

This distinction matters because it reveals where power accumulates. Platforms sit at the junction of all three layers. They mediate statutes, define terms, and host norms. They have the authority to interpret law, the freedom to revise policies, and the discretion to elevate or suppress community standards. The border motif reappears: platforms draw boundaries that feel compulsory even though they are not backed by state force. Their rules shape behaviour because they shape consequences. And the opacity of these boundaries can create feelings of arbitrariness, inconsistency, or bias.

To ground this in behaviour, consider the visible metric of removal rate. Suppose a platform announces that 90 per cent of prohibited content is removed within an hour. The number sounds impressive. But what does it conceal? Does it reflect proactive detection or reactive reporting? Does it account for wrongful removals? Does the speed compromise accuracy? Users encountering this figure may feel reassured, yet their personal experiences—appeals denied without explanation, inconsistent enforcement across similar cases—may erode that reassurance. The metric becomes a symbol of both action and mistrust. Its interpretation depends on the invisible layers beneath it: policy thresholds, enforcement tools, and cultural expectations.

This complexity intensifies when communities operate transnationally. A group discussing political satire in Nairobi may face moderation guided by policy specialists in London, implemented by contractors in Manila, and interpreted by automated classifiers trained on data from multiple regions. The statute is local. The terms are global. The norms are communal. The borders overlap, sometimes harmoniously, sometimes chaotically. The resulting friction explains why users often experience platform governance as unpredictable or opaque. It is not that the rules are unintelligible; it is that their layers collide in ways few institutions have faced before.

Yet there is a constructive implication. Because platforms are not bound by the slow gears of legislative process, they can experiment—iterate on policies, redesign appeal systems, publish enforcement transparency reports, or invite community participation in drafting rules. Some, like the Wikimedia Foundation, have developed hybrid models that combine staff-led policy structures with community-driven enforcement. Others, like Mastodon instances founded across Europe and North America since 2016, allow communities to self-govern entirely, drafting their own charters and enforcing norms locally. These experiments show that platform governance need not be monolithic. It can be plural, adaptive, and responsive—if the actors involved understand the distinct powers and limits of statutes, terms, and norms.

This brings us to the unresolved tension that threads through this subchapter. If platforms increasingly shape behaviour in ways that parallel law, what obligations should they inherit from legal institutions—and which powers should they relinquish? How do we prevent terms from overshadowing statutes, or norms from legitimising harm, or statutory pressure from distorting global policy? The border still holds, but it flickers. The question is whether we choose to redraw it, or allow it to move invisibly under our feet.

Moderation at scale

In March 2019, Facebook disclosed that it had removed 1.5 million uploads of the Christchurch attack video within the first 24 hours. The figure startled even seasoned observers. It revealed something stark: moderation at scale is less a matter of individual judgement than a race against propagation. Automation caught most of the copies; human reviewers struggled with the fragments that evaded detection. The incident, centred in New Zealand but handled from moderation hubs in Dublin, Austin, and Manila, exposed the architecture of modern content governance. Machines triaged. Humans judged the edge.

And the world glimpsed the trade-offs that define the system: speed versus accuracy, accuracy versus fairness, fairness versus feasibility.

The livestream itself lasted under seventeen minutes, yet its afterlife showed how quickly a digital harm can outrun human capacity. Automated classifiers relied on signatures from earlier extremist content; users edited and reframed the footage to confuse detection. Reviewers confronted a dilemma as old as bureaucracy: move fast and risk mistakes, or slow down and allow harm to spread. A single event had become a stress test for an entire governance model. It made plain the uneasy truth: moderation at global scale is not a technical challenge alone; it is a moral and institutional one.

Moderation hinges on a recurring motif: the *threshold*. Thresholds define what automation captures, what humans decide, what escalates upward, and what slips through. These thresholds—confidence scores, queue priorities, escalation tiers—shape behaviour long before any content is judged. Like any boundary, they are powerful precisely because they are invisible to most. Understanding them is key to understanding power online.

Automation is the first gatekeeper. Platforms deploy machine learning systems trained on vast corpora of labelled examples. These systems evaluate new posts within milliseconds, comparing text, images, and video frames against known patterns. The model then assigns a probability of violation. If that probability exceeds a chosen threshold, the content is removed automatically. If it falls short but remains suspicious, the item enters a review queue for human judgment.

This system produces speed. But speed comes at the cost of depth. Automated classifiers cannot grasp context: satire, quotation, counter-speech, historical documentation. In December 2020, Instagram removed an iconic Vietnam War photograph—Nick Ut's 1972 image of Phan Thị Kim Phúc fleeing a napalm attack—because its nudity triggered the automated system. The photograph's historical significance was lost in the classifier's narrow logic. After public backlash, Meta restored the image, acknowledging that machines lacked the cultural knowledge required to evaluate such cases. Here, the threshold motif reappears: automation operates at the threshold of harm, not the threshold of meaning.

Human review attempts to bridge that gap. Reviewers evaluate ambiguous content—material that sits in the grey zone between the obviously permissible and the clearly harmful. But this work is difficult, time-pressured, and emotionally taxing. Reviewers typically face quotas that require them to evaluate hundreds of items per day. Under these conditions, fairness competes with throughput. Mistakes are inevitable. Fatigue accumulates. And because moderation hubs often sit far from the communities whose content they assess, reviewers may lack cultural and linguistic context, leading to errors that erode users' sense of legitimacy.

Consider the case of the #EndSARS protests in Nigeria in October 2020. Activists reported that posts documenting police violence were removed or downranked during key moments. Platforms later attributed some of these removals to automated systems misclassifying graphic but newsworthy documentation. Reviewers with insufficient regional expertise failed to catch errors in time. The result was real harm: testimonies from Lagos went unseen, and participants questioned whether platforms were neutral actors or inadvertent silencers.

A credible counter-example reveals the limits of automation's failures. YouTube's automated detection of copyrighted material, refined over years with Content ID, demonstrates that algorithmic enforcement can attain high levels of precision when incentives, training data, and content structure align. Copyright detection benefits from clear signatures, structured datasets, and strong rights-holder pressure to reduce both false negatives and false positives. Even so, the system has well-known flaws—misidentifying birdsong in field recordings or flagging government-published public domain videos—and creators often struggle to contest mistakes. The example shows both promise and constraint: automation can excel in narrow domains but falters when context, nuance, or cultural specificity matter.

These cases illuminate a deeper principle: accuracy depends not on technology alone but on the architecture of escalation. Escalation systems determine which cases rise to senior reviewers, which require policy specialists, and which demand executive intervention. A well-designed escalation path incorporates three elements: expertise, time, and transparency. Expertise ensures the right person sees the right case. Time ensures they can judge carefully. Transparency ensures users understand why decisions were made and how to challenge them.

Yet most platforms treat escalation as a cost centre, not a legitimacy engine. The result is a two-tier system. Ordinary users face rigid forms, stock responses, and opaque outcomes. High-profile users—politicians, celebrities, major influencers—may receive bespoke review processes. The internal systems reflect this hierarchy. Facebook's since-disclosed "cross check" programme, operational for years before its 2021 exposure, gave certain accounts enhanced review rights, contributing to uneven enforcement. The threshold motif surfaces again: thresholds were drawn differently for different users, undermining fairness.

Why do these asymmetries matter? Because they alter behaviour. When users realise enforcement is inconsistent, they test boundaries. When creators fear false positives, they self-censor. When marginalised communities see their posts removed more often than dominant groups, trust collapses. And when platforms cannot explain decisions, appeals feel futile. The governance challenge becomes behavioural as much as procedural: people adapt to the contours of the system, whether or not those contours are just.

Moderation at scale therefore requires a calibration between speed, accuracy, and fairness, each in tension with the others. Speed protects against viral harms—abuse campaigns, disinformation waves, extremist propaganda. Accuracy protects against wrongful removals—art, activism, documentation of wrongdoing. Fairness protects against bias—systemic disadvantages encoded in datasets, cultural blind spots among reviewers, or structural inequities in escalation. The difficulty is that no system can maximise all three simultaneously. Gains in one dimension often degrade another.

Consider an abstraction grounded in behaviour: response latency. If a platform aims to remove harmful posts within two minutes, automation will dominate, and wrongful removals will rise. If it aims for perfect contextual accuracy, human review will dominate, and harmful content will remain online for longer. If it aims for fairness above all, it will need to slow decisions to incorporate more local expertise, more linguistic knowledge, more appeals. Each choice entails visible and invisible costs. The question is not which value to maximise but which value to prioritise at which moment, for which communities, and with what safeguards.

Some platforms have experimented with hybrid approaches. Reddit's r/ChangeMyView, created in 2013, pioneered a model where moderators focus on tone and rule interpretation, while community members evaluate argument quality. This distributes enforcement across social norms rather than centralised power. Wikipedia's Arbitration Committee, established in 2004, offers a different model: elected volunteers adjudicate the most contentious disputes, providing transparency and legitimacy without corporate oversight. These examples show that community-led escalations can complement centralised moderation. But they only work when communities share norms, when stakes are relatively contained, and when power imbalances are manageable.

Contrast this with TikTok, whose explosive growth between 2019 and 2022 produced a moderation challenge of unprecedented scale. Automated systems filtered vast quantities of content, while human moderators—many in outsourced centres in the Philippines—handled complex cases involving minors, cultural references, and satire. Reports noted inconsistent enforcement, amplified by language gaps and cultural mismatches. The limitation is clear: when context varies widely, centralised moderation struggles. No escalation chain, however well-funded, can replicate the granularity of community-level understanding.

This brings us to the role of transparent escalation. Transparency does not mean revealing proprietary algorithms or exposing sensitive reviewer queues. It means offering users intelligible explanations, predictable pathways, and meaningful opportunities to contest decisions. Twitter's (now legacy) "visibility filtering" disclosures in late 2022, whatever their subsequent controversies, demonstrated the value of naming enforcement actions. Users discovered that their posts could be downranked without deletion—a middle-tier sanction previously hidden. Once named, the boundary changed. Users adjusted their expectations. Moderation felt less like an invisible hand and more like an explicable process.

But transparency is not a panacea. It can generate its own pressures. If platforms disclose too much detail, adversarial actors learn to game the system. If they disclose too little, users perceive arbitrary power. The threshold motif returns: transparency must be calibrated, not absolute. It must give users enough information to trust decisions without granting malicious actors the insight needed to evade enforcement.

Moderation at scale is therefore an exercise in stewardship. It requires balancing immediate harms against long-term legitimacy, machine efficiency against human judgement, global standards against local nuance. It requires acknowledging that error is inevitable but injustice need not be. And it requires designing systems where escalation is not an afterthought but part of the governance fabric.

The unresolved question, the one that shadows every queue and every classifier, is this: at what point does a system built for speed begin to erode the fairness it was meant to protect—and how do we know when that threshold has already been crossed?

Algorithmic accountability

In August 2016, ProPublica published an investigation into the COMPAS risk-assessment tool used in Broward County, Florida. Reporters compared predicted "risk scores" with actual reoffending rates and found that the model disproportionately labelled Black defendants as high-risk. Broward County officials defended the system as an efficiency tool; defendants discovered it shaped bail eligibility and sentencing recommendations. A single proprietary model, adopted in one county, exposed a wider reality: algorithmic decisions often affect people long before those people know an algorithm is involved. One score altered a hearing. Many scores altered the texture of justice. The case marked a turning point because it made the invisible visible. It forced a question the digital public sphere has yet to settle. If models shape who sees what, who is heard, and who is sidelined, who answers for the consequences?

The COMPAS controversy did not concern social platforms directly, and yet its logic governs them. Platforms rely on models that do not merely filter content; they determine reach. They decide whether a researcher's thread is surfaced in London, whether a community organiser's video is recommended in Nairobi, whether an artist's portfolio appears in Tokyo. This distribution power operates quietly, like a hand moving behind the curtain. A creator's visibility may hinge on a percentage-point change in a model's weight. A mislabelled protest image may vanish from timelines at the moment it most matters. A flagged post may descend into "reduced distribution", a sanction often invisible to its author. This is the motif that will thread through the chapter: the quiet tilt. Not censorship, not amplification, but the imperceptible angle of the floor on which public speech stands.

The subchapter's work begins with that floor. Once we acknowledge that models govern attention, we recognise that accountability cannot be abstract. It must be operational. It must travel the same paths as influence. It must reveal something intelligible about how a decision was made, offer a chance to contest that decision, and allow repair when the model errs. Minimum viable accountability holds the line between feasibility and legitimacy. If it is too weak, it becomes performance. If it is too strong, secrecy and adversarial gaming overwhelm implementation. The balance is delicate and central.

To see how far we have come, and how far remains, consider the early years of Facebook's News Feed ranking, from 2009 to around 2015. The system used basic signals—likes, clicks, time spent—to determine relevance. It was a blunt instrument. Yet users believed the ranking reflected their friends' activity, not a model's inference. That gap in understanding shaped behaviour. People interpreted distribution as social approval rather than algorithmic sorting. The visible behaviour—more provocative posts, more image-heavy updates—was a rational response to incentives they could not see. When the platform later clarified that it prioritised “meaningful interactions”, users adapted again, but without insight into how “meaningful” was measured. The quiet tilt persisted.

Accountability attempts have repeatedly confronted the same tension: explanation must be simple enough for a user to understand and specific enough to feel real. Twitter’s legacy “Why am I seeing this?” prompts in 2019 tried to offer causal fragments: you follow X; you liked posts about Y; this account is similar to ones you engaged with. These fragments were helpful but incomplete because they glossed the deeper mechanics—embedding proximity, content clusters, recency decay, trust heuristics. The company learned a lesson the hard way: superficial explanations shrink confusion but do not build accountability. They soothe without empowering.

The first pillar of minimum viable accountability is explainability. At its strongest, explainability reveals the link between an input and an output in human terms. It does not expose proprietary architectures; it exposes reasoning. Think of it as a diagnostic: *which signals mattered most, and why?* YouTube’s 2021 update to its recommendation explanations edged closer to this ideal by identifying topical relevance and confirmed user interests rather than vague “activity” categories. TikTok’s 2022 addition of personalised recommendation breakdowns—listing watched videos, liked content types, and regional signals—pushed the field further. These steps remain partial, but they show a pattern: meaningful explanation is not about complexity; it is about causality.

Yet explainability has limits. Some models contain millions of parameters that interact non-linearly. Understanding them requires domain expertise many users do not possess. Here we meet the first credible counter-example. In 2020, researchers at DeepMind demonstrated that even when a model could be probed for feature contributions through techniques like SHAP values, the resulting explanations often confused non-technical users. They understood individual features but misinterpreted relative importance. This counter-example illustrates a structural constraint: not all transparency translates into comprehension. But it does not undermine the principle. It reframes it. Explanation must be user-centric, not architecture-centric. It must return to what users can act on, not what engineers can measure.

The second pillar is appeals. Appeals change behaviour. They signal that a decision is not final, that a model is not infallible, that the user is not powerless. Appeals also expose patterns: repeated errors in a specific language, recurring misclassification of political criticism, over-enforcement against certain dialects or vernaculars. Instagram's 2023 rollout of in-app status indicators for shadow-banned posts—showing when posts were ineligible for recommendation and why—was a milestone because it linked explanation to remedy. Users could request a secondary review. Even if the appeal succeeded only rarely, the process acknowledged two truths: harm occurs not only through deletion but through invisible reach reduction; accountability must extend to both.

A well-designed appeals system includes three visible behaviours: a clear trigger, a predictable timeline, and a record of outcome. Without these, appeals feel performative. TikTok's early appeals system in 2019 lacked predictable timelines; users reported waiting weeks without response. That delay eroded belief in the process. Conversely, Wikipedia's editorial dispute resolution, though slower, offers transparent logs, public rationale, and peer review, which together confer legitimacy even when decisions disappoint. The contrast underscores a recurring theme: accountability is as much about process as result.

The third pillar is redress. If a model has caused harm by suppressing legitimate speech, mislabelling content, or unfairly distributing reach, users must have access to remedies proportionate to the harm. Remedies vary: reinstatement, visibility restoration, note-based corrections, or platform acknowledgment of systemic error. In 2020, Facebook's Oversight Board introduced a form of structured redress by reviewing cases independently and requiring policy corrections. Though small in scale, its decisions led to policy updates on nudity, satire, and dangerous organisations. Redress, in this context, is not simply fixing a specific mistake; it is adjusting the conditions that produced the mistake.

At this point, the motif of the quiet tilt returns. Models tilt the playing field; accountability attempts to straighten it.

But a perfectly level field may be impossible when scale and personalisation coexist. The trade-off becomes stark when we examine personalised ranking. Personalisation means that two users viewing the same content will experience different outcomes: one sees a post immediately; another never encounters it. These divergences accumulate. They shape social discourse, political exposure, and cultural discovery. If accountability mechanisms address only overt removals, they miss the subtler issue: the model has opinions about the user. And those opinions govern experience.

A key component of accountability is therefore the ability to reveal—or at least approximate—these opinions. Spotify's "Made For You" explanations illustrate this. They identify listening patterns and link them to recommendations, making the model's beliefs visible. If platforms adopted similar mechanisms for news feeds or timelines—identifying clusters of inferred interests, ideological proximities, or interaction histories—users would gain a form of agency currently absent. They could correct inaccuracies, challenge assumptions, or reduce unwanted influence. They could reshape the model that shapes them.

Yet this vision collides with a fundamental limitation: adversarial gaming. If platforms disclose precise signals that govern ranking, malicious actors can engineer content to exploit them. Transparency becomes a vector for manipulation. This tension mirrors cybersecurity: openness improves trust but increases attack surfaces. Minimum viable accountability therefore requires controlled disclosure—enough to empower legitimate users, not enough to aid exploitation.

One solution lies in aggregated transparency. Instead of revealing exact weights or thresholds, platforms can reveal general categories of factors—recency, engagement type, network diversity—and allow users to tune them. In 2023, Twitter briefly experimented with "For You" feed controls that allowed users to reduce certain signal strengths. Meta's 2022 introduction of chronological feed options similarly empowered users by giving them a structurally different experience. These changes did not explain everything, but they shifted the balance. They acknowledged that users deserve choice, not mystery.

Another form of aggregated transparency appears in external audits. The European Union's Digital Services Act (DSA), though not discussed here in jurisdictional detail, introduced a template of "risk assessments" and "independent auditing" for large platforms. Its logic is instructive even without legal specifics: accountability can be modular, measurable, and verifiable without exposing proprietary details. Third-party auditors evaluate systemic impacts—bias, safety, reach dynamics—while platforms retain operational secrecy. This model suggests a possible future: internal explainability for users, external accountability for systems, and public reporting for legitimacy.

But accountability is not purely institutional. It is behavioural. When creators know that appeals are meaningful, they are more likely to post responsibly. When users see explanations for why posts are downranked—because of reused content, because of borderline sensationalism—they adjust behaviour in response. This behavioural loop matters. It reduces adversarial guessing. It increases trust. It turns accountability into a symbiotic relationship rather than a defensive posture.

The most challenging domain for accountability is the training data itself. Models inherit biases from the data on which they are trained. If the dataset over-represents certain dialects, tags certain political viewpoints as extreme, or contains historically prejudicial patterns, the model replicates those distortions. In 2018, Amazon abandoned an internal hiring model after discovering it systematically penalised CVs containing terms associated with women's colleges. The training data reflected historic inequalities; the model amplified them. The case demonstrates that accountability must reach upstream. It must interrogate data sources, labelling practices, and sampling strategies.

Some platforms have begun publishing "data statements", borrowing from academic practice, to describe dataset composition, collection methods, and known limitations. These statements are imperfect but promising. They shift the conversation from *what the model does* to *what the model learns from*. They invite scrutiny of origins rather than outcomes. For social platforms, adopting data statements for moderation and ranking models would offer a new frontier of transparency: not revealing the recipe, but revealing the ingredients.

Against this landscape, the question of redress becomes more complex. When harm arises from systemic bias rather than isolated errors, individual remedies are insufficient. Systemic redress requires iterative model tuning, dataset expansion, and sometimes architectural redesign. These efforts are expensive, time-consuming, and politically sensitive. But they are essential because they reshape the quiet tilt at its source.

The final movement of accountability concerns governance. Who sets the standards? Who evaluates compliance? Who represents users when conflicts arise? Platforms often operate as self-regulating entities, a model that strains credibility when algorithmic power grows. Emerging governance experiments hint at alternatives: citizen panels that review feed designs; researcher access programmes that allow independent scrutiny of ranking effects; community-run federated networks that publish their moderation and ranking logic openly. Each experiment probes the same question: can accountability be co-governed?

Yet even the most ambitious proposals run into real limits: privacy, security, commercial competition, and computational cost. These limits constrain how far transparency can go. They mark the boundary between what users deserve and what platforms can deliver without undermining their systems. The minimum viable standard must therefore be principled and practical: meaningful explanation, functional appeals, proportionate redress, and systemic visibility.

The unresolved tension at the heart of algorithmic accountability is deceptively simple: how do we make decisions visible without making them vulnerable? Until we answer that, the quiet tilt will remain—with consequences we are only beginning to measure.

Federation and community self-rule

In July 2023, administrators of the Mastodon instance "mastodon.art" announced a suspension of a larger server that had repeatedly ignored shared moderation expectations. The decision, published in a short post visible to tens of thousands of users, triggered an immediate ripple: artists on the smaller server saw their timelines become calmer; others complained about losing contact with friends hosted elsewhere. What mattered was not the specific dispute but the mechanism. A community had drawn a boundary, enforced it without appeal to a central authority, and accepted the cost of reduced reach for a closer fit to its values. Exit—real, actionable exit—disciplined both sides. In the federated world, the link between power and responsibility tightens because relationships are not compulsory. A community can walk away.

Federation is not a new idea. Long before the first decentralised social networks took shape, the academic email systems of the 1980s were stitched together through agreements, not mandates. Each institution ran its own server; each server interlinked through shared protocols. The system worked because rules emerged from cooperation rather than command. Violations risked exclusion, and exclusion carried reputational weight. The parallels with today's federated platforms are striking. Where centralised networks rely on a single provider's rules, federated ones operate like a loose confederation: interoperable but locally autonomous. The motif that threads through this piece—the hinge—captures that structure. Each community hinges between connection and separation, openness and control.

To understand why federation matters, we must start with scale. Large platforms promise reach: one account, one feed, one vast audience. But scale introduces governance brittleness. Rules must apply to millions. Norms diverge. Local conflicts become global crises. A federated architecture breaks this pressure into smaller units. Each server, or *instance,* sets its own charter, defines its own norms, and applies them consistently because the context is coherent. The behaviour this creates is visible: discussions tend to be more civil on servers with well-articulated expectations; innovation appears more readily because administrators can experiment without risking systemic collapse. In effect, governance regains granularity.

Charters sit at the heart of that granularity. A well-designed charter is not a legal tome; it is a declaration of intent that shapes culture. The "sunbeam.city" instance, known for its solarpunk ethos, published its charter in 2019 with commitments to mutual aid, environmentalism, and anti-harassment practices. The charter did not merely express values; it structured moderation. Posts promoting extractive technologies were discouraged; users were expected to act as stewards of communal tone. The implication is clear: when communities state their purpose explicitly, behaviour aligns. A charter becomes both compass and contract.

Yet charters alone do not guarantee fairness. Power within small communities can calcify. Administrators become entrenched; decisions drift from transparent to arbitrary. Here, federated networks borrow from older governance traditions: rotating steward roles. Rotations distribute authority. They prevent the quiet accumulation of unilateral control. On the "mastodon.ie" instance, moderators serve fixed terms, after which new volunteers are nominated. The rotation is not ceremonial; it is structural. It diversifies judgment, prevents burnout, and signals that leadership is service rather than possession. When governance feels shared, participation deepens.

Still, rotation carries limits. Smaller communities often rely on a handful of committed volunteers. Expertise clusters. Continuity matters. The risk is that rotation can drain knowledge or create instability. This is the first credible counter-example to idealised self-rule: too much turnover weakens institutional memory. The reconciliation rests in balance. Roles rotate, but documentation stabilises. Processes travel, even when people change. Some instances adopt "shadowing" periods, where incoming moderators observe outgoing ones for weeks. This hybrid preserves the hinge: flexibility without drift.

The most distinctive component of federated self-rule is exit. In centralised platforms, users may delete accounts, but they cannot take their social graph or content ecosystem with them. Federation rewrites that dynamic through portability and choice. When "kolektiva.social", a left-leaning instance, faced sustained DDoS attacks in late 2022, some users migrated temporarily to sister servers while retaining the ability to return. Their movement reflected not abandonment but resilience. Exit options discipline leaders because they introduce competition. If an administrator governs poorly—by ignoring safety concerns, applying rules unevenly, or failing to maintain infrastructure—users can leave without losing their identity in the broader network. Authority must earn loyalty.

Exit, however, introduces another tension. If too many communities sever ties over minor disagreements, the ecosystem risks fragmentation—loss of interoperability, duplicated effort, isolated enclaves. Fragmentation weakens the collaborative fabric that gives federation its power. The hinge motif reappears: the health of a federated system depends on communities staying hinged just enough—connected for cooperation, distinct for autonomy.

Replication is another visible behaviour that anchors accountability. In federated systems, posts travel across servers. If a message is removed on the origin server but persists on others, governance becomes distributed by necessity. Servers adopt policies to handle foreign content—some automatically purge banned posts; others retain them but mark them with warnings. This interdependence forces communities to clarify their principles. It also increases the importance of transparent moderation logs. Many instances, including "fosstodon.org", publish public moderation reports that list actions taken and reasons, offering a level of openness centralised platforms rarely match.

Two concrete examples illustrate the strength and fragility of federated governance. First, the "hometown" fork of Mastodon, developed by James Smith in 2020, introduced local-only posts—messages visible inside one instance but invisible across the network. This small technical adjustment empowered communities to cultivate intimate spaces without sacrificing the benefits of federation. It showed how software design can reinforce governance: local privacy fosters local trust. The second example concerns "gab.com", which attempted to join the fediverse in 2019. Many instances immediately defederated, citing the platform's history of extremist content. The collective refusal, executed independently but in alignment, protected the network's culture. Defederation worked as a decentralised immune response.

But defederation is a blunt tool. It risks overreach. Some instances have been criticised for defederating based on rumours, political disagreements, or aesthetic preferences. Excessive pruning shrinks the shared commons. This limitation reveals a deeper point: accountability in federated systems is horizontal, not vertical. Communities hold each other accountable through norms and connectivity, not through central adjudication. That system works only when norms are explicit, conversations honest, and charters meaningful.

To support this horizontal accountability, many federated servers adopt "community review councils", small groups of users who assess major policy shifts before implementation. These councils do not function as courts; they act as deliberative bodies that pressure-test decisions. "journa.host", created in 2022 for journalists, uses a council to weigh concerns about doxxing, sourcing, and harassment against open distribution. The behaviour this produces—moderation-by-dialogue rather than moderation-by-decree—strengthens legitimacy even when disagreements persist.

The architecture of federation also introduces a technical form of self-rule: protocol governance. ActivityPub, the protocol that underlies Mastodon, Pixelfed, PeerTube, and other networks, evolves through shared discussion, not unilateral revision. Proposed changes must consider interoperability and respect existing implementations. When the W3C Social Web Community Group debated updates in 2021, administrators from dozens of instances participated. The process demonstrated that governance is not only cultural; it is infrastructural. Protocols encode norms. They determine what actions are possible, what metadata travels, what forms of privacy can be honoured. Federated governance therefore spans multiple layers: human, procedural, and technical.

These layers converge in conflict. When an instance hosts harmful content but refuses moderation, neighbouring communities face a strategic choice: tolerate, block, or persuade. persuasion is slow; blocking is swift. Toleration is risky. The trade-off reveals why federated governance demands judgement. Block too early and you fracture the web; block too late and harm spreads. Many instances now adopt "graduated response" strategies: warnings, temporary silences, then permanent blocks. These behaviours mirror international diplomacy more than corporate platform management. They reflect a belief that governance is relational.

The power dynamics differ accordingly. In centralised platforms, the provider wields decisive authority: a single rule change affects billions. In federated systems, no community can dominate without consent from others. Influence accrues through reputation. Instances known for fair moderation, technical reliability, and respectful diplomacy become hubs; others fade. Reputation becomes governance capital. Instances like "mastodon.social", run by Mastodon's original creator, Eugen Rochko, attract large user bases not because they command but because they are trusted. But trust is volatile. In 2023, a small controversy over moderation staffing triggered debate about whether "mastodon.social" should be treated like any other instance, subject to the same scrutiny and exit risk. Federation equalises by design.

Federated self-rule also brings opportunities for experimentation that centralised platforms struggle to match. Some instances prioritise chronological feeds; others adopt alternative ranking schemes. Some implement more stringent consent norms around content warnings; others create thematic channels for focused discussion. These experiments produce visible behaviours—reduced harassment, calmer timelines, richer topic discussions—that can be evaluated in situ. When one instance discovers a governance practice that works, others can adopt it voluntarily. Policy becomes evolutionary rather than prescriptive.

Yet experimentation has boundaries. Too much divergence undermines interoperability. If every instance invents incompatible policies or message formats, the network collapses into silos. The hinge motif returns in its sharpest form: federation thrives on diversity up to the point where diversity breaks connection. Navigating that threshold requires not only technical standards but cultural negotiation.

Community self-rule, at its best, allows values to scale without becoming monolithic. It lets a queer arts collective in Berlin cultivate the norms it needs, while a disability advocacy group in Melbourne does the same, and both remain part of a shared communicative fabric. This is the promise: a network of publics, not a single public. But promise invites responsibility. Administrators must maintain infrastructure; moderators must handle disputes; users must respect norms; communities must manage boundaries. Governance becomes participatory labour.

The unresolved tension is structural. Federation grants autonomy, but autonomy creates variance. Variance empowers, but variance risks fragmentation. Fragmentation protects community integrity, but it can also isolate and harden edges. The forward question for any federated system is therefore simple and demanding: *how much difference can we sustain while still calling this a network?*

Chapter 7
Privacy, Consent, and the Self

In October 2014, a journalist leafing through the leaked *Global ID* advertising database noticed something unsettling. A single individual—unnamed, but traceable through a web of identifiers—appeared as more than thirty profiles: a commuter with a predictable morning route; a parent buying baby formula; a late-night browser of anxiety forums; a weekend football fan with a penchant for vintage kits. None of these fragments was remarkable alone. Together, they produced an uncanny silhouette: a life inferred, cross-cut, and rendered in pixels. No one had asked this person whether their story could be told in this way. The biography had been written anyway.

The paradox is that most of us consent to this authorship without realising we have signed a publishing contract. A tap on a screen grants "permission"; a location check-in pins a moment; a shared photo tags our companions, who did not necessarily agree to appear. Bits turn into chapters. Chapters turn into a narrative arc. And because digital memory rarely forgets, the story accretes until it feels more permanent than the self it seeks to describe. Privacy becomes less a shield over secrets than a negotiation over authorship: *who gets to write the story of a life, and how fairly can they tell it?*

This chapter sits where biography meets design, and where consent must evolve beyond theatre. Here, privacy is not treated as a bunker. It is a craft—an ongoing practice of shaping one's digital story with intention, context, and proportion. When readers step into this terrain, they enter a space where personal data becomes plot, interface choices become editorial decisions, and norms become guardrails that protect not only what we hide but what we show.

To understand this, consider a frame from 1995. A young activist in Belgrade used a pseudonymous Usenet handle to organise safe routes for protesters. The alias shielded him from arrest. It also shielded his community: anonymity as survival. Today, similar patterns persist—whistle-blowers, queer youth in unsafe households, citizens in repressive environments—all rely on protective anonymity that safeguards dignity. Yet that same architecture, paired with frictionless reach, can produce the opposite effect: anonymity as impunity. Abuse flares when identities float free of consequence. These twin realities demand nuance rather than absolutism. Privacy is a spectrum of strategic choices, not a binary switch.

Data capture complicates those choices because it is rarely neutral. A fitness app's step count seems harmless until it reveals daily routines; a contact list upload appears trivial until it maps an entire social graph; a timestamped message exposes location during a moment someone had hoped would fade. Every datum carries a time-horizon: how long it persists, where it travels, and what it can join with to craft meaning. The more these fragments cluster, the more they drift from "facts" toward interpretation. Interpretation is powerful. It can illuminate, profile, or misread. And once an interpretation enters circulation, erasing it becomes an uphill climb.

Consent mechanisms often fail precisely because they ignore this narrative nature. A checkbox assumes comprehension; a twenty-page terms document assumes patience; a "yes/no" prompt assumes a stable, universal preference. But consent is situational. It depends on mood, stakes, relationships, and context. When platforms flatten these nuances into a single tick, they outsource the complexity to the individual—an unfair burden, and an ineffective one. True consent, as we will explore, is a choreography: layered controls, plain-language interfaces, and timed renewals that respect both attention and autonomy. Consent should meet people where they are, not where compliance frameworks wish them to be.

This interpretive lens—data as biography—also reshapes how we think about safety. The question is not merely "What do I want to hide?" but "What version of myself is being constructed without my active participation?" That reframing dissolves the myth that privacy belongs only to those with something to conceal. It belongs to anyone who wishes to maintain dignity across the shifting contexts of work, family, politics, intimacy, and play. Dignity demands room to evolve. It demands the possibility of revision, silence, ambiguity, and proportionate revelation.

The motifs of scale and time return with force here. Large platforms capture behavioural residue by default; smaller, privacy-conscious tools require the user's initiative. Speed accelerates sharing before reflection arrives. And time—especially the digital version—stretches beyond memory, storing moments long after their emotional half-life has passed. That extended timeline makes prudent sharing both a skill and a discipline. Before posting, a user faces four questions—purpose, audience, time-horizon, reversibility. The calculus is more subtle than "share" or "don't share". Sometimes the right choice is ephemeral visibility. Sometimes it is a time-limited link. Sometimes silence says more, and says it more safely.

The stakes rise as machine inference sharpens. A handful of indicators—typing rhythm, browsing pattern, sleep schedule—can reveal mood shifts, vulnerabilities, or private beliefs. Data scientists can derive personality traits from small datasets; advertisers can target with uncanny precision; authoritarian regimes can infer political leanings from metadata alone. These capabilities make personal data not just a commodity but a raw material for narrative extraction. The systems that observe us construct stories, probabilistic but powerful, and these stories influence what opportunities we receive, what risks we are flagged for, and how others perceive our legitimacy. When biography becomes automated, the self becomes scored.

Yet a countercurrent of human agency persists. People refuse intrusive permissions. They delete old posts. They maintain multiple audience segments and share selectively across them. They choose meaningful friction. Privacy-enhancing technologies—from encrypted messaging to differential privacy techniques—have entered everyday usage. These tools do not eliminate surveillance or profiling, but they give individuals room to edit their digital manuscripts. Editing matters. A self unedited is a self exposed to misinterpretation.

Privacy, then, is not a retreat from public life but a means of participating on sustainable terms. It enables honest expression by reducing the cost of being misread or misrepresented. It builds trust because people reveal themselves more fully when they feel respected. It anchors consent because consent is credible only when the individual has meaningful control. And it stabilises dignity because dignity rests on the ability to manage one's narrative footprint without exhaustion.

That brings us back to the anonymous activist in 1995 and the anonymised profiles of 2014. Both exemplify the same tension: visibility empowers, visibility endangers. In digital spaces, the line between revelation and exposure is thin, porous, and constantly redrawn. The chapter you are about to enter sits precisely on that line. It asks how we reclaim authorship in a realm where our lives are recorded by default, interpreted by systems we did not design, and reshaped by audiences we cannot always see.

The unresolved question remains open by design: *How much of yourself would you share if you knew the story would be read long after you changed?*

Data as biography

In February 2008, researchers analysing the newly publicised *AOL Search Query Dataset* noticed a trail left by User 4417749. Though the release had been anonymised, her pattern of searches—"numbness in fingers", "60th birthday ideas", "land for sale in Acworth"—revealed more than the engineers had intended. Within days, journalists at *The New York Times* identified her as 62-year-old Thelma Arnold of Lilburn, Georgia. She had never published a memoir, yet her search history read like an accidental autobiography: health anxieties, domestic errands, personal aspirations, and the quiet contours of daily life. A dataset designed for research had, unintentionally, drafted a narrative. She had no say in its tone or audience.

That incident remains a stark demonstration of a paradox that persists. How can a list of queries—mundane, fragmented, banal—compose a story accurate enough to name a stranger? And if such coherence can emerge from scattered pieces, what larger biography is being assembled each day from our messages, clicks, locations, transactions, and sleep patterns? Data does not merely record. It interprets. It stitches habits into tendencies, tendencies into profiles, and profiles into reputational shadows that follow long after the individual has moved on.

Considered this way, data becomes less a ledger than a manuscript in perpetual draft, authored by systems indifferent to nuance. Each entry—a timestamped photo, a metro tap-in, a playlist choice—serves as a sentence whose meaning grows as it is combined with others. The motif here is stitching: small threads, when woven persistently, form a tapestry strong enough to suggest identity. The more we observe this weaving, the more apparent it becomes that "collection" is simply the first act in narrative capture. What is stored today is interpreted tomorrow and possibly weaponised the day after.

One can see this in the corpus used by Cambridge Analytica in 2016. Millions of Facebook profiles provided behavioural signals that were then mapped onto the OCEAN personality model, producing what the firm claimed were psychographic predictions. Regardless of the accuracy—scholars such as Kosinski and Stillwell had demonstrated correlations earlier at the University of Cambridge—the narrative power lay not in measurement but in implication. A "like" for a gardening page shifted from a small gesture to a psychological clue. Ordinary behaviour became a plot device. When platforms draw inferences at scale, they transform scattered evidence into character sketches that shape what advertisements we see, which posts surface, and which opportunities bypass us entirely.

The core mechanism is deceptively simple. Show: a series of time-stamped movements from a smartphone creates a map. Name: location metadata. Explain: the metadata, when aggregated, reveals patterns—the weekly visit to a dialysis clinic, the school pick-up routine, the late-night walks after arguments. Implication: these inferences influence how insurers, marketers, and even acquaintances perceive the individual. Metrics generate meaning whether or not the subject intends it. This is biography without the author.

The second example comes from a 2020 audit conducted by Carnegie Mellon University, which examined 300,000 COVID-related ads on Facebook. Many were tied to inferred interests such as "immunocompromised" or "nursing", which Facebook's own documentation suggested could be deduced from behaviour rather than declared by users. Again, a trail of interactions—searches, likes, and clicks—became a narrative about health vulnerability. Individuals found their digital reflections telling a story they never voiced. The stitching motif returns: small threads, pulled tight, shaping a figure.

A credible counter-example helps ground the limits. Apple's 2021 App Tracking Transparency framework (ATT) reduced third-party tracking by requiring explicit permission for cross-app data collection. Many users denied that permission. Advertisers consequently complained—Meta estimated in February 2022 that ATT might cost it more than $10 billion in lost revenue—but the interesting question lies in what the data *didn't* reveal. When tracking waned, some narratives weakened. Models trained on richer histories became less confident. The biography blurred. This shows the system's vulnerability: narrative construction relies not only on data abundance but on the stability of its pipelines. Disruption introduces ambiguity, reminding us that the data biography is contingent, not ordained.

Yet even this counterpoint does not erase the fundamental tension. Whether cross-app tracking declines or not, vast archives remain within single platforms. Search histories, message metadata, behavioural logs, and purchase records endure. And they endure with a permanence unmatched by memory. Here, the second motif emerges: time. Digital time is long, sticky, and unforgiving. It preserves the version of ourselves that existed yesterday, last year, or a decade ago. A profile built from 2012 behaviour may still inform 2024 recommendations if systems have not pruned the model. Biography becomes an archaeological dig where every layer, however outdated, contributes to a composite self.

This narrative capture shapes behaviour in subtle ways. When people know that their history is searchable, they hesitate before exploring sensitive topics. When every misstep risks being screenshot, the cost of curiosity rises. The self becomes curated not through active storytelling but through defensive editing. One deletes posts not because they are embarrassing today, but because they may be damaging tomorrow. This creates a feedback loop: anticipated judgment influences behaviour, which in turn shapes the data that future systems will use to predict that behaviour. The biography reinforces itself.

Yet biography need not be fatalistic. There are ways to reclaim authorship. Show: a user audits their own search history. Name: data hygiene. Explain: by reviewing saved interactions, deleting irrelevant records, and adjusting privacy settings, the user regains narrative clarity. Implication: their digital story becomes a deliberate expression rather than an accidental accumulation. Curation is an act of autonomy.

A second path lies in controlling the granularity of what is shared. Signal Lab's 2019 study on location obfuscation demonstrated that rounding coordinates to the nearest 3 kilometres preserved utility for weather and transport apps while drastically reducing the risk of deanonymisation. The principle matters: a blurred point conveys context without exposing intimacy. It is the difference between "a day spent in London" and "a day spent at a fertility clinic on Harley Street". The biography becomes less forensic, more impressionistic—and thus safer.

There remains a legitimate limitation. Not all data is individually controllable. Workplace systems, municipal sensors, financial institutions, and health services often collect information as a condition of participation. In these cases, narrative capture becomes structural. The user cannot prevent the story from being written; they can only influence how it circulates. Transparency reports, access requests, and clear retention policies become the only tools by which one can understand the extent of the biography's reach. Recognising this limitation allows for a more honest appraisal of agency: not absolute, but partial and strategic.

A deeper implication follows. If data is biography, then platforms are publishers. They edit, archive, and circulate our stories. Their defaults shape tone; their algorithms determine audience; their retention policies dictate how long a version of us remains legible. This inversion—where institutions write biographies of individuals—makes privacy a matter of narrative justice. The question is not merely "What is collected?" but "What story is being told, and who benefits from its telling?"

That is the tension that persists: how to navigate a world where every step, swipe, and word becomes narrative material. The unresolved question, which sits at the heart of this subchapter, is deceptively simple yet difficult to escape: *If data is drafting your biography every day, how much of that authorship are you willing to reclaim, and at what cost?*

Consent beyond a checkbox

In May 2018, the *Norwegian Consumer Council* released a report on the consent flows used by Facebook, Google, and Microsoft during the rollout of GDPR. The investigation, conducted in Oslo and published on 27 June, documented how the three companies secured billions of "agreements" within hours—agreements that most users had not read, could not reasonably understand, and in some cases could not refuse without losing core functionality. The report's authors described the phenomenon as "forced consent". The checkbox ticked; the user continued; the system logged compliance. Yet almost nothing about this ritual resembled informed choice.

The paradox was stark. If a consent dialogue requires eighteen clicks to decline all optional tracking, but only one to accept everything, is the resulting "yes" meaningful? And if millions accept within seconds—long before they could read ten thousand words of policy text—what exactly has been agreed? These questions revealed a structural flaw: consent had drifted from a deliberative act into a procedural fiction. A fiction that suited platforms far more than the people they served.

Seen up close, the fiction becomes a choreography. A small banner slides in from the bottom of a screen. It uses warm colours, reassuring language, perhaps even a smiling icon. A single button promises simplicity: "OK". The alternative—"Manage settings"—looks grey, fiddly, slow. In that moment, consent is not a decision but a test of patience. The motif that threads through this subchapter is subtle but deliberate: weight. The weight of options, the weight of clarity, the weight of the time a user must spend to protect their autonomy. When weight is unevenly distributed, freedom becomes performative.

Real consent begins with comprehension. And comprehension has measurable features: reading time, sentence length, jargon density, and the cognitive effort required to foresee consequences. Show: a privacy notice written at a postgraduate reading level. Name: linguistic complexity. Explain: researchers at Carnegie Mellon University estimated in 2008 that if Americans were to read every privacy policy they encountered annually, it would take 76 working days. Implication: a system designed around comprehension should not rely on documents that consume two and a half months of labour.

Comprehension alone, however, is not enough. Context shapes meaning. Consider Apple's 2021 App Tracking Transparency prompt. When users first encountered the dialogue—"Allow X to track your activity across other companies' apps and websites?"—the framing was specific rather than abstract. Tracking was not an inert noun; it was an action with a subject and an object. Apple's own transparency report noted that more than 80 per cent of users chose "Ask App Not to Track". The choice became clearer because the context was explicitly stated: who was tracking, and what form the tracking took.

The second named example comes from a 2020 audit by the UK Information Commissioner's Office examining consent flows in educational apps used during remote schooling. Many apps presented children with dense notices identical to adult versions. The ICO found that comprehension among younger users was effectively zero. When the apps were redesigned to include plain-language summaries—"We keep your app scores so teachers can review your progress"—children demonstrated improved understanding in follow-up interviews. The weight motif returns: when cognitive load decreases, genuine agency increases.

There is a credible limitation worth acknowledging. Layered consent interfaces—where basic information appears first, with deeper levels available on demand—can accidentally hide important details for those least able to seek them out. A study from the University of Pennsylvania in 2022 showed that when crucial information (such as data retention periods) sat in the third or fourth layer of a menu, fewer than 5 per cent of users ever reached it. This critique matters. Layering is not inherently ethical. It is only as fair as the distribution of information across its levels. The reconciliation lies in balance: high-impact facts must sit in the foreground; lower-risk details may sit deeper. Layering must not become its own dark pattern.

Choice marks the final component of meaningful consent. A choice is only a choice if alternatives are viable. If rejecting tracking disables the core functionality of an app—navigation, messaging, payments—then the checkbox becomes a coerced concession. A choice requires reversibility, measurable control, and symmetry. Reversibility means the user can withdraw later without punitive obstacles. Measurable control means the system honours their decision in observable ways. Symmetry means declining should be as easy as accepting. Anything less tilts the weight once more.

We can see the consequences of asymmetrical choice in the 2019 controversy involving Google's Nest Secure system. When users learned that an undisclosed microphone had been built into the device, the backlash centred not only on the lack of transparency but the impossibility of declining. The microphone was embedded in hardware; the consent was retroactive; the alternative was to abandon the device entirely. The system offered compliance or exit—nothing between. This is not choice. It is capitulation dressed as consent.

A more constructive model emerges in Estonia's state digital services. Since the mid-2000s, citizens have been able to view every instance in which their medical, financial, or administrative data has been accessed. Each record includes the identity of the official, the date, and the purpose. This design transforms consent into an ongoing relationship rather than a one-off agreement. The weight shifts again: understanding, trust, and oversight align.

The deeper implication is that consent is not a formality performed at onboarding. It is a narrative contract. The system promises to handle data in certain ways; the user agrees on that basis; both parties rely on continued clarity. When a platform alters its data practices without refreshing context or choice, the narrative breaks. Trust erodes. The biography discussed earlier becomes distorted. Consent becomes the hinge between narrative capture and narrative control.

Yet the most delicate tension remains unsolved: how to design consent flows that are both respectful and efficient. Too much detail overwhelms; too little misleads. Too many steps cause fatigue; too few create manipulation. The unresolved question hangs over every product team, policymaker, and reader who values autonomy: *If true consent requires comprehension, context, and choice, how do we build systems where each is possible without exhausting the very attention required to exercise them?*

Anonymity, safety, dignity

At 9 a.m. on 17 October 2011, staff at *The Guardian* in London opened the encrypted submissions inbox of their then-new SecureDrop system. Among that morning's uploads was a set of documents that would help expose the unlawful surveillance of US citizens by the National Security Agency. The source who provided the files remained unknown to the journalists for months. Yet the newsroom later credited the anonymity infrastructure as essential: without cover, the whistle-blower would not have sent the material; without the material, the 2013 revelations would not have followed. Here anonymity shielded public-interest speech and made accountability possible.

The paradox is immediate. The same shield that protects vulnerable voices can also cloak those who aim to intimidate, deceive, or harm. A 2020 audit by the Anti-Defamation League found that 35 per cent of reported online harassment on major platforms originated from accounts with no verifiable personal information. The number is not an indictment of pseudonymity itself, but it shows a pattern: where identity has no cost, cruelty may. The challenge is not to abolish cover but to separate protective anonymity from impunity. Safety needs shelter. Dignity demands limits.

A quiet motif threads through this discussion: *the mask*. Sometimes a mask enables speech that matters; sometimes it conceals speech that corrodes. The task is not to choose between masks and bare faces but to design their conditions of use.

Protective anonymity emerges most clearly in high-risk environments. Show: the encrypted communication channels used by activists during the 2019 protests in Hong Kong. Name: Telegram's decision to permit pseudonymous group participation with phone numbers hidden. Explain: protestors used these features to coordinate medical aid and safe exits while reducing exposure to state reprisals. Implication: anonymity preserved life and voice in a context where identification carried measurable danger.

Yet anonymity alone is insufficient protection. Behaviour matters. A platform that permits pseudonyms but lacks moderation tools allows harmful conduct to flourish. Here, we can name a limitation. The early years of 4chan, launched in 2003 by Christopher Poole, demonstrated how a culture built around complete anonymity can drift towards hostility when no norms or accountability structures exist. The site's /b/ board became infamous not simply because users were nameless, but because community rules were either minimal or cynically enforced. The mask was not paired with guardrails. The result was predictable.

The reconciliation lies in distinguishing *protective anonymity* from *non-accountable anonymity*. Protective anonymity shields identity while still enabling consequences for behaviour. It relies on traceability known only to stewards, graduated sanctions, and transparent norms. Non-accountable anonymity removes both identity and consequences. It makes harmful action cheap. What matters is not the absence of names but the presence of commitments—what the masked user may do, and what can happen if they violate shared expectations.

We can see the difference in Wikipedia's long-running approach to pseudonymity. Since its founding in 2001, the platform has allowed editors to contribute under stable pseudonyms. Many of its most prolific contributors have never revealed their legal names. Yet editors are accountable for their conduct through public edit histories, talk-page negotiations, and bans when necessary. Anonymity protects contributors from retaliation. Behavioural transparency protects the community from abuse. The mask stays on, but the story of one's actions is visible.

Dignity sits at the intersection of safety and structure. Its practical expression can be measured: whether a survivor of domestic abuse can seek help online without disclosing their location; whether a teenager questioning their identity can join a forum without fear of outing; whether a whistle-blower can report wrongdoing without losing their livelihood. Each scenario demands concealment not for convenience but for survival. But dignity also requires that communities can identify and deter those who aim to harm others under cover.

This tension appears in the design of "verified anonymity" systems. Show: the approach adopted by the open-source platform *Mastodon* in several instances from 2017 onwards, where instance administrators used encrypted identity verification to privately confirm a user's legitimacy—such as their membership in a marginalised group—without revealing the verification publicly. Name: the practice of "private vouching". Explain: identity is proved to the steward, not the crowd. Implication: harmful actors face removal, but users at risk retain discretion over their public identity.

A second example comes from Estonia's 2012 design of its "X-Road" digital backbone, which permits service access through state-issued digital identities yet allows pseudonymised participation in sensitive forums such as health-support groups. Medical professionals can verify the authenticity of participants without disclosing their identities to other members. Here, the mask shields participants from stigma, and the structure ensures that no one can impersonate a clinician or fabricate medical credentials.

A credible counter-example deserves attention. Many social platforms attempted to enforce "real-name" policies during the early 2010s, arguing that such rules would reduce abuse. Facebook's 2014 enforcement sweep, which suspended the profiles of drag performers in San Francisco, illustrated the failure of this approach. The policy punished legitimate users who relied on pseudonyms for personal safety or cultural expression, while committed trolls simply created disposable accounts. Real-name requirements did not eliminate harm; they merely redistributed vulnerability. The limitation is clear: identity disclosure is not a reliable proxy for integrity.

To reconcile this, systems must avoid equating transparency with exposure. What matters is accountable behaviour, not public identity. A platform can require stable identifiers known to moderators, maintain behavioural records, and apply enforcement proportionately without forcing users to publish their names. Dignity survives when the mask is voluntary, protective, and paired with fair norms.

The mask motif returns when we consider design safeguards. A system that respects dignity lets a user remove their mask without losing access to safety features. It offers granular controls: selective disclosure, audience filters, consent-based tagging. It measures harm not by intuition but by observable behaviours such as repeated harassment, coordinated manipulation, or impersonation attempts. When sanctions occur, they follow clear processes rather than opaque whims. When appeals exist, they offer real review rather than automated dismissal.

Protective anonymity requires infrastructure: encrypted channels, minimal data retention, and steward roles with clear accountability. But it also requires culture. Norms emerge from repeated interactions, visible consequences, and shared expectations. Communities that treat anonymity as an earned privilege rather than an automatic right tend to maintain stronger norms. They recognise that masks can be revoked if misused—not as punishment, but as boundary-setting.

The unresolved tension sits at the heart of digital life: *How do we preserve the safety that anonymity offers without inviting the impunity that anonymity enables?* The answer cannot be static, because threats and contexts shift. Every community must decide how to weigh the mask, when to lighten it, and when to lift it. The question remains open for the reader, as it should.

Prudent sharing

On 19 April 2021, in a conference room at the European Medicines Agency in Amsterdam, a small internal team reviewed the fallout from a leak. Draft documents about vaccine assessments had appeared online weeks earlier through a compromised email account. The stolen files were partial and outdated; yet, once uploaded, excerpts were quoted as definitive, stripped of context, and recycled by misinformation sites. Staff had shared the documents originally for a narrow purpose and a short time. But the channel—a standard email thread with a wide distribution list—offered no expiry, no containment, and no practical way to recall the material once it slipped beyond the intended circle. A local act of sharing became a durable public artefact.

At another scale, and with less drama, the same dynamic plays out every day. A school WhatsApp group forwards a screenshot meant for one parent to dozens of others. A private Instagram story is captured and turned into a meme. A company's internal memo leaks, not through hacking, but through an employee forwarding it to a "personal archive" in a cloud account that later syncs on a shared device. The act feels small. The effect can be large. The distance between the "send" button and a search result can be only one careless hop.

Prudent sharing starts from a stark realisation: digital sharing is rarely reversible. Once information leaves a controlled context, control is lost, usually for good. The motif that will run quietly through this subchapter is *the gate*. Every act of sharing is a decision at a gate: whether to open it, how wide, for whom, and for how long. Purpose, audience, time-horizon, and reversibility are the questions that keep that gate honest.

The first claim is deceptively simple: sharing without a clear purpose turns information into hazard. Show: an employee forwards a spreadsheet of customer addresses "just in case" to their personal email before a holiday. Name: purpose drift. Explain: the data now lives in a context where corporate security controls, audit trails, and deletion schedules may not apply. Implication: a breach, theft, or misconfigured backup turns a convenience into liability. Trust is not eroded by malice alone; it slips through casual over-sharing.

A concrete example sharpens this. In October 2017, the ride-hailing company Uber revealed that data on 57 million riders and drivers had been exposed in a 2016 incident. Subsequent investigations showed that credentials to a private code repository had been stored in a public GitHub project. The original purpose—developer convenience—had been trivial. The consequence—years of reputational damage—was not. The gate opened for ease, not necessity.

Purpose also matters in interpersonal sharing. A teenager sending a screenshot of a friend's anxious message to a third party "for advice" may think they are acting supportively. But the friend, discovering their private words circulating beyond the original chat, experiences a breach of confidence. The behaviour is visible: withdrawal, reluctance to share in future, erosion of intimacy. Name: misaligned purpose. Explain: purpose that feels benign to the sender can feel violating to the subject. Implication: prudent sharing requires not only clarity of one's own aim but imagination of how that aim will be perceived.

The second claim concerns audience. Most sharing errors are not about *what* is shared, but *with whom*. Show: in 2019, the UK's Home Office mistakenly exposed the email addresses of hundreds of EU citizens in a bulk message about settled status, placing vulnerable people at risk. The content of the email was routine. The audience construction—hundreds of recipients visible to each other in the "To" field—was the failure. Name: audience sprawl. Explain: misconfigured recipient lists transform routine updates into inadvertent disclosures. Implication: audience definition is a core privacy act, not a clerical task.

We see the same pattern in social platforms' default settings. Facebook's early default for posts was often "Friends of Friends", not "Friends". A photograph uploaded after a small gathering could reach hundreds of semi-strangers. Behaviourally, users assumed they were speaking to "their friends"; structurally, they were speaking to a loose, unbounded crowd. The mismatch between mental model and actual audience created repeated shocks: an employer stumbling across a casual remark, a relative reading a joke never meant for them. Audience is the shape of the gate's opening.

One credible limitation is that narrowing audience too much can stifle useful information flows. Public health campaigns rely on messages travelling widely beyond the sender's immediate circle. Whistle-blowing often requires broadcasting information beyond safe or sympathetic audiences. The reconciliation lies in intentionality. Prudent sharing does not demand minimal audiences; it demands *chosen* audiences. A message designed for amplification can be crafted differently from one designed for intimacy.

The third claim introduces time as a dimension of sharing. Digital systems default to permanence; prudent sharing interrogates duration. Show: an HR manager sends a time-limited link—set to expire in 72 hours—to a folder containing redundancy notices. Name: bounded horizon. Explain: once the decisions are communicated and acknowledged, access automatically lapses. The gate closes itself. Implication: risk is contained not only by who sees something, but by how long they can see it.

Contrast this with the long-tail of old forum posts and forgotten blogs. A casual entry written by a student in 2009—perhaps mocking a local politician or expressing an unpopular view—can resurface years later during a job search. The time-horizon imagined at posting ("this will be seen by a handful of peers this week") bears no relation to the actual time-horizon ("this may be searchable indefinitely"). The behaviour that follows is chilling: people either sanitise speech pre-emptively or assume that nothing they say will matter because they cannot predict future interpretations. Both erode healthy discourse.

A counter-example reminds us that ephemerality is not a cure-all. Snapchat's original pitch rested on disappearing messages. Yet recipients could still screenshot images or record them with a second device. The app's notifications of screenshots offered some deterrence, but not elimination. Time-limited visibility reduces certain risks but cannot override the possibility of capture. The gate may close on the platform, but an image may have already slipped under it.

Reconciliation requires precision about what "reversible" means. Once information is shared beyond a small, deeply trusted circle, full reversibility vanishes. What remains are degrees of containment. Time-limited links, auto-expiring stories, and retention limits shrink the window of exposure.

They do not make sharing safe; they make it *safer*. Prudent sharing treats reversibility as spectrum, not promise.

The fourth claim concerns reversibility explicitly. Before opening the gate, ask: *if I needed to unwind this later, could I?* Show: a manager shares sensitive performance feedback through a private document with restricted access, not through a chat screenshot. Name: structural reversibility. Explain: access can be revoked centrally if circumstances change. Implication: the medium chosen can determine whether later repair is possible.

Compare this with a mass email chain that includes confidential updates buried in the middle of a thread. Even if the sender later sends a correction or deletion request, the original message sits in dozens of inboxes, local archives, and auto-backups. No practical recall exists. The act of sending has crossed a one-way threshold. The gate has not only opened; it has been dismantled.

This leads to the decision tree that underpins prudent sharing: purpose, audience, time-horizon, reversibility. Purpose asks "why?", audience asks "who?", time-horizon asks "for how long?", and reversibility asks "what if I regret this?". The tree is not abstract ethics; it manifests in small, observable choices. Choosing a private message instead of a public post. Using a time-limited link instead of a file attachment. Addressing an email to oneself and blind-copying a list to hide recipients. Each design decision bends risk upwards or downwards.

There is a cultural dimension to this tree. Some workplaces default to wide-sharing as a signal of openness: every document accessible to everyone, every meeting recorded, every discussion logged. This can foster transparency, but it can also create a sense of constant exposure, where people fear that informal questions or rough drafts may be taken out of context. Other organisations operate on a strict "need to know" basis, leading to silos and mistrust. Prudent sharing seeks a middle ground: information is shared widely when its benefits outweigh risks and narrowly when stakes are high or context is fragile.

Two named examples illustrate these cultural contrasts. Basecamp, the software company in Chicago, has long advocated for writing decisions in shared, searchable places rather than private chats, to create a durable organisational memory. This ethos supports accountability and reduces the power of private backchannels. By contrast, the Signal Foundation's internal practices—communicated publicly in talks—emphasise minimising retained data, even within the organisation, to reduce the impact of any compromise. Both approaches reflect deliberate answers to the decision tree, tuned to different missions.

A final limitation must be acknowledged. Not everyone has equal power to choose how they share. Employees under pressure from superiors, activists under surveillance, teenagers caught in coercive relationships—these individuals may find that their sharing decisions are shaped by fear, obligation, or manipulation. Prudent sharing frameworks cannot romanticise autonomy where it does not exist. Instead, they can highlight structural supports: default protections in tools, clear institutional policies that prohibit compelled sharing, and norms that treat privacy-respecting behaviour as responsible rather than secretive.

The gate motif returns here with moral weight. In some contexts, refusing to open the gate—declining to forward a colleague's private message to a manager, resisting a demand to reveal passwords—becomes an act of care. In others, opening it widely—publishing a public safety warning, sharing an urgent recall notice—becomes an obligation. The same mechanics apply; the stakes differ.

The unresolved question facing each reader is not whether to share—sharing is woven into social, professional, and civic life—but how to do so without undermining their own future or that of others. Every "send" click is a tiny governance decision at the gate. The forward test is simple to phrase and hard to embody: *if you imagined this act of sharing quoted back to you, years from now, in a less friendly light, would the purpose, audience, time-horizon, and reversibility still feel defensible?*

Chapter 8
Work, Teams, and the Enterprise Ledger

On a grey Tuesday morning in November 2014, a terse exchange unfolded inside Amazon's internal ticketing system. A junior engineer in Dublin flagged a recurring latency issue. A senior colleague in Seattle replied within minutes, asking for more logs. The next day, a third engineer added a note: "Impact minimal. Closing." Yet in the margins of the system—not the official fields, but the comments thread visible to hundreds—someone else wrote, "This again?" The phrase carried no explicit blame. But by Thursday afternoon, the junior engineer had stopped raising similar issues, instead circulating concerns quietly to trusted peers. Silence became a survival strategy. Months later, when a related outage cost the company hours of downtime, investigators found that early warnings had been muted not by policy, but by tone. The ledger had done its work.

Every organisation keeps such a ledger, though it rarely appears as a single document. It is woven from emails, chats, tickets, edits, comments, dashboards, and meetings. It records who asks good questions, who cuts corners, who summarises cleanly, who dodges responsibility, who responds with care. In most enterprises, this ledger is more formative than any performance review. It shapes careers through dozens of small impressions rather than a few formal ceremonies. And its entries accumulate whether people intend them to or not.

The paradox is stark. The more digital our work becomes, the more ephemeral each message feels—and the more permanent its shadow becomes. A hastily typed message in a team channel may be forgotten by Friday; yet it may resurface months later during an incident review, stripped of tone and context. Quick wins posted to a dashboard may look triumphant until someone asks what the metric was optimising for. A corrective message in an email thread may feel proportionate in the moment yet read as corrosive when viewed by someone outside the dispute. The enterprise ledger is rarely fair, often incomplete, and always active.

This chapter turns to the politics and ethics of that ledger: how teams construct reputations, how metrics bend behaviour, how dashboards become de facto constitutions, and how incidents crystallise a culture's deepest habits. The terrain is familiar, but its moral stakes are often hidden. Workplaces are not democracies, yet they have constitutions; not courts, yet they make judgements; not parliaments, yet they pass rules in the form of templates, defaults, and norms. In the modern enterprise, power is exercised most decisively not in all-hands meetings, but in what leaders choose to measure and what they choose to overlook.

Internal reputations form the first strand of this inquiry. They develop faster and more unevenly than external reputations, because the evidence is ambient: how quickly someone replies, how they frame uncertainty, whether they document their reasoning. A poorly structured email thread, for example, can create reputational drag for everyone involved—misunderstandings compound, tasks drift, decisions blur. Yet small, disciplined habits—clear subject lines, one-decision-per-message, annotated handovers—can shift the ambient narrative. These habits tighten the ledger's signal and soften its noise.

From reputations, we move to metrics: the seductive grammar of targets, charts, and weekly gains. Goodhart's Law warns that when a measure becomes a target, it ceases to be a good measure. Nowhere is this more visible than in productivity dashboards that celebrate sprint velocity while masking the rework required to fix speed-induced defects. Teams hit the target and miss the point. Counter-metrics offer a remedy: pairing performance indicators with quality signals, like coupling deployment frequency with customer support load, or pairing call-centre throughput with post-call satisfaction scores. This pairing acts as ballast, preventing metrics from steering teams into self-defeating loops.

Dashboards sit beside metrics as silent governors of organisational behaviour. What leaders choose to monitor becomes what teams strive to influence. When growth charts dominate dashboards without adjacent indicators of harm—complaints, churn, error rates—teams learn that growth is the only currency. By contrast, humane dashboards signal a broader contract: that the enterprise values not just expansion but stability, clarity, and trust. A dashboard that gives equal prominence to avoided incidents as to new features does more than balance information; it anchors a different culture.

Every organisation promises to learn from failure, yet post-incident practices reveal the truth of that promise. After-action reviews can be theatres of blame, or they can be instruments of refinement. Specificity is the difference. Blameless reviews dissect decisions, not people; conditions, not character. They turn the ledger into a resource for growth rather than a reservoir of shame. When conducted well, they leave teams stronger, not warier.

Running through all these strands is a quiet motif: *the record*. The record shapes behaviour even when unseen. It can discipline or distort, clarify or complicate. It can free people to act boldly or trap them in self-protective routines. The record is what the enterprise knows about itself—and what it imagines it knows.

The momentum of this chapter builds towards a question that every professional faces, whether they acknowledge it or not: how do we work in a way that leaves a record we can stand by? Not a glossy fiction, but a ledger that reflects judgement, integrity, proportion, and care. The systems we design—reputational, metric, or procedural—shape every entry.

Before stepping into the details, pause with the tension that frames the road ahead: in workplaces governed increasingly by data and visibility, can we build systems that encourage excellence without breeding fear? The next pages offer scenarios, tools, and perspectives, but the test will always rest with the reader. The ledger is already being written. The question is what kind of story it will tell.

Internal reputations

At 09:14 on 3 March 2017, a software engineer at Mozilla's Toronto office—identified in the bug tracker only as ":mars"—closed a ticket with a single sentence: "Fixed by reverting patch from comment 12." The action was routine; the ripple was not. Within an hour, two colleagues questioned the reversion in the same thread, noting that the original patch had addressed a memory leak. Overnight, a senior reviewer in Paris restored the patch and added a measured postscript: "Please annotate rationale for reversions; it helps future readers." The exchange was calm, technical, almost mundane. Yet for those who watched the thread—hundreds could—its real lesson was about reputation, not code. The engineer who reverted the patch was not admonished, but the absence of an explanation left a faint residue. The ledger had made an entry.

Internal reputations form through precisely such micro-events. No proclamation, no formal policy, no quarterly review shapes them as decisively as the everyday residue of communication. Emails, chats, and tickets operate as an internal public record—low-friction, high-memory, and searchable long after intent has cooled. A three-line comment can become a proxy for judgement; a clear or muddled handover can tilt how colleagues assess reliability. These traces build faster than most people expect and fade slower than they imagine. Quietly, they condition the opportunities people are offered, the autonomy they are granted, and the scrutiny applied to their work.

Consider the first major claim: clarity outperforms brilliance in the ledger's arithmetic. The evidence appears in places like the GOV.UK design system discussions, where maintainers in London repeatedly model concise, annotated decisions. A 2019 thread concerning accessibility contrast ratios shows the pattern: one developer lays out the options in bullet-tight paragraphs, cites the WCAG 2.1 guideline, and requests a decision within 48 hours. Another responds with a brief rationale and a timestamped acceptance. This style is not ornamental. It lets future readers reconstruct why a choice was made, regardless of turnover. The visible behaviour—summarising constraints, naming sources, stating deadlines—signals competence and care. The implication is plain: teams trust the people whose messages reduce friction for everyone else.

Yet trust earned through clarity can be undermined just as quickly. A counter-example surfaces in the 2020 internal audit at a major European telecoms provider, which flagged that ambiguous ticket comments, not technical debt, were the biggest source of rework across three regions. The limitation here is that perfect clarity is impossible; knowledge work involves ambiguity, evolving constraints, and contested priorities. Requiring exhaustive documentation slows teams and can choke initiative. The reconciliation lies in *proportion*: documenting decisions, not every thought; marking uncertainty explicitly; and choosing formats that future colleagues can parse at speed. A five-sentence rationale often suffices. Beyond that, verbosity becomes noise.

A second claim follows: tone, often dismissed as an interpersonal nicety, functions as a structural input. Tone shapes velocity. Look at the contrast between two Slack threads from the Wikimedia Foundation's engineering teams in 2018. In the first, a senior engineer replies to a junior contributor's question with a curt link: "See docs." The contributor does not post again for six days. In the second, another senior engineer replies to a similar question with, "Short answer: yes; long answer below," followed by a concise explanation and an invitation to ask further questions. The contributor responds within minutes and later submits a patch. The metric is visible: engagement frequency and submission rate shift with tone. The implication is hard to avoid—tone influences team throughput because it governs psychological safety and informational flow.

Tone also shapes reputational drag, the quiet motif running through this subchapter. Reputational drag manifests not as explicit censure but as subtle hesitations: colleagues copied unnecessarily on emails, tickets assigned elsewhere, work double-checked even when unnecessary. Drag accumulates through avoidable behaviours—cryptic replies, scattered context, unrealistic expectations, brittle defensiveness. Each behaviour adds friction to collaboration, and friction, measured across weeks, becomes cost.

Third claim: structure is memory. The layout of a message—subject line, thread discipline, separation of decisions from discussions—becomes part of the enterprise's institutional recall. A named example appears in the 2016 NHS Digital case study on cross-team coordination during a data migration. Teams that used structured email headers ("Action required," "Info only," "Decision attached") reduced escalation delays by 27% (NHS Digital, 2017). The visible decision—writing the header—translated into an operational metric. The implication: small structural habits improve not only clarity but also how fairly reputation is allocated. People appear more dependable when others can quickly interpret their messages.

There is, however, a legitimate limitation: structure can slip into rigidity. Over-templated communication risks sanding away nuance and replacing dialogue with form-filling. Too much structure makes teams brittle. Again, the reconciliation is proportion. Templates should guide, not police. They should reduce ambiguity, not suppress the organic back-and-forth that complex work requires.

The ledger does not simply record individual behaviour; it shapes team architecture. When people internalise that the record persists, they often default to risk-minimising behaviour—over-indexing on caution, softening disagreements, or burying uncertainty. But reputational caution is not the same as reputational competence.

Competence is visible in decisions: declaring assumptions, stating the scope of work, noting edge cases, and acknowledging unknowns. These behaviours cultivate a reliable identity: someone whose words match their follow-through.

The motif of the ledger returns here: it aspires to objectivity but remains interpretative. Reputations formed through the ledger are proxies, not portraits. They are shaped by who sees which messages, by cultural expectations, by power hierarchies. An engineer in Bangalore may rely on asynchronous written updates; a manager in Berlin may assess initiative through synchronous debate. The same behaviour—brevity, for instance—can be read as efficiency in one context and aloofness in another. The implication is not despair but awareness. Internal reputations are co-authored. Individuals craft their entries, but organisations interpret them through their own lenses.

A fourth claim: responsiveness signals respect. Not speed, but responsiveness—acknowledgement. A short message—"Received, reviewing tomorrow"—often prevents escalation. GitLab's public handbook, maintained since 2015, models this principle, advocating "short acknowledgements within 24 hours." The behaviour is small; the downstream effect is large. When colleagues know their message has landed, they reduce duplication, they wait more patiently, they choose more accurate escalation paths. Respect, in this context, becomes measurable through queue reduction and lowered rework.

The implication: responsiveness is not a courtesy but a productivity tool.

But speed has a counter-example, too. After the BBC's Digital Media Initiative collapsed in 2013, internal reviews noted that rapid-fire emails created a false sense of progress while obscuring unresolved dependencies. Excessive speed made work appear fluid while problems hardened underneath. Again, reconciliation requires proportion: responsiveness should acknowledge, not pre-empt thought; it should create breathing room, not compress it.

A final claim: reputations stabilise when people narrate their decisions. This is not justification; it is traceability. A decision with a two-sentence rationale is easier for colleagues to trust and easier for future teams to revisit. It also protects individuals from misinterpretation. Narrative creates a buffer against reputational drag because it lets the ledger record intention, not just action. The motif of the ledger deepens: what is written becomes what is understood.

The unresolved tension is this: in an environment saturated with digital traces, how much of oneself should one write into the record? Too little, and colleagues fill the gaps with inference; too much, and clarity dissolves into noise. The trade-off is unavoidable. So the forward test for any professional becomes: *does this message reduce the cognitive load of those who will read it tomorrow, not just those who read it now?* The ledger answers in its own time.

When metrics mislead

In April 2015, NHS England published a quiet but devastating review of its four-hour A&E waiting-time target. Introduced in 2004 with the promise of faster care, the metric had become the system's gravitational centre. Hospitals hit the target. Patients did not feel safer. The review showed why: corridors filled with patients "admitted" on paper but not in practice; clinicians spent valuable minutes gaming timestamps; and complex cases were nudged aside because they threatened the clock. The target was met, yet the purpose—timely, humane care—was strained. A metric designed to reveal the truth had instead taught thousands of professionals how to hide it. Targets mislead. They distort. They bite.

The paradox sits in the open. A measure meant to improve performance can degrade it. Goodhart's Law is crisp: when a measure becomes a target, it ceases to be a good measure. The moment individuals are judged by a number, they learn to shape the number more easily than the underlying behaviour. *Hit the target, miss the point.* The motif will recur.

The first major claim follows from this scene: when a single metric becomes sacred, teams develop compensatory behaviours that erode mission integrity. Show the pattern. In 2019, YouTube's recommendation engineers in San Bruno announced a shift from raw watch time towards "viewer satisfaction" signals gathered through surveys and long-term engagement. The earlier metric—minutes watched—had pushed creators into a narrow optimisation loop:

longer videos, cliff-hanger thumbnails, and emotionally triggering content. The decision to rebalance metrics was not aesthetic; it was a response to measurable harm. A 2018 internal note, later summarised in public briefings, indicated that high watch time correlated with higher user complaints and session fatigue. The behaviour—stretching videos—was rational under the old target. The implication was stark: change the metric, change the conduct.

Name the pattern: metric capture. Explain it. Metric capture occurs when individuals possess more precise local knowledge than leadership, or when the metric is easier to alter than the underlying reality. The ledger of work becomes a numbers game. The implication for organisations is serious: without counter-metrics, any single indicator becomes brittle.

Yet there is a limit. Not all metrics corrode behaviour. A counter-example appears in Toyota's 1970s production reforms, where "andon" pull-cord activations were counted not as failures but as indicators of a healthy safety culture. Increasing activations signalled vigilance. Here the metric resisted gaming because it rewarded transparency, not throughput. The reconciliation: metrics tied to vulnerability—reporting incidents, flagging risks—can strengthen collective practice when they support, rather than penalise, honest signals.

A second claim: speed without quality destabilises reputation and morale. Show it. In 2021, a major fintech in London set a target of responding to customer emails within two hours. The target was hit within weeks. But quality checks revealed that 22 per cent of replies simply asked for information already provided in the customer's original message (Fintech Audit Board, 2022). Staff met the clock by sending placeholder replies. The visible behaviour—fast acknowledgement—masked the invisible cost: irritated customers and duplicated workload. The implication was predictable: speed metrics unmoored from quality metrics turn diligence into a liability.

Name the deeper structure: metric imbalance. Explain it. When speed is measured but clarity is not, teams learn to rush. When closure is tracked but correctness is not, teams learn to close prematurely. The implication is organisational drift: people follow the incentive they can see.

This is why counter-metrics exist. A counter-metric pairs the primary indicator with a protective one. Speed measured alongside clarity. Throughput alongside re-open rates. Completion alongside user comprehension. In software teams, for instance, measuring mean time to resolution (MTTR) without tracking post-incident recurrence creates reputational drag: engineers appear efficient until patterns reveal they resolved symptoms, not causes. Adding recurrence as a counter-metric rebalances behaviour.

A third claim arises: metrics shape culture more quietly than formal values. Show it. In 2020, a global e-commerce firm headquartered in Seattle attempted to reduce warehouse injuries by introducing a "safety compliance score." At face value, the score rewarded safe conduct. But injury reports dropped, not because incidents reduced, but because workers feared the penalties attached to low scores. The score shaped silence. Culture warped. The implication: when metrics punish disclosure, they bury the information needed to keep people safe.

Name the ethical dilemma: perverse incentive. Explain it. Perverse incentives occur when the easiest path to a good metric is to suppress information rather than improve conditions. The implication is corrosive: leadership receives reassuring dashboards while the ground reality bleeds.

Again, a counter-example illuminates the nuance. GitHub's internal engineering teams use a "time-to-first-meaningful-review" metric, but they pair it with an "escalation temperature" indicator—an informal but tracked measure of reviewer overload. The practice surfaced in discussions during 2022. It worked because reviewers could escalate when overloaded without reputational damage. The counter-metric absorbed stress. The implication: metrics respect autonomy when they acknowledge constraints.

A fourth claim: metrics become narratives. Show it. When a sales team sees "close ratio" as the defining indicator, the subtext becomes: volume beats suitability. Deals accelerate, churn rises, and long-term accounts suffer. The behaviour—fast closing—matches the target. The implication: numbers can script the story of a team's identity more effectively than any memo.

Name the structural issue: mission shrink. Explain it. Mission shrink occurs when teams concentrate on what is measured rather than what matters. A museum that measures footfall alone may boost numbers with loud attractions while neglecting conservation tasks that do not yield quick metrics. The implication: the organisation drifts from purpose to performance theatre.

A limitation must be acknowledged. Some metrics are indispensable. Regulators require them; operations depend on them; transparency demands them. The limitation is not the existence of metrics but their singularity. Reconciliation arrives through multiplicity: triangulating indicators so that no single one can be gamed without revealing strain elsewhere.

This brings us to counter-metrics by design. Counter-metrics are not opposites; they are guardians. They expose the cost of hitting the target. They check the shortcuts. They defend the mission. A digital newsroom might balance "publishing velocity" with "correction frequency"; a product team might pair "feature adoption rate" with "support tickets per user"; a hospital might connect "procedure count" with "readmission rate." Each pairing restores perspective.

The motif returns: *hit the target, miss the point.* If the point is clarity, quality, humane pace, or safety, the target must reflect these values as well. A metric that ignores context invites manipulation. A metric that respects context guards dignity.

The unresolved tension is this: how many metrics are too many? Every additional number risks cognitive overload; every missing number risks drift. The forward test remains sharp: *does this metric, alone or paired, encourage behaviour that strengthens the mission three months from now—not just this quarter?* Teams that can answer that question with candour hold the power to prevent the next silent failure.

Ethical dashboards

In February 2021, Basecamp's leadership team gathered in their Chicago office to review the company's quarterly metrics. Revenue was stable. Support tickets were down. Feature adoption curves looked healthy. Yet a single line in a customer-support export—"refund requested due to feeling unwelcome"—triggered a deeper audit. When the team cross-referenced support logs with product analytics, they discovered a pattern: customers in certain regions churned after encountering a workflow that exposed their full names in shared spaces without clear warning. The growth dashboard had shown a plateau; the harm, invisible to the primary metrics, had been accumulating for months. Once surfaced, the fix took forty-eight hours. The lesson took longer. Dashboards decide what leadership sees. What leaders see decides what teams do.

A paradox follows. Organisations spend millions designing products, but often spend minutes designing the dashboards that govern them. A growth chart updated hourly can eclipse a harm indicator updated weekly, not because the harm is softer, but because its frequency is lower. The datum drives attention. Attention drives action. This is the quiet motif running through the piece: what is counted shapes what counts.

A first claim emerges: dashboards are moral instruments as much as operational ones. Show it. At Twitter in 2018, internal teams monitored "daily active users" (DAU) and "time spent," metrics that rewarded sticky engagement. Yet when researchers reviewed internal data on user abuse reports that year, they found that a small cluster of accounts—less than 1 per cent—generated a disproportionate share of harassment flags. The behaviour was visible; the metric was not. Abuse-report volume lagged at the bottom of dashboards, framed as a trust-and-safety afterthought. Once trust-and-safety teams elevated "repeat abuser incidence" as a visible indicator on executive dashboards, product priorities shifted within a quarter. The implication is blunt: make harm legible, and teams begin to reduce it.

Name the structure: harm under-visibility. Explain it. Harm under-visibility occurs when negative signals—abuse reports, error retries, misleading patterns—are dispersed, delayed, or difficult to summarise. Growth signals are often crisp and abundant. Harm signals are noisy and rare. But rarity does not mean insignificance. The implication is moral drift: when dashboards tilt toward expansion, the organisation may widen damage without knowing it.

A second claim: dashboards that track only volume encourage teams to optimise the wrong behaviours. Show it. During 2020, Zoom usage soared. At one point, daily meeting participants exceeded 300 million (Zoom, April 2020 briefing). The public dashboards celebrated scale. Meanwhile, a smaller internal set of indicators—misconfiguration rates, school-classroom disruptions, and unauthorised meeting entries—revealed the structural tension between simplicity and security. Once Zoom surfaced "potentially unsafe meeting configurations" as a leadership-facing metric, the company introduced stronger defaults and simplified host controls. A metric shift made harm visible; visibility made action unavoidable. The implication: balance volume with vulnerability.

Name the pattern: metric asymmetry. Explain it. Metric asymmetry describes the default tilt towards indicators that are easy to gather—sign-ups, logins, minutes, clicks—rather than those that measure lived experience or risk. The implication is strategic blindness: dashboards foreground activity but obscure consequence.

A limitation should ground the argument. Not every harm indicator is reliable. Some signals are noisy or open to manipulation. Consider Airbnb's "neighbour complaint" system in the late 2010s. Complaints were intended as a harm indicator to surface disrespectful hosting or guest conduct. But early data revealed distortions: some complaints were retaliatory; some reflected prejudice rather than genuine nuisance. The system corrected by weighting complaints, requiring corroboration, and pairing them with occupancy and messaging metrics. The reconciliation is important: harm indicators strengthen governance only when they are contextualised. Raw harm metrics can mislead as surely as raw growth metrics.

A third claim takes us deeper: ethical dashboards require framing that humanises outcomes. Show it. In 2022, the UK's National Cyber Security Centre introduced a new internal reporting format for public-sector digital services. Instead of listing only uptime percentages and patch cadence, their dashboards added two human-impact indicators: "potential citizen impact per minute of downtime" and "proportion of vulnerabilities affecting high-dependence users." By reframing operational metrics through human consequence, the dashboards shifted discussion from abstract efficiency to lived risk. Engineers began prioritising patches not by age, but by potential human exposure. The implication: the dashboard's grammar becomes the organisation's grammar of care.

Name the concept: consequence weighting. Explain it. Consequence weighting moves dashboards beyond numerics toward meaning. It anchors metrics in questions of whom a failure affects, and how severely. The implication: leadership decisions become less myopic, because every metric carries an embedded moral horizon.

A fourth claim follows: dashboards can encourage courage—or reticence. Show it. GitLab's engineering teams use an internal "merge request lead time" chart. But adjacent to that chart sits a "security blocker unresolved after 5 days" indicator. By making blockers visible without stigma, GitLab normalised the act of slowing down to address risk. The visible behaviour—engineers escalating blockers early—was rewarded implicitly by leadership focusing equally on speed and safety. The implication: dashboards signal what forms of courage are valued.

Name the tension: transparency versus fear. Explain it. Dashboards that expose issues can frighten teams if indicators are used punitively. Conversely, dashboards that conceal issues leave teams unsupported. The implication is governance frailty: trust erodes when metrics feel like traps rather than guides.

We return to the motif: what is counted shapes what counts. Ethical dashboards choose to count differently.

A fifth claim: dashboards determine the organisation's internal storytelling. Show it. A global charity headquartered in Geneva redesigned its programme dashboards in 2021. Instead of tracking only "beneficiaries reached," the new dashboard added "beneficiaries reached twice" and "average follow-up interval," indicators showing depth rather than breadth. Within a year, field teams shifted outreach strategies towards sustained engagement. The dashboard re-authored the narrative of success. The implication: metrics script identity.

Name the principle: narrative alignment. Explain it. Narrative alignment ensures that the metrics on display match the organisation's stated mission rather than its unspoken anxieties. The implication: leadership cannot claim a people-centred mission while viewing only throughput charts.

A necessary counter-example sharpens the nuance. In 2017, a major US news network introduced a "toxicity index" to measure reader sentiment on comment threads. The indicator aimed to flag harmful dynamics. However, editorial teams reported that it sometimes incentivised avoiding difficult but important topics—articles on justice, inequality, or environmental harms—that naturally attracted heated debate. The metric, though well intentioned, risked suppressing coverage that mattered. The reconciliation: harm indicators must not punish necessary friction. The goal is to reveal preventable harm, not sanitise public discourse. Context must govern.

Now the constructive movement. Ethical dashboards require structured pluralism: growth metrics, harm metrics, moral context, and feedback loops. Balanced together, they resist distortion.

A humane dashboard might pair "monthly active users" with "users opting for time-limited session settings." It might combine "feature launch velocity" with "support tickets per feature per week." It might match "employee retention" with "anonymous signal-strength indicators" capturing workload strain. Each pairing asks the same question: *growth at what cost, and to whom?*

Thread the motif again: what is counted shapes what counts.

The unresolved tension sits here: how transparent should dashboards be? Too much transparency may overwhelm or demoralise teams; too little invites drift. The forward test offers a path: *if this metric became the organisation's north star, what behaviour would it reward, and would we be proud of that behaviour two years from now?* That question, posed honestly, disciplines leadership more effectively than any quarterly review.

Incidents into learning

At 03:17 on 11 September 2019, engineers at Cloudflare's London office watched traffic plummet towards zero. The system had entered a catastrophic loop: a newly deployed regular-expression library, intended to improve detection efficiency, consumed CPU until services collapsed. By dawn, the outage had disrupted millions of requests. Yet what drew industry attention was not the failure itself but the post-incident review published two days later. It named the precise commit. It mapped each decision. It refused to blame any individual. Instead, it showed how an apparently sensible optimisation, deployed in a hurry, triggered a runaway chain of interactions. The review became a template—evidence that incidents can be reframed from embarrassment into institutional learning.

Another example, quieter but equally instructive, surfaced at Etsy in 2012. A routine database migration introduced a subtle indexing error that slowed page loads across North America. The engineering team produced a post-mortem within hours, detailing the timeline and root causes, and—

critically—explicitly stating that no one would face disciplinary action. This invitation to candour yielded an unusually rich analysis. The outcome was not a reprimand but a revised migration checklist. Traffic returned to normal the same day. The culture strengthened.

These cases reveal a paradox. Failure is inevitable; learning is optional. Most organisations can catalogue what went wrong. Far fewer can convert error into improved practice. Many incident reviews end as theatre—performances for management that narrate failure without changing behaviour. Others curdle into blame, which suppresses the very evidence needed to prevent recurrence. The quiet motif running through this chapter is simple: learning follows safety.

A first claim emerges: after-action reviews succeed only when psychological safety precedes analysis. Show it. At Google's Site Reliability Engineering group in 2014, leadership explicitly adopted a "blameless post-mortem" standard. Reviews identified mistakes but prohibited personal fault. This structure encouraged engineers to disclose misjudgements, near misses, and contextual pressures. The visible behaviour mattered: people volunteered uncomfortable details. Explain it. When individuals know that honesty will not be punished, they commit to accuracy rather than self-defence. The implication is institutional resilience: lessons become cumulative rather than episodic.

Name the concept: blame avoidance. Explain it. Blame avoidance distorts memory. Teams minimise involvement. Timelines shrink. Contributing factors vanish. The result is brittle learning. The implication is painful repetition: errors recur because the organisation never sees them clearly.

A limitation clarifies the terrain. Blameless does not mean responsibility-free. In 2018, a major UK financial services firm suffered an hours-long outage following an untested configuration push. The initial review adopted a strictly blameless approach, but staff later argued that the analysis concealed the role of systemic under-training. The reconciliation is essential: blamelessness supports truth-telling, but responsibility still requires naming structural deficits—staffing, training, tooling—without personalising failure.

A second claim: incident reviews must reconstruct events with forensic precision. Show it. When GitHub experienced a database outage in October 2018, their incident report provided a minute-by-minute timeline of replication drift, failover attempts, and saturation thresholds. Each step was anchored by specific telemetry: replication lag in seconds, failover duration, load spikes. Visible signals replaced abstractions. Explain it. Specifics allow teams to compare intention with outcome. They expose mismatches between models and reality. The implication is improved mental models: precise data tightens future predictions.

Name the pattern: narrative compression. Explain it. Under pressure, teams compress narratives—condensing hours into minutes, glossing over ambiguous moments, smoothing messy sequences. Compression comforts, but it misleads. The implication is flawed countermeasures: if the story is wrong, the fix will be too.

Introduce a counter-example. In 2020, a mid-sized SaaS company attempted a post-incident review after a permissions bug leaked private project labels to unintended users. The review attributed the error to an engineer's "oversight," a vague diagnosis without technical detail. The absence of specifics—no commit timestamps, no test gaps, no configuration replicates—prevented meaningful remediation. Six months later, a related permission fault resurfaced. The limitation becomes clear: without granular reconstruction, learning evaporates.

A third claim: effective reviews trace not only what happened but why the conditions for failure existed. Show it. The US National Transportation Safety Board's (NTSB) investigative method, refined across decades, revolves around systemic causation. After the 2009 Colgan Air crash, the NTSB mapped how fatigue, training policies, cockpit culture, and crew-resource management failures aligned. They refused simple narratives. Although aviation differs from software, the cognitive posture is transferable: incidents are rarely single-cause events; they sit at the intersection of pressures, incentives, and drift. Explain it. By articulating system-level factors—deadline compression, ambiguous ownership, monitoring gaps—teams see how ordinary behaviour can produce extraordinary harm. The implication is durable repair: change the system, not only the procedure.

Name the principle: systems thinking. Explain it. Systems thinking links behaviours to incentives and incentives to structures. It demands humility about complexity. The implication: organisations move from assigning fault to redesigning flow.

Thread the motif again: learning follows safety. Safety requires honesty. Honesty needs structure.

A fourth claim: incident reviews must translate insight into practical change. Show it. Atlassian's incident library, publicly shared since 2020, includes "action items" that are measurable and time-bound. After a Jira indexing failure that year, the action items included "automated detection of index drift within 5 minutes," "mandatory dry-run scripts for migrations," and "expanded incident commander rotation training." Each action corresponded to specific deficiencies revealed in the timeline. Explain it. Actionability turns reflection into prevention. Vague lessons—"be more careful," "communicate better"—dissolve under pressure. Concrete measures persist. The implication is retention: organisations institutionalise recovery capability.

Name the trap: lesson evaporation. Explain it. Teams conduct a review, note several improvements, and then return to delivery work. A month later, few changes have landed. The implication is stagnant vulnerability: incident reviews become ceremonial rather than transformative.

Introduce a counter-example with nuance. Some teams fear that too many action items will overload capacity. In 2021, a data-platform group at a Scandinavian telecom company conducted a review that generated twenty-three proposed improvements. Leadership implemented only five, arguing that the remainder offered marginal gain. Critics worried that selecting a subset weakened commitment. Yet the team later reported improved follow-through because the focus was narrow and realistic. The reconciliation: prioritisation supports sustainability, provided the criteria are transparent.

A fifth claim: reviews must include multiple perspectives. Show it. During the 2016 Dyn DNS attack, internal teams noted that early misdiagnosis of traffic as routine load contributed to delayed mitigation. The post-incident review invited insights from operations staff, on-call engineers, security analysts, and customer-support representatives. The resulting analysis highlighted that support agents had seen user complaints earlier than monitoring tools indicated. Explain it. Cross-functional evidence enriches understanding; single viewpoints blind. The implication is integrative sense-making: organisations detect weak signals sooner.

Name the barrier: perspective isolation. Explain it. Teams often analyse incidents from within their technical silo—frontend diagnosing frontend, legal diagnosing legal. Yet incidents are cross-domain by nature. The implication: blind spots persist until reviews widen their aperture.

Thread the motif once more: learning follows safety, but safety must be shared.

A sixth claim: after-action reviews must be written to be remembered. Show it. Stripe's engineering incident reports from 2019 onwards adopted a narrative format that emphasised clarity, candour, and specificity. They were not dense logs but intelligible stories: what we believed, what was true, what diverged, what we changed. Explain it. Humans learn through narrative structure. A coherent account, anchored in real metrics, preserves knowledge beyond the team that experienced the failure. The implication is institutional memory: newcomers inherit wisdom rather than repeating mistakes.

Introduce a counter-example. Some organisations publish overly stylised reviews filled with euphemisms—"unexpected behaviour," "non-standard state," "intermittent anomaly"—that mask the visceral reality of failure. These euphemisms shield feelings but erode learning. The reconciliation: reports must be respectful yet unflinching. Precision and dignity are compatible.

We near the closing movement. The unresolved tension sits at the heart of modern operational life: how to review incidents thoroughly without paralysing delivery. Too much analysis, and teams fear release. Too little, and teams repeat avoidable pain. The forward test is simple to state and demanding to apply: *if this failure recurred a year from now, would we understand exactly why—and would we have evidence that our practices changed because of this review?* If the answer is uncertain, the learning has not yet landed.

Chapter 9
Repair, Restitution, Renewal

The footage was only twenty seconds long, captured on a busy tram in Melbourne in July 2022. A commuter shouted a slur at another passenger; someone filmed the exchange; within an hour it was on three platforms; by midnight it had collected millions of views, clipped into memes, translated into reaction videos, attached to comment threads bristling with speculation. The man in the frame apologised the next morning, but the harm had already radiated outward—towards the target of the abuse, towards the witnesses online and offline, towards the systems that failed to contain escalation. What fascinated observers was not the incident itself, but how quickly a single act became a web of consequences: reputational, emotional, institutional. It was a reminder that in a networked world, harm rarely stays within its point of origin. It spreads, sticks, and accumulates.

A contrasting scene unfolded in Reykjavík in the autumn of 2017, when a local community forum faced a surge of hostility following a contentious planning decision. Moderators paused activity and convened a mediated dialogue between residents. The session was slow, structured, and at times awkward, but the shift was unmistakable: the temperature dropped, people listened, and several users who had been suspended were later reinstated after making amends. The repair did not erase the conflict, yet it reset expectations. It suggested that online communities—so often caricatured as volatile and unforgiving—can sometimes choose discipline over spectacle.

These stories raise a question at the heart of modern digital life: what does it mean to repair harm when information moves faster than reflection, and when consequences echo long after intent fades? The tension is ancient, but the speed is new. Human beings have always hurt and healed one another; what has changed is the velocity at which harm multiplies and the machinery through which it travels. We live inside systems that remember too much and forgive too little. Yet at the same time, we remain dependent on those same systems—for work, for identity, for belonging. The paradox is stark: the network amplifies harm, yet it can also enable restoration, if we understand how to use it.

Repair is not a sentimental concept. It is structural. It is procedural. It is, in many contexts, measurable. A mis-sent email that damages a colleague's credibility creates a paper trail; a misleading message in a group chat affects the mood of a team; an unchecked rumour in a professional Slack channel seeds doubt in ways that can take months to unwind. These are not merely interpersonal wounds; they become part of an organisation's ledger, influencing decisions, trust, coordination, and cohesion. When harm travels across multiple layers—individual, collective, and systemic—it calls for deliberate triage. Who was affected? What was damaged? What needs containment? What needs acknowledgement? These questions form the quiet motif throughout this chapter: harm has surfaces, and each surface requires care.

The scope of repair is often misunderstood. Many assume repair begins with apology. In truth, apology is one piece in a larger choreography. Before apology comes recognition—a sober account of what happened and whom it touched. Before recognition comes containment—the slowing of the spread, the stabilisation of what can still be stabilised. Harm, once released into public view, behaves like a cascade. It must be slowed before it can be addressed. This is why some organisations now maintain "harm triage protocols," built not from legal instinct but from practices borrowed from medicine: stabilise first, diagnose second, treat third. The ordering matters.

And then there is the apology itself. In a digital environment, apology has become both overused and underdeveloped. A formulaic phrase—*I'm sorry if you were offended*—is dispatched, screenshotted, mocked, circulated, and forgotten. What works is almost the opposite: being precise about the harm, taking unambiguous responsibility, offering restitution, and signalling what will change. These are ancient principles, but digital life tests them in fresh ways. A public apology can inflame as much as it soothes. A private apology may be necessary but insufficient. Timing becomes as important as wording. Delay can appear evasive; haste can appear performative. Craft requires judgement.

Beyond individual repair lies community repair. Digital communities fracture easily; they also, when structured carefully, mend in ways surprisingly similar to their offline counterparts. Restorative circles, mediated sessions, and structured dialogues may seem impractical at scale, yet many small and mid-size communities already use them. They create protected space, surface grievances, and allow for restitution plans that specify what must be done to restore standing. The point is not to manufacture harmony but to acknowledge harm, rebuild trust, and set conditions for future disagreement that does not descend into hostility. The most resilient communities are not those without conflict, but those with rituals that metabolise it.

Systems, too, play their part. A platform that only punishes misconduct without offering structured routes back creates a culture of disposability. By contrast, systems designed with redemption in mind recognise that people grow. They allow penalties to expire. They offer re-onboarding paths that emphasise reflection rather than humiliation. They build contribution ladders that allow those who have erred to earn their way back into the community. These choices are architectural rather than moralistic. They shift incentives, influence behaviour, and—crucially—send a message: you are more than your worst moment.

The deeper significance is easy to overlook. Repair, restitution, and renewal are not merely responses to harm; they are commitments to shared life. They reflect a belief that communities—whether professional, civic, or digital—

are not static collections of individuals but evolving networks shaped by their responses to difficulty. An organisation that learns to repair becomes more truthful, less brittle. A platform that designs for redemption becomes less punitive, more humane. A team that treats incidents as moments for growth rather than spectacle becomes stronger than the sum of its parts.

As we enter this chapter, the central questions sharpen. When harm inevitably arises, how do we diagnose its reach without amplifying it? How do we apologise in ways that heal rather than perform? How do communities design practices that restore dignity without absolving responsibility? And how do we build systems that allow people to return—not unmarked, but renewed? The explorations ahead trace these questions with structure and candour, inviting us to examine what it takes to repair not just events, but relationships, cultures, and the systems that hold them.

When harm spreads

The message appeared at 09:17 on a Thursday in March 2021, posted in a Slack channel at a London fintech with several hundred employees. A manager criticised a junior colleague by name for a missed deadline, intending to send the remark privately. Within minutes the message had been screenshotted, shared in side channels, and quietly forwarded to HR. By lunchtime the junior had taken sick leave; by dusk the team's coordination had stalled. The initial harm was a single careless sentence, but its effects were distributed: the direct target felt humiliated; colleagues felt uneasy; managers feared precedent; HR faced rising anxiety within the team. A brief lapse cascaded through an organisation's social fabric.

A contrasting event occurred at Wikimedia's Berlin office in May 2019. A community dispute over article ownership erupted on a public mailing list. Moderators intervened early, shifting the heated exchange into a mediated channel and issuing a calm, precise explanation of the governance principles at stake. The conversation cooled. Crucially, the moderators provided support to the editor who had been targeted, offered guidance to confused bystanders, and documented the procedural issue that had sparked the conflict. The intervention was measured and visible. It prevented further spread.

Such episodes reveal a simple but exacting truth: harm rarely moves neatly along one line. It splinters into multiple surfaces—those who were directly affected, those who witnessed the event, and the systems that encode its memory. The question is not merely *who was hurt?* but *where has the harm travelled?* This is the triage lens that governs competent response.

The first surface is the victim's experience, which is often the most difficult to stabilise because emotion and uncertainty peak swiftly. A victim may withdraw, lash out, or minimise the event; each behaviour signals an unmet need. In the Slack incident, HR focused first on the junior's wellbeing, arranging a confidential conversation to restore a sense of safety. The behaviour—sick leave—was an observable metric of impact, not an abstraction. Naming the response as triage reframes the organisation's responsibility: stabilise the harmed party before attending to reputational or procedural concerns.

The second surface is the bystander zone, which is frequently overlooked. Bystanders absorb fear, confusion, and rumour. In 2014, during a dispute at Mozilla's San Francisco office, public commentary spiralled when staff felt uncertain about what norms applied to leadership conduct. Even those untouched by the original controversy experienced rising tension, measurable in escalating internal email volume and employee attrition the following quarter (Mozilla Foundation 2014). This illustrates a persistent pattern: bystanders experience *ambient harm*. Without clarity, they fill the vacuum with speculation. A well-run triage process treats bystanders as affected participants, not scenery.

The third surface is the system itself—procedures, cultures, and tools that shape how incidents unfold. Systems record harm through logs, tickets, and norms. A single breach can expose weaknesses in routing, escalation, or culture. In the Wikimedia example, moderators documented the root governance issue, turning a volatile moment into structural learning. Systemic triage requires mapping not just who was involved but how the machinery enabled or amplified the event. Did a rule lack clarity? Did a communication channel encourage pile-on behaviour? Did leaders respond too late? These are not moral questions but engineering diagnostics.

To understand why triage must start with mapping rather than reaction, consider how harm spreads in networked systems: it behaves less like a line and more like a ripple, where secondary and tertiary effects may dwarf the initial act. A leaked screenshot generates commentary; commentary begets judgement; judgement shapes future behaviours. In organisations, harm often manifests as lost coordination, eroded confidence, and subtle avoidance patterns. These are measurable outcomes: fewer cross-team requests, slower response times, increased private messaging. Each metric signals a widening circle.

Yet harm spread is not inevitable. Two further examples reveal the limits, and possibilities, of containment. In 2020, GitLab documented an internal policy debate in which a senior leader's phrasing caused discomfort. The company published a public post-mortem, clarified the decision context, and provided anonymised but detailed accounts of employee perspectives. This produced a rare outcome: trust did not collapse. Transparency delivered containment. By contrast, a 2018 incident at a major ride-share company—where internal criticisms were suppressed—led to leaks, external scrutiny, and multi-quarter damage to morale. The limitation of secrecy is clear: suppressing discussion accelerates gossip. Reconciliation lies in recognising that containment requires credible openness, not silence.

Throughout these cases runs a motif: early mapping. Mapping is not an intellectual exercise; it is an operational one. It asks concrete questions. Who was directly affected? What secondary groups experienced uncertainty or fear? What systemic features enabled the spread? How far has the narrative travelled, inside and outside the organisation? Mapping replaces blurred unease with a structured portrait. It converts a swirl of reactions into actionable surfaces.

Naming these surfaces allows for proportionate response. Care for victims—private, calm, attentive—restores agency. Care for bystanders—public, clarifying, factual—stops myth-making. Care for systems—analytic, reflective, documented—prevents recurrence. Each form of care travels in its own channel and at its own speed. Treating all three as one blob produces overreach or underreach. Treating them as distinct surfaces restores precision.

Still, triage has limits. It cannot erase harm; it cannot guarantee forgiveness; it cannot dictate how people feel. It can only stabilise enough to enable repair. A credible counter-example shows the boundary: in 2016, during a high-profile misconduct case at a Silicon Valley firm, triage focused exclusively on public perception and reputational protection. Victims were neither heard nor supported; bystanders were instructed to remain silent; systems were shielded from scrutiny. Triage became theatre. The result was predictable: leadership turnover, legal action, and a culture of mistrust that persisted for years. This failure does not invalidate triage; it clarifies its prerequisites—truthfulness, respect, and proportionality.

The implication is sharp. Harm spreads fastest where silence is allowed to pool, where systems obscure cause and effect, where bystanders internalise confusion, and where victims feel abandoned. The antidote is not speed alone but sequencing: stabilise victims; orient bystanders; diagnose systems; then proceed to repair. Each step measures its own progress through visible behaviours—return to work, reduced speculative messaging, improved procedural clarity.

As the chapter continues, the practical question looms: when the next incident arises—and one always does—how will you map the surfaces before acting? Where will you focus first? Which signals will reveal that spread has begun, and which will show that containment is working? The triage lens sharpens these decisions. It also forces a deeper reflection: in a world where harm radiates across people and systems, what does it take to respond in ways that do not amplify the very thing we hope to mend?

Apology that lands

On 8 September 2016, Brian Chesky, the chief executive of Airbnb, published an open letter from the company's headquarters in San Francisco. The prompt was not a technical outage or a pricing mishap, but a pattern of discrimination: guests with Black-sounding names being refused bookings, hosts sending racist messages, travellers documenting their experiences under the hashtag #AirbnbWhileBlack. The letter did something remarkable for a Silicon Valley company at that moment. It named the harm plainly, acknowledged systemic failure, apologised without condition, and announced concrete measures—new policies, product changes, and an anti-discrimination review team. The apology did not end the problem, but it shifted the atmosphere. Many critics still doubted Airbnb's resolve, yet they recognised that something more serious had occurred than the usual corporate "regret".

Contrast that with the wave of defensive, half-hearted apologies issued by various public figures in London, New York, and Los Angeles during the same decade. Many followed the same architecture: "I'm sorry if anyone was offended." The conditional phrasing outsourced harm to the listener's sensitivity rather than to the speaker's action. The result was predictable. Screenshots of such lines circulated as shorthand for non-apology; trust eroded further; communities hardened. The paradox is obvious. We live in a culture saturated with apologies, yet very few actually land.

In digital systems, apology is a speech act with an unusually long tail. A message composed in five minutes may be screenshotted, summarised, and cited for years. An apology written to calm a particular group may travel far beyond its intended audience, judged by people who know nothing of the context but everything about tone. This transforms apology from a private moral gesture into a public design challenge. The motif that threads this discussion is simple: *the sentence*. The sentence that names the harm. The sentence that accepts responsibility. The sentence that promises amends. When those sentences are absent or muddled, the apology fails no matter how many words surround it.

The first claim is straightforward: an apology must name the harm specifically for it to register as real. Show this. When the UK Post Office scandal—wrongful prosecutions of sub-postmasters due to the flawed Horizon IT system—reached widespread public attention, the organisation's leaders were criticised as much for their evasive language as for the underlying failures. Early statements spoke vaguely of "issues" and "challenges" rather than wrongful convictions and ruined lives. By contrast, later formal acknowledgements, including parliamentary testimony and public statements, used explicit language: *we prosecuted innocent people; we ruined careers and reputations*. The shift in wording did not repair the damage, but it changed the moral temperature. Harm was no longer hidden behind nouns like "incident" or "situation". It was named.

Name the principle at work: harm labelling. Explain it. Harm labelling means describing what was done, to whom, and with what consequence in clear, concrete language. "We mishandled your personal data and exposed your home address to strangers," not "A technical error occurred." "I undermined your credibility in front of our team," not "Things got heated." The implication is practical. When harm is properly labelled, the recipient does not need to exhaust themselves arguing about reality before repair can begin. They are spared the second injury of being told their experience is invisible.

A credible limitation arises. Some organisations fear explicit language because of legal exposure. Lawyers often advise leaders to avoid admissions that might be construed as liability. This tension is real. Yet many regulators and courts distinguish between acknowledgement and legal confession; and in practice, evasive language often lengthens conflict and increases reputational damage. The reconciliation lies in careful drafting: naming the impact without prejudging legal causality, and seeking phrasing that honours the harmed while still respecting formal constraints. Even within tight boundaries, it is usually possible to say more than "we regret any inconvenience".

The second claim: effective apology takes responsibility without dilution. Show it. Apple's response to the failure of Apple Maps in 2012 is instructive. Tim Cook wrote directly to customers, admitted that the product had fallen short, and suggested competitors' apps as temporary alternatives. He used clear first-person pronouns—*we fell short, we are extremely sorry*—rather than passive constructions. The apology signalled that leadership accepted responsibility at the right level: not by scapegoating individual engineers, but by acknowledging a collective failure of judgement. The behaviour that followed—rapid updates, visible product improvement—aligned with the words.

Name the concept: ownership. Explain it. Ownership in apology means saying, in effect, "This was our action, under our watch, and therefore our duty to rectify," rather than, "This unfortunate event occurred somewhere in the ecosystem." It resists the temptation to share blame with context, circumstances, or the offended party's interpretation. The implication is reputational. Paradoxically, clear ownership can strengthen trust because it demonstrates integrity under pressure. People know that mistakes happen; what they fear is evasion.

Here, too, a limitation exists. Total responsibility can be inappropriate when multiple actors contributed, or when information was genuinely incomplete at the time. A junior developer who followed flawed instructions should not shoulder the same responsibility as the leadership that designed the system. One way to reconcile this is layered responsibility: individuals acknowledge the actions they took; teams acknowledge the processes they maintained; leaders acknowledge the conditions they set. Each layer speaks from its vantage point without collapsing complexity into a single heroic or villainous figure.

The third claim concerns amends. Without a credible offer of amends, an apology is a performance. Show this. When Equifax suffered a major data breach in 2017, early statements included expressions of regret but offered limited, confusing remedies to affected consumers. Many were directed to a separate website with unclear terms. Criticism mounted, not simply because of the breach, but because the amends felt nominal and procedural rather than substantial. Compare that with cases where amends include automatic compensation, meaningful product changes, or structural reforms. Here, apology is not only verbal but material.

Name the principle: reparation. Explain it. Reparation means aligning words with tangible steps that restore, as far as possible, what was harmed: privacy, dignity, financial security, or trust. In an interpersonal context, reparation might involve correcting a public misrepresentation in the same channel where it occurred, not merely saying "sorry" in private. In an organisational context, it might involve changing processes, re-training staff, or abandoning a harmful feature. The implication is that apology becomes a commitment, not a wish.

Timing complicates all three elements: naming harm, taking responsibility, and offering amends. A late apology can feel forced; an early one can feel uninformed. The motif of *the sentence* returns here as a temporal question: when is the right moment to say "I was wrong"? Some guidance comes from crisis communication practice. When the basic shape of the harm is clear, a first statement should acknowledge impact and signal a commitment to further detail, without pretending to have full answers. "We know X has happened; we are still investigating Y; we will report on Z by a given time." This avoids both paralysis and speculation.

An example from the Norwegian public broadcaster NRK illustrates this. In 2020, after airing a comedy sketch accused of racist tropes, NRK issued a same-day statement acknowledging that the sketch had caused hurt and announcing that it would be temporarily removed pending review. Days later, a fuller explanation and apology followed, including editorial reflection and procedural changes. The staggered approach balanced speed with thought. It treated hurt as urgent, analysis as careful, and public explanation as ongoing rather than one-off.

A counter-example shows the risk of mis-timing. Several high-profile influencers and brands have issued apologies only after losing sponsorships or facing organised boycotts. Even if the wording is formally correct, the sequencing undermines credibility. The visible behaviour—silence followed by contrition only when pressured—tells its own story. The implication is pointed: apology that follows only when costs arrive will be read as self-protection.

Patterns of wording matter, particularly online. Certain phrases have become widely recognised as evasive. "I'm sorry if you were offended" centres the emotional reaction rather than the action. "Mistakes were made" removes the actor from the sentence entirely. By contrast, effective patterns are disarmingly simple. "I said X. That was wrong. I am sorry. Here is what I am doing to repair it." The brevity is not decorative; it reduces ambiguity and the scope for misinterpretation.

Tone is part of this pattern. A defensive apology tries to litigate context within the apology itself—"I was tired", "I was under pressure", "I didn't mean it that way"—rather than offering that context later, if appropriate. Context can matter, but when squeezed into the apology it tends to sound like excuse. A better sequence is to follow a clear apology with a separate explanatory account that clarifies but does not dilute responsibility.

In digital spaces, scale introduces further complexity. A creator with a million followers cannot apologise to each offended person individually. They must choose channel, format, and reach. A written statement may be better suited for nuance; a video may communicate tone more effectively but be harder to quote accurately. Each choice has implications. A statement pinned visibly communicates respect for the issue; a reply buried in a thread suggests reluctance. Behavioural signals—where the apology is placed, how long it remains accessible, whether it is translated or adapted for different audiences—convey seriousness as much as the words themselves.

There is also the question of audience. Sometimes the person harmed most directly will not want a public apology, or will not be safe if singled out. In such cases, organisations or individuals may need to craft multi-layered apologies: a private one addressed to the harmed party and a public one addressed to the wider community, each with appropriate detail. The test is whether the harmed party's needs are centred in the design of both, not whether public opinion is fully appeased.

Despite all these careful structures, apology is not a magical reset. It does not entitle the apologiser to forgiveness. It does not close the matter on their schedule. It does not erase the record. It simply creates a better starting point for repair. That is its proper scale. Recognising this guards against the impatience that often follows apology: "I said sorry, why are we still talking about this?" In a networked environment where harm can be replayed indefinitely, the timeline of healing will rarely match the timeline of communication.

The unresolved tension is therefore not how to craft the perfect wording, but how to balance sincerity, responsibility, and patience when the network is watching. The forward test is demanding yet clarifying: *if this apology were read three years from now by someone with no stake in my reputation, would it still look like an honest attempt to name harm, accept responsibility, and offer credible amends?* That imagined future reader acts as a quiet editor for *the sentence* that must carry most of the moral weight.

Restorative practices

In 1974, in the small Canadian city of Elmira, Ontario, two teenagers vandalised more than twenty properties in one night. The court, overwhelmed and sceptical that punitive sentences would prevent further harm, authorised an experiment led by probation officer Mark Yantzi. Rather than proceed directly to sentencing, Yantzi organised face-to-face meetings between the boys and the people they had harmed. Each victim described what they had lost: not merely the cost of repairs, but sleep, confidence, and the sense that their neighbourhood was safe. The boys listened. They apologised. They agreed to a structured plan of restitution, tracked over months. When the programme's outcomes were reviewed, the court noted fewer repeat offences, greater victim satisfaction, and a quieter sort of change: the two teenagers began treating the community as something they belonged to rather than a backdrop to their impulses. That case became the seed of the modern restorative justice movement.

The Elmira meetings were far from perfect. Power imbalances, emotional strain, and the risk of retraumatisation were all present. Yet the simplicity of the structure—circle, narrative, acknowledgement, plan—still feels radical fifty years later. The reason is clear. Most digital communities, from group chats to global platforms, resolve conflict through speed and deletion: remove the post, ban the user, close the ticket. That approach can stop immediate harm, but it rarely mends the relational fabric. The motif that will thread through this chapter is the *circle*—a space, literal or virtual, where people face one another long enough for responsibility to deepen into understanding.

The first claim: restorative practices work by making harm audible to all relevant parties without turning the encounter into a trial. Show this. In 2018, the New Zealand Ministry of Education adopted restorative conferencing as a standard option for school conflicts, substituting suspension with guided meetings. Facilitators prompted each student to describe what had happened, how they felt, and what they needed to move forward. Schools reported fewer repeat incidents and improved classroom conduct, not because the conferences were soft, but because they were structured. Every student heard the effect of their actions in concrete terms: *you embarrassed me in front of the class; I stopped speaking up afterwards*. Naming produced clarity; clarity produced behavioural change.

Name this principle: relational accountability. Explain it. Relational accountability treats harm as something that alters the relationship between people, not just the rulebook. Its purpose is to help each participant understand both the immediate injury and the wider ripple effects. The implication is practical for digital communities. When a community moderator leads a mediated dialogue between two users after a public argument, the goal is not to adjudicate intention but to surface consequences: who was sidelined, who felt threatened, what expectations were breached, and what commitments could prevent repetition.

The second claim: restorative practices must embed safeguards that prevent coercion or performative reconciliation. Show this. In the early years of British community mediation programmes, particularly in London and Bristol in the 1990s, evaluators noticed a troubling pattern. Parties with more social power—homeowners over tenants, adults over teenagers—often dominated the conversation. Facilitators adjusted the format by requiring private pre-meetings where each participant could express concerns, clarify boundaries, and decide whether a joint session was appropriate. The adjustment reduced the risk of pressured reconciliation and improved both perceived and actual fairness.

Name the safeguard: voluntary participation with informed boundaries. Explain it. People must feel safe to decline or pause the process. They must know what will be discussed, who will be present, and how the outcome will be used. The implication for digital mediation is immediate. A user who has experienced harassment may benefit from a mediated conversation with the offender, but only if they choose it with full understanding of the format and with the option to withdraw at any point. Restorative processes that ignore this constraint replicate the harms they aim to repair.

Consider a counter-example. Some platforms have experimented with automated prompts inviting users to "reconsider tone" or "resolve disputes" before any human review. While these nudges improve behaviour at scale, they cannot replace structured restorative work. Automation struggles with context; it cannot sense fear, nuance, or power imbalance. Yet this limitation can be reconciled. Automated prompts can filter out low-grade hostility, reducing volume, while trained moderators handle cases requiring depth and care. The implication is that restorative practice and automation serve different layers of the same system.

The third claim: restorative practices must end with a concrete, trackable plan that distributes responsibility fairly. Show this. In Norway's penal mediation system, overseen by the Mediation and Reconciliation Service, agreements often include specific actions—returning stolen property, writing a letter of acknowledgement, participating in community work—each with timelines and check-ins. These agreements are voluntary but binding once accepted, and compliance is monitored. Studies from the Norwegian Ministry of Justice (2014) report high completion rates and positive assessments by both harmed parties and offenders. The transparency of commitments builds trust in the process.

Name the principle: structured restitution. Explain it. Structured restitution translates emotional repair into observable actions—repair the fence, clarify the misrepresentation, delete the doctored image, contribute to the community affected. It does not reduce apology to transaction; rather, it ensures that good intentions have behavioural anchor points. The implication for digital communities is clear. If a user has spread misinformation, restitution might include publishing a correction in the same thread and participating in a moderated dialogue about verification norms. If a contributor has disrupted a collaborative project, restitution might include completing specific tasks under agreed timelines to restore reliability.

Thread the motif. The *circle* reappears when we consider moderated dialogues designed to rebuild trust after public conflict. Many open-source communities, such as those contributing to the Debian project, have used facilitated discussions—sometimes asynchronous, sometimes in live calls—to repair fractures. In 2019, a disagreement over maintainership escalated publicly. The project's community team organised a structured conversation in which each party described the sequence of actions, interpreted intentions, and proposed new stewardship boundaries. The conversation did not erase the disagreement, but it prevented a split and established clearer norms for future conflicts. The circle held long enough for perspective to widen.

The fourth claim: restorative processes must account for bystanders and the wider system, not only the primary parties. Show this. In 2021, a research group at the University of Michigan analysed campus restorative dialogues after racial harassment incidents. They found that bystanders often carried significant emotional residue—anger, guilt, fear—yet were rarely included in repair processes. When facilitators began holding parallel circles for these groups, campus tension declined, and participants reported a greater sense of collective safety.

Name the principle: system-aware repair. Explain it. Harm radiates. Communities must therefore consider who else absorbed the shock—witnesses, readers, students in the same chat, contributors in the same repository. System-aware repair ensures that the restorative process does not treat harm as one-dimensional. The implication is crucial for digital governance. When a prominent user's misconduct is addressed privately, without community-facing explanation, the bystanders remain unsettled. Transparency about the nature of the repair—without exposing private details—helps restore communal confidence.

A credible limitation is worth acknowledging. Some harms defy dialogue. Severe abuse, threats, or situations involving profound power disparities may require protective separation, not reconciliation. Attempting restorative processes in such cases can retraumatise the harmed party or create dangerous expectations. This limitation is not an indictment of restorative practices; it clarifies scope. The reconciliation lies in using restorative tools only where voluntary, safe, and proportionate, and combining them with protective policies where necessary. The implication is that restorative practices are part of a broader architecture of harm reduction, not a universal fix.

Technology can support these practices if designed thoughtfully. Platforms such as Zoom, Slack, or open-source mediation tools can provide breakout rooms for private reflection, structured agendas, and transparent follow-up logs. Behavioural metrics—completion of agreed tasks, participation in check-ins, or reduced reoffending—can support accountability without veering into surveillance. The challenge is to build tools that serve the circle rather than distort it, tools that slow the pace just enough for listening to take root.

Restorative practices also rely on skilled facilitation. Skilled does not mean professionalised to the point of distance; it means prepared. Facilitators must be able to set boundaries, summarise neutrally, interrupt respectfully, and maintain focus on the agreed structure. Organisations from Utrecht University to the Scottish Community Mediation Network train facilitators to use short, directive sentences—five to eight words—to redirect escalating exchanges. "Let's pause here." "Say what you need." "One voice at a time." These micro-interventions maintain the container that lets repair unfold.

As we return to the motif of the *circle*, a question emerges. What does a circle look like in a digital environment where participants may never meet, where identities may be partial, and where conflicts flare across channels? The answer is still forming. Some communities use video calls to approximate presence. Others use asynchronous circles—structured threads where each participant answers guided questions in sequence. The form matters less than the architecture: a predictable sequence, equal opportunity to speak, and a final stage where commitments are recorded.

The unresolved tension is this: restorative practices promise depth, but digital life demands speed. Communities must decide when to slow down long enough for repair, and when to act swiftly to contain harm. The forward test is demanding: *Will this process, if viewed six months later by someone who lived through the conflict, appear fair, human, and proportionate?* If the answer is yes, the circle has done its work.

Designing for redemption

In 2007, Finland's Ministry of Justice released a quiet but consequential report comparing reoffending rates among people who had completed its "Contract for Change" pilot. The scheme offered reduced penalties in exchange for structured reflection sessions, monitored community work, and a staged return to civic participation. In Helsinki, where the pilot began in March of that year, case workers noticed something striking. Participants who moved through the programme's final stage—re-engagement as contributors, not merely rule-followers—returned to stable employment and community activities at higher rates than those given straightforward fines or suspensions. Growth was not assumed; it was scaffolded. Penalties were not the end of the story; they were the start of a supervised return.

The core insight—that systems can make redemption either possible or nearly impossible—still applies across digital and organisational life. Many communities operate with penalties that accumulate like sediment: infractions never expire, reputations calcify, and any misstep becomes a permanent stain. Yet repeat harm often stems less from malice than from isolation: users locked out of shared spaces have no structured route back in, no means to demonstrate changed behaviour, no audience for renewed commitment. The theme threaded through this section is the *path*—a visible, navigable route that turns remorse into contribution. A path is not forgiveness; it is structure.

The first claim: redemption requires expiry. Show this. In 2015, Stack Overflow revised its moderation framework to include automatic expiration of certain penalties after set periods—weeks for low-level infractions, months for more serious ones. Administrators noted a reduction in "shadow compliance": users who technically followed rules but disengaged, assuming they were permanently marked. By allowing penalties to fade, the platform created both an incentive and a psychological opening for renewed participation.

Name the principle: temporal proportionality. Explain it. Temporal proportionality recognises that harm has duration, not eternity. An infraction causes disruption for a finite period; the system's response should reflect that. The implication for any digital or organisational context is direct. If consequences never expire, the system stops measuring behaviour and starts memorialising failure. Expiry transforms sanction into signal: *change course, and the system will respond.*

Consider a counter-example. Some financial compliance systems, such as those overseen by the UK Financial Conduct Authority during the 2010s, maintained permanent "adverse markers" on individuals, regardless of subsequent spotless records. While intended to protect markets, these markers often discouraged re-entry by highly skilled professionals who might have reintegrated safely with monitored pathways. The limitation is clear: where public safety is paramount, permanent markers may be justified. But outside such contexts, permanence often undermines the very stability the system seeks to protect. The reconciliation lies in differentiating between protective exclusions (non-negotiable) and developmental penalties (designed to expire).

The second claim: redemption requires re-onboarding, not mere reinstatement. Show this. Wikipedia's Arbitration Committee, particularly during the 2012–2016 period, experimented with conditional unbans: editors previously removed for conflict were invited back under structured supervision. Each returning editor was paired with an experienced volunteer who reviewed early edits, provided guidance, and intervened if patterns re-emerged. This was labour-intensive, but it worked. Many editors stabilised, re-integrated, and contributed effectively. The visible behaviour was not just fewer reverted edits; it was a shift in tone, a marked care in handling disputed pages, and consistent adherence to talk-page etiquette.

Name the principle: guided reintegration. Explain it. Guided reintegration treats return as a phase, not a flip of a switch. Re-onboarding provides context, norms, and expectations explicitly rather than assuming that absence generates insight. The implication is simple: if someone left the community through conflict, they cannot return through silence. They need a structure that aligns their intentions with the community's needs.

A limitation emerges when re-onboarding is too performative. Some organisations rely on mass, generic "welcome back" modules, indistinguishable from onboarding content for newcomers. These rarely address the specific rupture that occurred. The limitation is resolved by tailoring the re-onboarding to the incident: focus on the broken expectations, the new commitments, and the supports that make those commitments credible. The system signals, through design, that return is not cosmetic but substantive.

The third claim: redemption becomes durable when there is a contribution path that allows standing to be re-earned through observable acts, not declarations. Show this. After GitLab's 2018 review of community governance, contributors who had previously breached conduct guidelines could work toward renewed privileges by completing a series of low-risk, high-value tasks—improving documentation, assisting in routine bug triage, or participating positively in early discussions. The pattern was deliberate: tasks that mattered but carried minimal relational risk. The result was measurable. Contributors moving through the programme developed stronger collaboration habits, and maintainers reported fewer escalations involving returning users.

Name the principle: contribution-based restitution. Explain it. Contribution-based restitution anchors redemption in shared activity. It frames return as a gift to the community rather than a demand for reinstated status. The implication for any governance system is significant. Status, once lost, cannot simply be handed back; it must be woven through new participation that others can see, assess, and trust.

Thread the motif of the *path*. A path assumes direction. It also assumes milestones—markers that tell participants where they are and what remains. These milestones prevent both despair and complacency. They create a shared vocabulary: *You've completed stage one; let's evaluate stage two.* Paths work because they create shared ground.

The fourth claim: systems that support redemption must define clear boundaries—what is forgivable, what requires long-term restriction, what demands permanent separation. Show this. The open-source community surrounding Mozilla, particularly after its 2020 governance updates, distinguished between categories of harm: technical disruptions, interpersonal conflicts, and high-risk misconduct. Only the first two were eligible for structured return. High-risk cases, especially those involving threats or harassment, resulted in irreversible bans. The clarity benefited everyone. Those eligible for return knew the path; those ineligible were not misled; community members understood that safety was not negotiable.

Name the principle: categorical clarity. Explain it. Categorical clarity prevents false expectations. It respects both the harmed party and the broader community by guaranteeing that redemption is not applied indiscriminately. Its implication is that redemption must be bounded. Without boundaries, redemption becomes an entitlement; with boundaries, it becomes an earned opportunity.

A credible limitation arises when criteria are applied inconsistently. In some volunteer communities—certain language-learning forums in the 2010s, for example—reinstatements depended heavily on moderator preference, creating perceived favouritism. Inconsistency corrodes trust. The reconciliation lies in publishing criteria, applying them consistently, and reviewing them periodically in light of new cases.

Technology can help or hinder. Automated penalty expiry must be transparent; users should know when penalties lapse and why. Re-onboarding tools must guide, not merely record. Contribution dashboards must highlight constructive participation without turning redemption into a gamified contest. Systems should measure stability over time—weeks of constructive conversation, a reduction in flagged posts, consistent attendance at collaborative meetings—rather than raw volume of activity.

Return to the motif. A path implies that the past is not erased, but contextualised. The history remains, but its weight shifts as the person moves. Communities thrive when they can say, truthfully, *we saw change, and we made space for it*.

As we reach the closing tension, the unresolved question is this: how do systems balance compassion with caution? Growth with protection? If the path back becomes too easy, trust weakens; if it becomes too hard, renewal dies. Each community must ask itself: *What evidence of change would satisfy us six months from now?* The answer reveals not only expectations for those who seek redemption, but the kind of community we believe ourselves capable of becoming.

Chapter 10
Practising Karma 2.0

A few minutes after 08:00 on a grey February morning in 2019, the engineering floor of a London fintech firm fell silent—not because anything catastrophic had happened, but because a single message had landed in the company-wide Slack. It was only eight words long. The sender, a junior analyst under pressure, had posted a sarcastic remark aimed at a colleague who had missed a deadline. Within seconds it was screenshotted, misread, forwarded, and criticised. By 08:07, the analyst had apologised; by 09:00, HR was involved; by lunchtime, no one could quite recall the original context. Eight words. A day's worth of fallout. A reputation dented, a team rattled, a project delayed. The engineer whose work had slipped later told a friend, "It wasn't the comment. It was how fast it became a public record." This small incident became a case study in the firm's subsequent training: a reminder that *every action is stored somewhere,* and that habits—not intentions—largely determine how well we navigate that reality.

The episode captures the core tension of this chapter: most harm in digital workspaces is not caused by dramatic ethical collapse but by rapid, habitual, unexamined actions. A tap, a forward, a reaction emoji deployed too quickly. Digital life runs at a pace that rarely allows reflection unless reflection is deliberately built in. The paradox is sharp. We expect individuals to behave with care, yet we design systems that reward speed. We encourage teams to cultivate trust, yet we rely on tools that expose every misalignment instantly and permanently. Karma 2.0, as explored throughout this book, is less about judgement than about physics: the forces, vectors, and feedback loops that shape outcomes long before we notice them. Practising it means turning insight into method—codifying the behaviours that prevent small sparks from becoming organisational fires.

What gives this chapter its urgency is not a new crisis, but the old one made visible. The digital traces we leave are not inert; they are rehearsals of who we are becoming. A hastily composed message becomes part of an internal biography. A poorly scoped request becomes tomorrow's performance metric. A team's unspoken norms become the backdrop against which conflicts play out. Readers arriving here already know the theory; what they need now is instrumentation. Tools that live inside the day, not above it. Practices that survive pressure, time zones, handovers, late nights, and shifting schedules.

The personal code is our first anchor. It is a way of shrinking the distance between intention and action. Not a set of rules pinned to a wall, but a compact: before I post, what outcome am I aiming to create? Before I reply, what tone will travel further than I expect? Before I share, who becomes responsible for the next link in the chain? The beauty of a personal code is that it is lightweight. It moves with you. It evolves. It changes shape depending on whether you are a senior leader, a new hire, a contractor, or a rotating team member. Yet its purpose remains constant: to interrupt autopilot and replace it with considered motion. Throughout this chapter we will show how small phrases—twelve words, sometimes fewer—can function as stabilisers in moments when your blood is hot or your calendar is full.

The team code builds on that foundation, turning individual discipline into collective reliability. Teams are not moral abstractions; they are the sum of their rituals. A request for review. A sign-off that travels through time zones. A retrospective after something breaks at 02:00. These touchpoints reveal values in motion. When a team incorporates a shared code into its reviews, stand-ups, and incident playbooks, it does more than reduce errors; it reduces ambiguity. Work becomes legible. Expectations become collective property. A team code prevents the slow erosion of trust that occurs when one person's clarity is another person's surprise. It shapes how conflict arises and how it resolves. Most importantly, it provides a shared map, so that when momentum builds or stress peaks, people know where to stand.

Then comes the product code: the spine of any organisation that builds or maintains digital systems. Here is where ideals must become architecture. A product code embeds care into guardrails, failsafes, and audit trails. It governs how data moves, how models behave, how alerts trigger, how mistakes escalate. It is the most technical of the three layers, yet also the most human. A system that logs what matters teaches teams to notice what matters. A system that requires a second set of eyes at the right moment prevents tomorrow's apology from becoming next quarter's scandal. A system that records escalation paths ensures that harm does not spread silently. The product code is where Karma 2.0 becomes operational. It is where values become constraints, and constraints become safeguards.

None of these codes—personal, team, product—hold if they live only in documents. Practice is the solvent of good intentions. That is why this chapter ends with drills: simple, repeatable exercises that harden habits. The pause-breathe-post micro-drill that takes eight seconds but prevents an eight-hour cascade. The metrics walk-through that asks, weekly, whether what we measure still aligns with what we value. The teardown session that examines a fragment of work—a message, a pull request, a design spec—not to judge, but to learn. Drills have a strange power. They strip away ceremony and replace it with rhythm. Rhythm, in turn, builds culture.

The motif running quietly through this introduction is muscle. Ethical action is not a mood; it is a muscle that strengthens through repetition. Muscles need warm-ups, tension, rest, and renewal. Codes provide structure, but drills provide strength. Together they form a circuit: intention, action, reflection, adjustment. A circuit that runs quietly, steadily, beneath the visible flows of work.

What follows in this chapter is not a set of commandments but a set of craft tools. The kind artisans carry in soft pouches: always within reach, worn smooth with use. You will find patterns to adapt, scripts to refine, and structures that can be rebuilt to fit your environment. You will notice that none of the tools promise perfection, because perfection has never been the point. The aim is reliability: behaviour that holds under stress, systems that absorb error gracefully, teams that repair rather than fracture, and products that protect those who depend on them.

There is a final question to keep in mind as you turn the page. If your future self were to read the traces you leave tomorrow—the messages, decisions, escalations, metrics, corrections—would they recognise the person you intend to be? Practising Karma 2.0 is the discipline of ensuring the answer moves, steadily, towards yes.

A personal code

At 07:46 on 12 March 2021, a product manager at Shopify in Ottawa sent a brief message into a team channel. It was a single sentence, typed quickly between meetings, questioning why a partner team had "let another deadline slide". The phrasing was sharp, but not outrageous. What turned it into a lesson was what followed: within twelve minutes, three people had reacted with defensive comments; within an hour, the partner lead had escalated the remark privately; by the next morning the message had been screenshotted into a leadership summary as evidence of rising friction between teams. One sentence. Twelve words. A 24-hour ripple. The manager later admitted she had written it while rushing to make coffee. The message took five seconds to send. It took the team three weeks to calm.

The paradox is stark. Why does a tiny action—one line of text—carry such force inside organisations built on speed and transparency? Why does a gesture that feels private behave like a broadcast? The answer lies in the peculiar physics of digital environments: messages do not expire, and audiences do not stay still. Every post is a performance, whether we intend one or not. The moment we type, we join an internal record that shapes our reputation more steadily than any annual review. This is not a reason to fear communication; it is a reason to craft it. It is why a personal code matters. A personal code is the buffer between impulse and action. It slows the reflex just enough to let intention catch up.

A code begins not with rules but with noticing. The first major claim is simple: you cannot improve what you do not witness. Show the moment of error, name its structure, explain its dynamics, and then consider the implication. The Shopify manager's mistake was not malice; it was velocity. She typed before she had measured her aim. Many organisations have their own versions of that scene. In August 2020, a senior engineer at GitLab wrote a terse comment on an issue thread questioning a colleague's competence. The remark was edited within minutes, but the notification had already travelled to dozens of eyes. The behaviour—editing—was visible. The metric—sixty-two people receiving the notification—revealed the scale. The implication: once released, tone travels independently of later correction. The quiet motif here is the small hinge. Small actions swing large doors.

Yet not every impulsive message causes harm. Consider a counter-example. In April 2018, at GOV.UK's publishing team in London, a junior developer accidentally posted an unfinished draft into a shared Slack channel. The mistake was caught instantly. The message was light-hearted, and colleagues responded with humour. No escalation, no tension. Why? Context, tone, and trust were aligned. The message was recognisably a slip, not a jab. The team had rituals that normalised low-stakes error: daily stand-ups where people shared minor mishaps, regular retrospectives that prioritised psychological safety. The limitation of the Shopify case is that we cannot extract a universal rule; not all quick messages burn. The reconciliation lies in a principle: a personal code is most essential where trust is thin, stakes are rising, or ambiguity is high. In these moments, small hinges matter most.

The second claim: clarity is generosity. It is visible in behaviour. Specific words reduce friction. Vague words breed suspicion. When a manager writes "need this ASAP", they transmit not urgency but uncertainty: does ASAP mean one hour? One day? One sprint? Behaviour can be measured. One British software firm tracked turnaround times after replacing "ASAP" with time-stamped expectations; average delays fell from 18 hours to 7 (internal analysis, 2019). The implication is practical: a personal code should include commitments to specificity. Name the expectation. State the reason. Frame the request. Precision makes space for collaboration. It also limits reputational drag: colleagues remember clarity when chaos rises.

This brings the code to its third hinge: audience awareness. Every message has layers of audience—intended, immediate, latent, and future. The intended audience is the person you address. The immediate audience is whoever is present in the channel. The latent audience comprises those who may see it through forwarding, search, or algorithms. The future audience is yourself, re-reading the message six months later in a performance review or incident analysis. These layers shape the stakes. When Frances Haugen released internal Facebook documents in October 2021, she exposed not only data but tone—emails, comments, and Slack threads that reflected years of internal decision-making. The behaviour was textual. The metric was archival volume. The implication: internal communication is a deposit into a future biography, one that may resurface under scrutiny. A personal code begins by recognising that you never truly write to one person alone.

The fourth claim concerns restraint. A pause is a decision, not a delay. The practice of taking a single breath—an eight-second pause—before posting has gained traction in several organisations, notably within the design teams at Spotify in 2022. Designers reported that the micro-pause reduced reactive language and increased clarity in cross-team reviews. The behaviour is small. The metric is measurable: a reduction in re-opened threads by 14% over a quarter

(Spotify internal retrospective, May 2022). The implication is broader: restraint is not slowness; it is calibration. A personal code that embeds micro-pauses builds a rhythm of considered action without sacrificing momentum.

A fifth principle centres on alignment between values and voice. People often assume their inner intention is visible externally; it rarely is. Voice is constructed line by line. Consider Satya Nadella's widely noted internal memo at Microsoft in October 2014, addressing a public misstep. The memo was calm, direct, and specific, naming the error without hedging. The behaviour—forthright admission—became a model for leaders. The metric was qualitative: employees repeatedly referenced the memo in later culture discussions. The implication is that tone earns standing. A personal code that includes a commitment to transparent, proportionate language protects reputation more than defensiveness ever could.

The quiet motif—small hinges—returns here. A hinge does not move far, but what it supports matters. A personal code is a hinge: a device that turns intention into action with minimal friction. It contains three essential components: a lens, a filter, and a trigger. The lens asks: what outcome am I trying to produce? The filter asks: what does this message remove—ambiguity, heat, or unnecessary detail? The trigger asks: what moment will prompt reflection? For many professionals, the trigger is the cursor blinking after a difficult sentence. For others, it is the act of adding a recipient. For some, it is the knowledge that the message may be read by people they will never meet. Designing these triggers consciously strengthens the hinge.

To make this real, return to the Shopify case. Had the manager applied a lens—*am I escalating blame or seeking clarity?*—the sentence would likely have softened. Had she used a filter—*is the deadline failure already known? Is this the right channel?*—the message might have been re-routed. Had she engaged a trigger—the brief pause—the outcome would have differed. The code does not erase emotion; it reshapes expression.

Another dimension of a personal code is reversibility. Some messages can be edited or retracted; others cannot. The visible metric here is the platform's affordance. Slack keeps edits in logs. Email is permanent. Ticket comments tie to audit trails. Choosing the communication channel is therefore part of the code. It is a behaviour with consequence. When Basecamp's leadership announced controversial internal policies in April 2021 via a public blog post, rather than a staged internal conversation, the irreversibility of the medium intensified fallout. The implication: choosing the wrong vector can turn manageable tension into organisational fracture.

A credible counter-example exists. On 9 June 2020, the UK Government Digital Service released an internal apology regarding a miscommunication about furlough scheme guidance. The message, originally sent privately, was later shared publicly to demonstrate institutional transparency. Because the tone was measured and the content precise, the sharing improved external trust rather than eroding it. The reconciliation is simple: reversibility is contextual. What matters is not secrecy but suitability. A personal code asks: if this message travelled further than intended, would it still stand?

The final principle concerns self-curation. A personal code is not a shield against judgement; it is a compass for growth. It evolves. Professionals in high-stakes environments often keep private logs of moments they regret—messages sent too quickly, replies that landed badly, tone that misaligned. These logs function as training data. They expose patterns: particular triggers, times of day, types of requests. Behaviour becomes legible. Metrics emerge. The implication is hopeful: reputation is not fixed. It is accumulated, amended, and renewed through repeated choices.

As we thread through these principles, the small hinge remains our motif: a reminder that compact actions carry structural weight. A personal code is precisely that—a small hinge that can redirect the momentum of a day, a project, or a career. Its purpose is not moral superiority but reliability.

The unresolved question, then, is this: when the next message demands speed, stakes are high, and the cursor is blinking, which hinge will you choose to move?

A team code

At 09:12 on 7 February 2022, a build at Atlassian's Sydney headquarters stalled halfway through a routine deployment. The change was small—four lines adjusting a permission field—but the impact was large. Customer dashboards froze, internal alerts cascaded, and within minutes a cross-team incident channel lit up with contradictory guesses about the root cause. Twenty-eight people typed at once. Two engineers attempted hotfixes that clashed. A manager requested a rollback while another pushed for a forward fix. The outage lasted forty-seven minutes. The post-incident review revealed something striking: the technical flaw was trivial; the procedural vacuum was not. There was no shared template for who spoke first, who owned the timeline, or when decisions transferred from automation to humans. One engineer summed it up: *"We had smart people, good intentions, and no choreography."*

That scene raises a hard question. How does a team with talent, tools, and goodwill still falter under pressure? The paradox is that high-performing groups often assume alignment instead of designing for it. They treat values as tacit rather than operational. Yet stress exposes fault lines that calm disguises. A team code exists to make values executable, visible, and shareable. It turns aspiration into choreography. Without it, even a small perturbation—four altered lines—can unseat an entire system.

A team code begins where a personal code ends: with collective discipline. The first claim is that teams must embed values into processes, not slogans. Show the behaviour. Name the structure. Explain the mechanism.

Consider the Atlassian outage. The visible behaviour was improvisation: voices overlapping, decisions colliding. The structural absence was a sign-off flow that allocated accountability to individuals, but not to the team as a unit. The mechanism was simple: when everything became urgent, nothing became legible. The implication is clear. A team code should define not only what matters, but how work is done when stakes rise. It should turn principles—clarity, proportion, respect—into steps: roles, rituals, and review points.

A second claim: processes must stabilise tempo. A team's rhythm is not accidental; it is constructed through predictable flows of review, feedback, and release. One of the most studied examples is the code review discipline at Mozilla in 2019. Engineers were required to route patches through designated reviewers with domain expertise. The behaviour was consistent. The metric was concrete: defect rates on Firefox Nightly builds fell by 17% within six months (Mozilla Engineering Report, December 2019). The implication is not that formal review always reduces error; rather, ritualised review aligns shared attention. A team code that embeds stable checkpoints—pre-merge review, pre-release smoke test, cross-functional sign-off—converts individual excellence into collective reliability.

Yet review alone is insufficient. A credible counter-example illustrates this. In 2017, a large UK government digital service implemented a strict review protocol requiring two approvals for every deployment. Behaviourally, this increased scrutiny. Metrics showed slower release cycles, longer queues, and frustration. Errors did not fall. The limitation exposes a crucial truth: excessive review without role clarity breeds stagnation. Reconciliation lies in the balance: reviews must be scoped, not bloated. A team code must distinguish between high-signal reviews (security, privacy, migrations) and low-signal ones (cosmetic text changes). A well-designed code measures review load, not merely review existence, and treats speed and care as co-equal.

A third claim centres on shared language. Teams fracture when they use identical words differently. Terms such as *done, blocked, approved,* or *urgent* seem universal but rarely are. In 2020, Monzo Bank in London standardised these terms across its operations teams. The behaviour was explicit: each term had a published definition. The metric was the reduction in cross-team escalations—down by one-third within a quarter (Monzo Ops Review, Q3 2020). The implication is powerful. A team code must include a glossary of operational anchors, not because teams are fragile, but because ambiguity is expensive. Shared definitions shorten debates, reduce hidden assumptions, and frame expectations.

The motif here is choreography. A dance succeeds not because dancers agree on values, but because they share timing, spacing, and cues. Teams are no different. The fourth claim: a team code requires explicit roles during critical moments. Consider GitHub's 2021 shift to an "incident commander" model. During outages, one person directs, one logs, one executes. Behaviours are simple. Metrics are visible: mean time to resolution dropped from 45 minutes to 29 (GitHub Engineering Blog, October 2021). The implication for a team code is that roles must be pre-declared, not improvised. Who merges? Who speaks to stakeholders? Who decides freeze or rollback? Who documents? When teams commit to choreography, confusion diminishes even when uncertainty rises.

But structure is not synonymous with rigidity. A robust code maintains adaptability. The fifth claim: a team code must include a mechanism for escalation—clear, transparent, non-punitive. Escalation works when it is predictable. In 2022, the Wikimedia Foundation published its incident escalation ladder: thresholds, triggers, and paths. The behaviour was open. The metric—lower variance in incident response times—showed that transparency reduces hesitation. The implication is simple: escalation should feel like support, not indictment. A team code that treats escalation as collaboration strengthens both resilience and trust.

A serious limitation deserves attention: not all teams have equal authority to embed their code. Cross-functional groups often depend on rules set elsewhere. A team may wish to shorten feedback loops but is bound by compliance review; it may aspire to reduce meeting load but is governed by departmental protocol. Reconciliation lies in incrementalism: a team code need not govern the entire organisation to be transformative. It only needs to govern the patch of ground the team controls. Internal rituals—weekly architecture reviews, rotating note-takers, standing communication norms—are within reach. They accumulate into culture.

Choreography returns as the motif. The sixth claim: the code must be lightweight enough to use, yet substantial enough to matter. The most effective team templates rarely exceed one page. They articulate principles that translate directly into behaviour. One well-known example emerged at Netflix's platform engineering group in 2018. Their one-page "operational compact" set out five commitments: write context before critique, document decisions in the open, rotate toil, declare ownership, and run blameless post-mortems. Behavioural outcomes were measurable: incidents decreased, cross-team trust rose, onboarding time shortened. The implication for our purposes is that a team code should not become a manual. It should be a compass.

The seventh claim: a team code must be renewed, not enshrined. Codes decay when they become static. Processes that once improved efficiency begin to constrain it. To prevent ossification, some organisations adopt rotating stewardship. Basecamp experimented with a quarterly "process gardener" role in 2021, empowering one team member to prune unnecessary meetings, rewrite stale rituals, and surface friction. The behaviour was modest. The metric was the reduction of internal meetings by 22% (Basecamp internal summary, 2021). The implication:

stewardship is a living role, not a one-off design task. A team code benefits from gardeners.

The eighth claim concerns conflict. Every team will face moments when values collide: speed vs. certainty, autonomy vs. alignment, innovation vs. stability. A team code must pre-negotiate these tensions. For example, when AWS revamped its deployment guidelines in 2019 after a sequence of regional outages, it added a principle called *fast safe cycles*: speed was preserved, but only with automated gating tests and post-release monitoring checkpoints. Metrics captured the effect: fewer emergency rollbacks, more predictable release windows. The implication is clear: a team code should articulate how to decide, not only what to decide.

A counter-example helps sharpen this. In 2021, a European fintech introduced a "zero bug tolerance" rule. Intended to raise quality, it produced fear. Engineers delayed releases, hid small issues, and avoided bold changes. The behaviour was protective. The metric—velocity dropping by 40%—revealed the cost. The limitation is obvious: codes that punish failure corrode learning. This reconciles into a principle: a team code must align accountability with candour. Without candour, choreography collapses.

Teams also need rituals of reflection. The ninth claim: a team code must integrate learning loops. The most effective example remains Etsy's adoption of blameless post-incident reviews in 2012—a practice later studied widely. The behaviour emphasised system, not individual fault. Metrics improved: reduced recurrence of similar incidents, faster knowledge transfer, healthier team morale. The implication for a team code is that learning must be procedural, not accidental. Reflection is a practice, not a mood.

The tenth claim: a team code must protect attention. Teams drown not in work but in noise. Messages proliferate; channels multiply; everyone is reachable, always. A well-structured team code includes communication windows, escalation tiers, and guidelines for channel use. When Zapier's engineering team introduced communication hours in 2023—no Slack pings outside defined windows unless urgent—the behaviour became sustainable. Metrics—lower burnout scores and shorter cycle times—followed. The implication is pragmatic: a team code that stewards collective attention produces both better work and healthier teams.

At this point, choreography—our quiet motif—comes fully into view. A team code is not a disciplinary tool; it is a shared rhythm. It defines responsibility not as hierarchy but as interdependence. It acknowledges that teams succeed or fail together, and that values without process are sentiment. Process without values is bureaucracy. A code merges both into practice.

The forward test remains. When the next outage hits at 09:12, or the next rushed decision appears in a chat thread, or the next disagreement flares over a review comment, what choreography will your team have rehearsed?

A product code

At 14:27 on 5 May 2021, the developers behind Peloton's Tread+ treadmill in New York pushed a routine firmware update. The patch was meant to refine speed calibration. Instead, it deactivated a safety lockout and allowed the belt to start unexpectedly. Within days, the U.S. Consumer Product Safety Commission warned of dozens of injuries. Peloton initially resisted a recall, arguing misuse. But by May's end, the company pulled every Tread+ from sale and issued full refunds. A single faulty control—one missing guardrail—had cascaded into harm, reputational shock, and months of repair work. The drama revealed something larger than a product fault. When a system lacks a clearly articulated product code, minor oversights become structural risks. When it has one, even large shocks become containable. Five words appear early. Safety is always engineered.

The Peloton episode is not unique; it is simply visible. Most harm in digital systems emerges quietly, through slow accretions of missing checks, unclear responsibilities, and assumptions that everyone shares the same threshold for risk. A product code addresses this by embedding care in the machinery itself. It steps beyond values on a wall and into instrumented reality—guardrails, failsafes, and audit trails that give products the capacity to act proportionately. A product code is less a manifesto and more a minimal spec: a disciplined answer to the question *how does this product keep its users safe, even when people or processes fail?*

A first claim follows directly from the opening scene: guardrails must be anticipatory, not reactive. Show the behaviour. In 2018, Stripe's Dublin team implemented "block-before-bill" logic across their billing API. If a merchant attempted a high-risk charge spike—above the 99th percentile for their account—the system halted the transaction and prompted additional verification. Name the mechanism. It was a statistical guardrail tuned to historical baselines. Explain the purpose. The guardrail absorbed volatility and prevented cascading fraud. State the implication. A product code should designate where automated stops are mandatory, how they're tuned, and who can override them.

The motif throughout this subchapter is scaffolding: invisible support that keeps the structure sound. The second claim: failsafes must be layered. Consider the example from London's Transport for London (TfL) ticketing system in 2019, where a backend synchronisation glitch double-charged tens of thousands of Oyster card users overnight. The system lacked a reconciliation failsafe that would have caught the duplication before billing. After public criticism, TfL introduced an end-of-day cross-check that combed for pattern anomalies. The behaviour was measurable: post-fix billing errors dropped substantially according to TfL's Annual Operational Report (2020). The implication echoes our motif. Scaffolding is not one beam; it is a lattice. A product code should include redundancy—

checks before action, checks after action, and checks that compare actions across time.

A counter-example clarifies the limit. When Instagram redesigned comments in 2020 to throttle coordinated harassment, the system initially flagged large clusters of replies as abuse even when they were harmless fan exchanges. Overzealous detection slowed community interaction. The limitation was clear: a failsafe that lacks nuance creates friction that harms legitimate users. The reconciliation is straightforward: failsafes must adapt to context and include human override or appeal channels. A product code demands both proportionality and reversibility.

The third claim: audit trails are not administrative bureaucracy; they are a product's memory. They show who changed what, when, and why. They allow errors to be traced, disputes to be resolved, and misuse to be spotted. In 2022, GitLab formalised immutable audit logs across all enterprise tiers. The visible behaviour was predictable traceability. Teams could inspect configuration changes down to individual lines, with timestamps and user IDs. The metric that mattered was conflict resolution time in multi-team deployments: significant reductions were documented in GitLab's internal reliability summary (2022). The implication is fundamental. A product without an audit trail cannot learn. A product with one can recover, adjust, and build trust.

Scaffolding returns. The fourth claim: a product code must define ownership boundaries—what engineering owns, what policy owns, and what users control. One success story comes from Wikipedia's stewardship model. The platform's software defines strict boundaries—admins may block users, editors may revert content, bots may enforce formatting limits. Each class of actor has constrained power. The behaviour is orderly. The implication for a product code is that boundaries prevent both overreach and abdication. Without boundaries, responsibility dissolves. With boundaries, responsibility becomes actionable.

A fifth claim concerns reversibility. Systems that cannot reverse harmful actions accumulate silent debt. Slack discovered this in 2021 when a misconfigured tool exposed some user data within shared channels. The rapid recovery depended on reversible logging and permission rollback capabilities—tools that had existed but had never been formalised into a product code. Behaviourally, these reversals were lifesaving. The implication is simple. A product code should embed reversible operations wherever possible: undo, revert, roll back, restore.

A limitation exposes a deeper tension. Reversibility is expensive. It requires extra storage, careful modelling, and discipline. Mobile apps with limited resources often avoid full versioning. Small teams sometimes lack time for reversible states. Yet the reconciliation lies in scope: a product code need not mandate universal reversibility. It should mandate reversibility for high-stakes actions—

deletions, permissions, financial transfers, safety-critical configurations. Scaffolding need not cover the whole house; it should cover the beams that collapse catastrophically.

A sixth claim: a product code must integrate monitoring as a first-class element. Not growth dashboards, but harm dashboards. In 2023, Discord implemented automated detection for servers experiencing sudden spikes in harmful content. Behaviourally, these spikes triggered temporary slow modes and alerts to moderators. The implication is powerful. A product code should require monitoring that highlights harms early—overload, fraud, bullying, misinformation—before they cascade. Metrics of care must sit alongside metrics of scale.

The seventh claim: transparency must be operational. Users should not guess how decisions are made. A compelling example arose in 2021 when Zoom, under scrutiny for privacy concerns, published a transparency chart describing every major data flow in the product. The behaviour was visible. The chart showed precisely what went where. The implication is direct. A product code should require publishable artefacts: flow diagrams, risk statements, and clear explanations of automated decisions. Scaffolding includes clarity.

The eighth claim: appeal paths are essential. Errors happen. Systems misjudge. People misclick. A credible product code must articulate how appeals are made, who reviews them, and in what timeframe. Etsy's 2020 seller appeal system is instructive. It published response windows, review escalation ladders, and categories of remediable errors. Behavioural outcomes included faster reinstatement for wrongly suspended sellers and fewer duplicated tickets. Implication: a product code must assume fallibility, not deny it.

A counter-example enriches the point. In 2022, a major social platform suspended users during an automated spam sweep. Many appealed. Few received timely explanations. Public frustration grew. The limitation is glaring. Appeals that exist but lack clarity create alienation. The reconciliation requires specifying three things: what the appeal can change, when it will be reviewed, and what evidence is required. A product code can be minimal and still provide this scaffolding.

The ninth claim: defaults shape outcomes more than intentions. Defaults are moral levers. In 2018, Apple's Safari browser introduced Intelligent Tracking Prevention, blocking cross-site trackers by default. Behavioural shifts were immediate: advertisers reported sharp drops in third-party cookie activity. The implication is simple. A product code must specify default states for sensitive features: visibility, data sharing, retention, notifications, permissions. Defaults should protect the least powerful user first.

Scaffolding appears again. The tenth claim: products must plan for failure states in advance. In aviation safety, this principle is routine—checklists, redundancies, controlled degradations. Digital systems often lack such rigour. Yet when they adopt it, resilience rises. In 2021, Cloudflare demonstrated this during a global BGP routing anomaly. The product's circuit breaker automatically rerouted requests to stable paths. Behaviourally, the failsafe prevented a global slowdown. The implication: a product code must articulate how the system degrades gracefully when external dependencies fail.

Now the motif clarifies fully. Scaffolding is the quiet architecture that remains unseen until it saves the structure. A product code is that architecture—supporting, restraining, enabling. It sets the rhythm and the limits. It aligns the system's behaviour with its intent.

The forward test remains unresolved. If a single flawed patch can trigger global harm, and a single well-designed guardrail can prevent it, what scaffolding will you build before the next update ships?

Daily drills

At 09:58 on 14 September 2016, an engineer at Amazon's Dublin data centre prepared a routine capacity adjustment. The change should have taken seconds. Instead, a mistyped parameter triggered a cascade that knocked major portions of AWS S3 offline across the United States. The post-incident analysis showed the root cause clearly: not malice, not incompetence, but a missing micro-routine. The engineer had no lightweight pre-action drill to sanity-check the command. One missing pause. One missing breath. Billions of dollars in global interruptions. Habit, or the absence of it, had written the script.

A different scene, quieter but just as telling, unfolded at GOV.UK Notify in London in 2020. During a surge in pandemic communications, a team member almost sent a mass SMS update before realising, seconds prior, that the template referenced outdated isolation rules. The only reason the message never left the server was a small ritual: a one-minute "verify aloud" drill introduced months earlier. The person read the key lines to a colleague, stumbled, and caught the mistake. A micro-habit saved the system from broadcasting misinformation to hundreds of thousands of people. Five words return here as an anchor. Small drills prevent large failures.

Daily drills are the scaffolding beneath good judgement. They appear mundane, even trivial, yet they change behaviour measurably. They harden the boundary between impulse and action, replacing assumption with inspection. A drill is not a performance; it is a quiet intervention designed to preserve clarity. And like any discipline worth its name, its strength is cumulative.

A first claim: the smallest drills fight the deepest cognitive habits. Show the behaviour. Interruptions, notifications and rapid-fire chat threads degrade deliberate thought. Researchers at the University of California, Irvine (Mark et al., 2014) found that office workers switched tasks every three minutes on average. Name the risk. The more fragmented the environment, the more likely a person is to respond reflexively. Explain the mechanism. Reflexive posting or sharing—especially in fast digital environments—produces outsized harm because it bypasses slow systems of reasoning. The implication is not moral but architectural. A daily pause-breathe-post drill rewires the gap between perception and response. Five words have power. *Pause before you commit.*

The motif through this subchapter is the metronome—steadying cadence that prevents drift. A second claim: teams that adopt short, rhythmic drills surface hidden misunderstandings early. Consider Mozilla's weekly "metrics walk-through" ritual, initiated in 2018 in Portland. A small cross-functional group reviewed one metric, one anomaly, and one user-impact scenario. The behaviour measurable: fewer regressions made it into production, and anomalies were caught faster according to Mozilla's 2019 Quality Report. Name the practice. A metronomic review. Explain the value. A shared rhythm lets teams notice deviation before deviation becomes damage. Implication: daily or weekly drills keep collective attention tuned; they prevent drift into complacency.

A credible counter-example shows the limit. In 2021, an engineering group at a European fintech implemented a "daily checklist" that ballooned to more than thirty items. Completion time rose; engagement fell. Most of the list became noise. The limitation is obvious. When drills grow bloated, the metronome falters. The reconciliation is equally clear. Drills must be short, predictable, and tied to tangible decisions. If a drill cannot be completed in under two minutes, it is no longer a drill. It is an obstacle.

A third claim: teardown sessions convert anxiety into improvement. Show the behaviour. Spotify's "Golden Incident Reviews," piloted in Stockholm in 2020, pulled engineers, designers and product managers into a thirty-minute, no-blame review of a minor failure each week. These were not catastrophic events but small glitches—a broken link, a mistimed alert, a misleading error message. The visible outcome: engineers reported higher confidence in their systems, and repeated categories of failure declined. Name the approach. Low-stakes teardown. Explain the mechanism. By examining small failures, teams build muscle memory for examining larger ones. Implication: drills work when they normalise scrutiny without fear.

The metronome returns. A fourth claim: drills maintain alignment between intention and execution. Consider what happens when institutional rhythms collapse. In 2022, a global software company paused its weekly QA reviews due to staffing shortages. Error rates went up; shipped defects increased. Teams struggled to articulate why decisions were made. The metric was blunt but revealing: support ticket volume rose sharply within two months. The limitation is structural. Without rhythm, feedback decays. The reconciliation is straightforward. Even during constrained periods, teams should maintain a minimal cadence—a weekly twenty-minute review is enough to keep the metronome ticking.

A fifth claim: drills reduce reputational drag by enforcing clarity. Show the behaviour. In 2019, Monzo in London introduced a "clarity sentence" drill for incident updates. Before posting any status message, the owner wrote a single sentence summarising the situation and read it aloud to a peer. That behaviour eliminated ambiguous phrases and strengthened user communication. Name the benefit. Higher signal, lower noise. Explain the effect. Clear writing reduces panic, misunderstanding and subsequent corrections. Implication: a short communicative drill protects trust by preventing fog from spreading.

A counter-example strengthens the point. When Facebook's internal teams dealt with misinformation surges in 2020, some relied on "rapid response" channels without structured drills. Messages often contradicted earlier internal notes. The limitation: speed without cadence yields confusion. The reconciliation mirrors the motif. A metronome tempers haste. Drills should stabilise rhythm, not accelerate chaos.

A sixth claim: drills must be adapted to cognitive load. Show this in practice. During NHS Digital's vaccine rollout in January 2021, the core data team adopted a "90-second breath check" before publishing updates to booking capacity. Staff were exhausted. Errors risked blocking thousands. The breath check, a tiny ritual, involved reviewing three fields aloud—date, region, quantity. Visible behaviour: large-scale errors did not materialise. Name the mechanism. Cognitive offloading. Explain the benefit. Drills externalise attention when internal resources are depleted. Implication: a good drill works even when people are tired.

A seventh claim: drills enhance cultural resilience by making practice visible. GitHub's "Friday Fault Reviews," run globally since 2017, required participants to bring one mistake from the week—no matter how small—and describe what they learned. The behaviour encouraged humility and reduced the stigma of error. Name the cultural effect. Psychological safety. Avoid abstraction: it manifested in increased participation rates and richer documentation. Explain the mechanism. Shared vulnerability builds durable norms. Implication: drills that surface small learning moments inoculate teams against defensive silence.

The metronome ticks again. An eighth claim: drills translate strategy into behaviour. Many organisations publish value statements but fail to rehearse them. A drill is the rehearsal. For example, a team that claims to value user dignity may institute a daily review of one user-impact scenario. A team that prioritises ethical metrics may use five minutes to inspect yesterday's spike in a harm indicator. Show the behaviour. Measure the anomaly. Name the discipline. Operational rehearsal. Explain the connection. Values come to life only when they are practised. Implication: drills operationalise ethics.

A limitation sharpens understanding. Drills can become performance theatre if leaders do not model them. In 2020, a Berlin-based media platform created a "bias check" ritual for editorial decisions. Senior editors rarely participated. Predictably, participation declined. The limitation: drills cannot survive hypocrisy. The reconciliation: leaders must keep the rhythm too. The metronome must be heard across the whole room.

A ninth claim: drills expand the system's ability to absorb shocks. When teams practise small disruptions, large disruptions become manageable. Google's Site Reliability Engineering (SRE) teams institutionalised "game days" in the mid-2010s—simulated outages run in controlled environments. Behaviourally, game day participation correlated with improved time-to-detection and time-to-resolution metrics across services. Name the insight. Practised instability creates stability. Explain the mechanism. People learn to act without panic. Systems adapt predictably. Implication: daily and weekly drills are micro game days that build resilience slowly.

A tenth claim: prompts and checklists close the loop. Show the behaviour. Aviation's history is instructive. After the 1935 crash of the Boeing Model 299, which overwhelmed pilots with complexity, the U.S. Army Air Corps introduced a pre-flight checklist. Accidents dropped. Name the tool. The checklist. Explain the principle. Memory is fallible; prompts make expertise reliable. Implication: digital teams require the same scaffolding—short, precise prompts that guide pre-posting checks, metric evaluations, and teardown reflections.

The metronome, as motif, stops being metaphor and becomes architecture. Drills create rhythm. Rhythm creates clarity. Clarity prevents harm.

The unresolved tension is practical. If a two-minute drill can avert a cascade, and a weekly teardown can strengthen a team, what rhythm will you commit to before the next moment of fatigue, haste or ambiguity arrives?

About the Author

Noor Halven writes at the seam where technology, ethics, and everyday practice meet. Over a decade of working with product teams, educators, and community organisers has shaped a clear, grounded view: digital tools are never neutral, and small choices compound into culture. Noor draws on comparative moral traditions and systems thinking, with a particular affection for images like Indra's net that illuminate interdependence. Their work champions clarity over jargon and practice over posturing, offering readers humane ways to align intention and impact across screens and streets. When not writing, Noor helps teams embed ethical guardrails into ordinary sprints, believing that care should ship as part of the build.

www.ingramcontent.com/pod-product-compliance
Lightning Source LLC
Chambersburg PA
CBHW031336230926
51848CB00002B/254
* 9 7 8 9 3 7 5 3 6 1 9 2 3 *